The Borrowing Process

The Borrowing Process: Public Finance in the Province of Canada, 1840–1867

Michael J. Piva

University of Ottawa Press

© University of Ottawa Press, 1992
Printed and bound in Canada
ISBN 0-7766-0343-4

Canadian Cataloguing in Publication Data

Piva, Michael J., 1946–

The borrowing process: public finance in the Province of
Canada, 1840–1867

ISBN 0-7766-0343-4

1. Finance, Public — Canada — History — 19th century.
I. Title.

HJ8512.P49 1992   336.71'09'034   C92-090122-0

This book has been published with the help of a grant
from the Social Science Federation of Canada, using funds
provided by the Social Sciences and Humanities Research
Council of Canada.

Text and cover design: Judith Gregory

To Jonas and Maxim

Contents

Tables and Figures

Introduction

This book has been a long time coming, but then again when work began on this project I had not intended to study public finance. Rather, I was interested in trade and trade policy in mid-nineteenth-century Canada and in particular the impact of the Galt tariff. Unknown to me at the time, Ben Forster was beginning work on a related topic. Our research, as is now clear, took decidedly different paths because we began with different initial questions. Analyzing the political influences brought to bear on William Cayley and Alexander Galt, Forster would later comment that "substantial analysis of the fiscal position of the union of the Canadas remains to see the light of day."[1] I, meanwhile, started with the assumption that one needed to know much more about the fiscal position of the Union before one would be able to say anything new about the Galt tariff and its impact. Intending to write about trade, I wandered into R.G. 19, the records of the Department of Finance at the National Archives, looking for necessary background information on public finance. I never got back to my study of trade, although it took a very long time before I realized how pronounced was my shift in topic and intent.

As one would expect, R.G. 19 contains an enormous amount of material. There is no finding aid for this material. For some topics, access to relevant information is relatively easy. For those attempting to reconstruct a general overview of public finance, however, the organization of the material leaves much to be desired. For example, letters to and from the province's financial agents are contained in separate volumes; this requires one to go through three or four volumes simultaneously to reconstruct the flow of events and information. Moreover, letters to and from these agents concerned the execution of policy decision without providing much information about the processes of policy formation. One found letters despatching debentures but rarely containing information on why the government was increasing its debt. There are, in addition, many volumes containing more general correspondence and in these could be found intriguing little clues about issues of major significance scattered, it seemed, at random in letters to local customs agents dealing with the fine points of bureaucratic administration. I soon found myself collecting pieces of a jigsaw puzzle without knowing quite what I was looking for, because, as I kept reminding myself, I was not interested in public finance, I was interested in trade. Like it or not, I was collecting a lot of information on public finance without being entirely sure if it added up to anything. One way to find out was to ask my peers. I proposed giving a paper to the Canadian Historical Association (CHA).

For that paper I took the material in hand and tried to write a narrative on the processes that led to the compounding public debt problems faced by Canada at mid-century. Luckily the CHA asked Peter Baskerville to comment on this early effort. Baskerville was unaware of my "hidden agenda" and treated the essay at face value as a fairly unimaginative narrative on the growth of the public debt between 1848 and 1856. He asked, among other things, why I had begun the analysis with the crisis of 1847–1849 and why I believed this had been such an important turning point. Baskerville, of course, was right: the problem I was describing had a longer history about which I knew too little. It was at that point that my research ceased to be background for an analysis of Canadian trade and trade policies and became a study of government finance in the Union period.

My detailed study of public finance during the Union has not led to a fundamental alteration in the way I have always approached the Union period. It has, however, led to a number of findings which I believe add to the standard interpretation of the economic history of the period. Although a careful reading of the secondary literature indicates as much, the degree to which nearly all the problems associated with public finance revolve around one issue — transportation — is striking. Although some contemporaries quibbled about details, there was a remarkable consensus about the general need for the state to aid construction of canals and railways. Commitments to state-aided transportation projects created financial problems which in turn circumscribed all other policy discussions. Canada, to cite the obvious case in point, could never develop a commercial policy to deal with purely trade problems because tariff policy could not be divorced from fiscal policy. Trade was often the last thing considered by the Canadian government when it defined policies.

This led to a second surprise: from the perspective of government finance, changes in party, government, and minister made remarkably little difference to the basic economic orientation of the Canadian state during this period. Responsible government brought continuity rather than change. There is no indication at all in the records of the Department of Finance that a major shift in political power occurred in 1854. Despite all the turmoil and political instability between 1858 and 1864, and despite the grand pronouncements of Ministers of Finance such as William Howland that they intended to proceed in new directions, it was business as usual in the actual management of the public purse. In this context it was only fitting that after Confederation Sir Francis Hincks should return to the Finance portfolio in an essentially Tory cabinet, having spent all of his previous ministerial life as a leading Reformer. Similarly it is no surprise that men like Galt made their way from *Rouge* to *Bleu* by way of Finance. There certainly were issues that divided Canadians and their politicians, but in the main such issues did not, despite Grit rhetoric, involve public finance in any fundamental way.

A final point deserves comment. Since the seminal work of H. A. Innis, most of us take for granted that, relative to the United States, the Canadian state played a critical interventionist role in economic development. This work suggests that, if anything, we have underestimated the importance of the state during the Union period. The critical role played by the state went far beyond building canals, aiding and encouraging railways, or even, as some would have us believe, fostering infant industries through tariff protection. Peter Baskerville shows, for example, that the state did not only supply funds and help create a favourable financial environment for railway development; "[T]he Canadian state acted as a conduit for the transferral of managerial techniques deemed appropriate for an industrializing economic order."[2] The importance of the state involved as well more general contributions to the functioning of the provincial economy.

During the Union period Canada remained an export-led staple-dominated economy producing raw materials, primarily wood and grain, for external markets. This export-led economy, however, imported more than it exported. The consumption of those imports helped raise the standard of living and increased the rate of growth. Without the state this economy could not have functioned the way it did. It was the state that brought in the capital, which in turn allowed Canada to pay for those imports. Two critical institutions, the government and the railways (and the latter might not have been there but for the encouragement of the former), provided the fuel that drove the Canadian economic engine. There was simply no comparable economic institution; in terms of the amount of capital involved all other economic organizations pale into insignificance. Without dwelling on ahistorical concerns about supporting current standards of consumption and investment by mortgaging the economic future of generations to come, it is difficult to imagine what Canada might have been like had the state not acted as it did. Precisely because the state played such a critical role in the economy, essentially facilitating capital imports which helped balance trade deficits, an understanding of the economic history of the province must include an analysis of public finance.

Although I have accumulated many debts trying to complete this project, I am not sure who to thank. My experience with scholarly journals had made me very aware of the flaws of the peer review process. This book has made me equally aware of its advantages. Without doubt the two single most positive influences on this book were the two anonymous reviewers chosen by the University of Ottawa Press and the Social Sciences and Humanities Research Council. Although I did not always agree with the observations and suggestions made by these two critics, I shall be forever grateful for the care and attention both gave to the task. Both reviews were thorough, detailed, and, most importantly, constructive. Both were models of professionalism. I may not have incorporated all their suggestions, but the manuscript has benefitted in countless ways from their contributions.

One critic I do know. Various sections of the arguments contained in this manuscript have been presented as conference papers; Peter Baskerville has commented on most of those efforts. I have always found his observations pertinent and perceptive; his criticisms have always been constructive and useful. If I remain occasionally obtuse, I nonetheless thank Peter for always keeping me on my toes. I would also like to thank Chad Gaffield who offered excellent counsel at a critical moment.

Thanks are extended as well to the staffs of the National Archives of Canada, the University of Ottawa Library, and the University of Ottawa Press, particularly Jennifer Wilson and Janet Shorten, for their courtesy and their help. The Social Sciences and Humanities Research Council provided funds for a leave fellowship which allowed me to do much of the research on this project. In addition, this book has been published with the help of a grant from the Social Science Federation of Canada, using funds provided by the Social Sciences and Humanities Research Council of Canada.

I extend as well a special thanks to Catherine Wilkins who has helped keep body and soul together for many years. Finally, there are Jonas Piva and Maxim Piva to whom this book is dedicated. They have become a part of the book in ways they will never imagine.

Notes

1.   Ben Forster, *A Conjunction of Interests: Business, Politics, and Tariffs, 1825–1879* (Toronto, 1986), 40, note 35.

2.   Peter Baskerville, "Transportation, Social Change, and State Formation, Upper Canada, 1841–1864," in *Colonial Leviathan: State Formation in Mid-Nineteenth-Century Canada*, edited by Allan Greer and Ian Radforth (Toronto: 1992), 248.

Glossary

Bank note: A note issued by a bank undertaking to pay the bearer the face value of the note on demand. The issue of bank notes was restricted and regulated by legislation.

Bill of Exchange: A promissory note used in international trade by which the drawer makes an unconditional undertaking to pay a drawee a sum of money at, most commonly, some future date, usually 30, 60 or 90 days. In this sense a Bill of Exchange is simply a post-dated cheque or draft and, like a cheque or draft, it can be endorsed for payment to the bearer or any named person other than the drawee. Once it has been accepted and endorsed by the drawee, the bearer might not want to wait for payment and might sell the Bill (hence "commercial bills" or "commercial paper") in a money market, usually at a small discount. Since Bills of Exchange are post-dated, their sale represents a short-term loan from the purchaser to the bearer; the discount represents interest on that loan. In the United States, Bills of Exchange are often called "notes."

Coupon: In the nineteenth century, debentures were issued with coupons for interest payments attached. Each coupon was individually signed and dated at regular intervals and could be redeemed at face value. For example, a £100 debenture which ran for 20 years and paid interest at 6 per cent per annum on 1 July and 1 January would include 40 coupons worth £3 each, dated at six-month intervals. When due, each coupon could be "clipped" and redeemed. Since each coupon would be redeemed at par, the effective rate of interest would vary considerably with the actual price paid for the debenture. Thus, a payment of £6 per annum on a £100, 6 per cent debenture purchased at 85 (see "Quotations") would represent an effective rate of return of about 7 per cent.

Debenture: A fixed-interest security issued by limited companies or governments in return for long-term loans. Interest is paid at specific intervals (see "Coupons"). Usually, the term of the loan is specified, and at maturity the loan is repaid in a single lump sum at the full nominal value of the security. Occasionally, as was the case with British Consols, debentures could be irredeemable. There can be mortgage debentures secured by a mortgage on specific assets or floating-charge debentures. In the latter case interest must be paid whether the company makes a profit or not. In the event of non-payment, debenture holders can force liquidation, and their claims rank ahead of all shareholders. In the nineteenth century debentures issued by governments were occasionally referred to as "bonds," a name that became far more common during the twentieth century.

Discount: A negative difference between the current price or value of a security or currency and the par, or face, value of that security or currency.

Draft: The nineteenth-century name for a cheque, a draft was an order written by the drawer to a commercial bank or a central bank to pay on demand, after a specified date, a specified sum to the bearer. In the nineteenth century drafts were most frequently post-dated, that is, they were to be paid in 30, 60 or 90 days. Government drafts written on British commercial banks or the Bank of England for payment in England were always post-dated.

Nominal price [value] vs. actual price [value]: Technically, the "nominal" value or price of a security or currency equalled the par value or price. For example, the currency of account in Canada prior to 1858 was £ cy whose value relative to £ stg had been fixed by legislation. Although the "nominal" rate of exchange was always used by government accountants when valuing assets and liabilities, exchanging currency for sterling in financial markets always involved the payment of sometimes substantial premiums or discounts. Barings and Glyns often used the term "nominal" in the more usual sense of a price "existing in name only," rather than in the more technical sense of par value. Reports of "nominal prices" referred to unrealistic quotations in the market at which no sales either had been made or could be expected to be made.

Par: The nominal face value of a security or currency. Prices for securities and currencies were most frequently expressed as an index, with 100 being par (see "Quotations").

Preference shares: Holders of preference shares take precedence over the holders of ordinary shares, but their claims rank behind those of debenture holders when an issuing company is liquidated. Unlike debentures or securities, preference shares do not pay fixed rates of interest, although they usually entitle holders to fixed rates of dividend payments as well as a share of residual profits.

Premium: A positive difference between the current price or value of a security or currency and the par, or face, value of that security or currency.

Quotations: In the nineteenth century, the price of a security was always expressed as an index, with 100 representing par value. Both market quotations and actual sales were reported in this fashion. Thus, when Barings and Glyns reported selling debentures at 103, they received £103 for each debenture with a face value of £100. Thus, a price of 103 meant that the purchaser had paid a 3 per cent premium on the debenture. Alternatively, a price of 98 meant that the purchaser had bought the debenture at a 2 per cent discount.

Sinking Fund: Most long-term loans contracted through the sale of debentures were for fixed terms. Debtors frequently amortized such debts by making regular payments to a "Sinking Fund." Those payments would be calculated so that, together with interest, enough money would be accumulated in the Sinking Fund to repay the debt in full at maturity. Sinking Funds, meanwhile, were in most cases assets controlled by the debtor; moneys held in a Sinking Fund could be invested at the discretion of the owner of the asset. Occasionally, some creditors could contractually require the debtor to create such a fund and could either restrict or control the investments of accumulated assets.

Sterling (stg)/Halifax currency (cy): Despite the importance of imperial spending in the economic development of British North America, Sterling (£ stg) was never adopted as the currency of account in the colonies. At the time of Union the currency of account in Canada was based upon Halifax currency (£ cy), created in 1758 when the Nova Scotia legislature rated all Spanish dollars of 420 grains at 5s. This exchange rate meant that £1 cy equaled $4. Britain, meanwhile, had since 1703 valued the dollar at 4s 6d. The relative value of each currency to the dollar established a nominal exchange rate of £111.11 cy to £100 stg. In 1825 and again in 1838 the British lowered the exchange rate of the dollar, first to 4s 4d and then to 4s 2d. On this basis the relative value of the two currencies meant that £120 cy now equalled £100 stg. The currency laws in the new Province of Canada recognized this change and established a new exchange rate in which the British sovereign would be valued at £1 4s 6d cy making the exchange rate £121.67 cy for each £100 stg. Despite the legislative change the older rate of £111.11 cy to £100 stg continued to be used in government bookkeeping; most private transactions followed suit and used the older rate until 1858 when the government adopted a decimal currency based upon the dollar.

Chapter 1
Financing the Union:
The Problem

"Our state wagon is in the mud, & we are
not sure that Hercules, alias John Bull,
will come to our aid. Under any
circumstances we are at any rate bound to
put our shoulders to the wheel, resolutely,
& at the same time appeal to generous
John, & he may come to our relief."
— John Macaulay, 1838[1]

For many British North Americans 10 February 1841 was just another day. Most awoke early and set about their daily labours far from the roar of cannon in Montreal and Toronto. Those cannon signalled that this was no ordinary Wednesday. At 12 noon a Royal Proclamation joined the old provinces of Upper and Lower Canada in a new legislative union. In Montreal loyal British merchants loudly proclaimed their support for the Union while unrepentant French Canadians grudgingly accepted their fate. The mood in Upper Canada, meanwhile, seemed surprisingly ambivalent. Sir George Arthur commented that

> there existed so much actual despondency in Toronto, I considered it better to get up as much form and circumstances about the Proclamation as I could at the moment, and I am told it gave general satisfaction. I had no alternative but this course or to fall in with the prevailing melancholy mood of the City.[2]

Many viewed the Union as more necessary than desirable. Others undoubtedly went about their business and paid little or no attention.
 A combination of factors had convinced colonial authorities and provincial politicians, if not British North Americans at large, that union was indeed necessary. One of the more important was the problem of economic development. The near-unanimous opinion of the commercial and political elite suggested that rapid economic growth could

best be fostered by improving the commercial potential of the St. Lawrence river system. If some doubted the ability of the two provinces to
develop the river jointly, all agreed that singly neither possessed the
resources to accomplish the task.

The essential economic unity of the St. Lawrence system and
the need to canalize that waterway lay behind the original petition for
union forwarded to the Colonial Office by Montreal merchants in 1822.[3]
Uninterested in union, the Upper Canadian elite shared the desire for
transportation improvements. Undaunted by its meagre financial
resources the provincial government committed itself to large-scale
public works programmes. That the financial commitment might
become greater than Upper Canada's ability to pay became painfully
obvious during the commercial depression of 1837. Near-insolvency in
Upper Canada, combined with political unrest and rebellion in both
provinces, ensured a more sympathetic hearing for the old cry for union.

The economic motives of the Union, as well as the highly
contentious nature of provincial politics, surfaced quickly when
recently elected Members of the Legislative Assembly (MLAs) gathered
in the new capital of Kingston. They met for the first time on 14 June
1841 with the still indisposed Governor General absent. Austin Cuvil-
lier was unanimously elected Speaker. There followed a three-hour
debate over whether the Assembly, having not yet met the represent-
ative of the sovereign, had the power to adjourn.[4] After a long and
acrid debate the Assembly finally voted 47–27 to adjourn.

In a somewhat better mood, the Assembly reconvened the
following day to hear the Speech from the Throne. On this occasion
Lord Sydenham, looking "rather weak and languid,"[5] managed to
attend the Legislative Council. His short speech singled out the
"improvement of navigation" as his government's first priority. He went
on to observe that

> [t]o undertake this successfully, large funds will undoubtedly be required,
> and the financial condition of the Province, as it stands at present, would
> seem to forbid the attempt.[6]

Intended only to inaugurate the first session of the new Canadian
Parliament, these words proved far more prophetic than Sydenham
could have imagined. The 26-year history of the Union would witness
an unending struggle to find the "large funds" needed for ever more
expensive public works projects.

If the political history of the Union begins with the rebellions
in Lower Canada, the financial history begins with the public debt
crisis of Upper Canada. Lower Canada, which possessed a larger population and a more developed economy, entered the Union indebted

for only £114,000 stg, nearly all of it owed to its own citizens.[7] Upper
Canada, on the other hand, brought debts of £1.2 million stg.[8] The
largest portion of this debt was of recent vintage and was held by a
very few London bankers.

During the early years of settlement, the governments of
both Lower and Upper Canada had been able to finance their programmes — both public works construction and special programmes
such as compensation for war losses — out of the capital resources of
the province. The government raised necessary funds by selling debentures to local investors. This system worked as long as capital demands
remained moderate, but this ceased to be the case in the 1830s.
As capital requirements increased, John Henry Dunn, the British-
appointed Receiver General in Upper Canada, suggested that it would
be to the advantage of the province to tap London capital markets.[9]
With this in mind Dunn penned a circular note in April 1833 to several
London banking houses asking for tenders on four loans worth nearly
£250,000 cy.[10] At the same time Jonas Jones, President of the Board
of Commissioners which supervised the construction of the St. Lawrence canals, journeyed to the United States in an effort to raise money
there.[11]

The Upper Canadian government intended to do two things
with these new loans: pursue additional public works and "transfer"
the provincial debt to London. Dunn believed debentures paying
5 per cent interest could be sold in London; the proceeds from these
sales could then be used to call in and redeem outstanding 6 per cent
currency debentures. This would substantially reduce the cost of
servicing the existing public debt.[12] The province might profit as well
from an expected premium on the sale of its debentures, a profit that
would further reduce the effective rate of interest on the loan. In addition the sometimes substantial premium paid for sterling Bills of
Exchange sold in Canada and drawn on the proceeds of debenture sales
would add to the advantages of the loans. To avoid purchases of sterling
exchange to pay interest, some of the moneys would remain on deposit
in London.[13] With so many advantages Dunn refused to be deterred
when neither Jones' trip to the United States nor his own circular
letter produced the desired results. Instead Dunn journeyed to London
to negotiate personally these new loans.[14]

In London Dunn signed an agreement with Thomas Wilson
and Company for £200,000 stg.[15] This agreement bound neither party
until the Assembly passed enabling legislation authorizing the issue
of sterling debentures payable in London. Although Wilsons expected
Dunn to secure the passage of such legislation immediately upon his
return to Upper Canada, he did not present the question to the

government until February 1834. A month later he notified Wilsons that appropriate legislation had passed and the first £20,000 stg worth of the new debentures would be forwarded as soon as possible.[16] The exact relationship between the province and Wilsons, meanwhile, remained ambiguous.

Normal practice for negotiating loans called for the sale of debentures to the public through authorized agents and brokers, and for the payment of interest and eventual redemption through these same agents. Agents were usually paid a commission on each of these transactions, the original sale, the payment of interest, and the redemption of bonds. The British government relied upon the Bank of England, but the province had no bank of issue to use as a financial agent. Dunn, as Receiver General, sold domestic currency debentures to the public directly, while interest was paid at his office. The province had no agent in London. Although Dunn had been appointed by, and in theory was responsible to, the Lords Commissioners of Her Majesty's Treasury, there was no connection between the colonial Receiver General and the Bank of England. Dunn believed an essential part of his agreement with Wilsons was the establishment of a provincial agency in the British capital market. Indeed, when he notified Wilsons of the passage of legislation in March 1834, he commented that "I consider this transaction the commencement of a large business. . . . I have appointed your House as [our] agents, and which has been stated to the government."[17] The legislation authorizing the loan, however, did not provide, as Wilsons pointed out in protest, for the payment of a commission on either the sale of debentures or the payment of interest. Wilsons were not, in fact, the financial agent of the province for this loan; the company had simply purchased Canadian securities. To Wilsons Dunn noted the distinction, as well as his preference that Wilsons be an agent taking a commission rather than a creditor. He went on to observe that "I have no power, nor have I any authority in alluding to such an arrangement [agency], but it is a matter of future consideration for the proper authorities."[18]

Wilsons were, as Dunn acknowledged, a creditor; the company purchased £200,000 stg debentures from the provincial government at par. The province could sell Bills of Exchange drawn on Wilsons at its discretion up to £200,000 stg, but the debentures themselves were the property of Wilsons and part of the company's assets. When Wilsons periodically sold those debentures in the London market, the premium — about 2 per cent — belonged to the company.[19] However, Wilsons did act as agent without commission for the payment of the interest on those debentures sold to third parties. This was, as Lord Glenelg, the Colonial Secretary, later observed, a highly irregular arrangement. It would also in time prove a source of considerable embarrassment to Upper Canada and its Receiver General. Wilsons were not simply a "depositor in trust" but, as Glenelg pointed out, "the absolute Purchasers and Proprietors of the Debentures lodged with them." Those debentures were part of the assets of Thomas Wilson and Company.[20]

Before these problems were realized, Dunn negotiated a second, larger, loan. Immediately after the completion of the first agreement with Wilsons, Dunn began drawing on funds deposited in the provincial account in London. By late 1834 money was again running short, and in January 1835 Wilsons renewed an earlier offer to "advance" the province any funds required in exchange for debentures at par. The company would leave the question of commission open to the Legislature for consideration.[21] In early 1835 the provincial Legislature authorized a new £400,000 stg loan to be raised in London "for the purpose of prosecuting public works in progress and cancelling all the public debt now due."[22] If the government encountered delays negotiating this loan, the act provided that £100,000 could be raised domestically by the sale of shorter-term — six months to five years — 6 per cent debentures.

The Bank of Upper Canada offered to purchase £30,000 stg on condition that such debentures would not be redeemed in less than three years. Dunn was unimpressed. He believed this sum — itself insufficient to meet the government's needs — was all that could be raised domestically. The nominal quotation, meanwhile, for Canadian 5 per cents in London stood at 103, although there was no demand at that price. This convinced Dunn that the province could do better than Wilsons' offer to purchase at par. Under the circumstances he suggested that the government accept Wilsons' offer for £100,000 stg at par to cover immediate needs, and that he proceed to London to seek competitive, and hopefully higher, bids for the remaining £300,000 stg.[23]

Dunn addressed a circular letter in May to Baring Brothers and Company, Reid Irving and Company, Gould, Dowie and Company, Thomas Wilson and Company, Edward Ellice and Company, Gillespie, Moffat, Finlay and Company, N. Rothschild and Company, Mr. Daniel Bell, and Robert Sheddon and Sons. He got no encouraging responses. Few London companies would lend money to the province at 5 per cent, nor, as Gillespie, Moffat, Finlay and Company pointed out, did they wish to act as unpaid agents for the province since the legislation authorizing the loan provided no commission for the sale of debentures or the payment of interest.[24] In Dunn's words, he "found considerable reluctance amongst the monied Houses to have anything to do with the Loan."[25] He was, however, able to convince Baring Brothers and Company to share equally in the loan with Thomas Wilson and Company.[26] As in the case of the previous £200,000 loan with Wilsons in 1834, Barings and Wilsons purchased these debentures at par and any profit from resale belonged to the companies; they remained creditors rather than "agents."

Having successfully negotiated £400,000 stg debentures in London, Dunn then found that relations between him and his bankers began to sour. Neither banker would be paid a commission on the sale of debentures, although both would profit as long as they could sell the bonds in the market at a premium. But Dunn did not need all this money immediately; he intended to draw funds as required over the course of the next several years, and no interest was to be paid until the money was actually drawn. Dunn, then, was in no hurry to send the debentures to Wilsons and Barings, and this delay caused considerable irritation to both, particularly as the quotation for Canadian securities fell with the increased political unrest in British North America.

Wilsons had already advanced the province £100,000 stg in early 1835 even before the final deal with Dunn was completed in July. In February 1836 they had still not received the £100,000 stg balance for which they had contracted. Barings, meanwhile, had received none of the debentures due their house despite the July 1835 understanding that the bonds would arrive "as soon as possible" and certainly before the end of the year. Both insisted that any further "unreasonable delay may defeat all the calculations of profit."[27] Dunn replied that the debentures would be sent immediately, claiming that his five-month personal illness had prevented him from "doing as I engaged" and sending the debentures sooner.[28] With the construction season now open, Dunn also began issuing drafts on both Wilsons and Barings, drafts that continued to be issued regularly throughout 1836 and into May 1837.[29] At that point, in the spring of 1837, Wilsons informed Dunn that there might be trouble honouring the Receiver General's drafts on London.

The government intended to use these loans to support its public works programme while reducing expenditures by "transferring" the domestic debt to London where interest rates were lower. The latter objective was partially met. In January 1836, after the agreement for the second loan of £400,000 stg had been finalized but before the final £300,000 stg debentures had been shipped to London, £202,000 cy of the total outstanding debt of £378,850 cy held in the province had been redeemed. At this point the public debt held in Canada stood at £178,850 cy and the debt held in Britain at £241,600 stg. The sterling debt then ballooned as the Receiver General issued drafts on Wilsons and Barings, yet there was to be no further reduction in the currency debt held in the province. Indeed, the currency debt increased to £195,830 before the end of the year.[30] With a rapidly increasing public debt, the province would face a financial crisis in mid-1837 triggered by the panic in the United States and the suspension of specie payments in that country.

Two events, as Peter Temin has shown, produced the panic.[31] The Bank of England, however inappropriately, blamed its rapid depletion of specie reserves in 1836 — the Bank lost £3.5 million in gold that year — on an outflow to the United States. The Bank believed this resulted from an overextension of credit to that country. To stop this loss, the Bank raised its discount rate, which hit 5 per cent in August 1836. More significantly for our purposes, the Bank refused to discount Bills of Exchange drawn on several "American Houses," as those counting houses involved in the Anglo-American trade were known. Baring Brothers and Company, one of those "American houses," survived the panic by immediately placing severe limits on new credit accounts in its American business. Here was the source of Barings' increasing impatience at the delay in receiving Canadian debentures. Other houses, and in particular the "Three Ws" (as Timothy Wiggin and Company, George Wildes and Company, and Thomas Wilson and Company came to be known), were slower to react.

The Bank of England had taken this action because it was convinced that the large outstanding credits in the United States were the source of its problems; its policies proved effective, as the discount rate in Boston and New York reached 2 per cent per month by late 1836. By early 1837 most of the American houses in Britain were in severe financial difficulties; they found it increasingly difficult to collect outstanding arrears in the United States, which in turn made it impossible to remit funds to meet obligations in Britain.

In early 1837 cotton prices in England began to fall following a second poor crop year. This was accompanied by a sharp rise in the price of foodstuffs. The decline had immediate repercussions in New Orleans and New York. Foreign accounts had to be paid in either sterling exchange or specie, and the drop in the price of cotton made it even more difficult to acquire sterling exchange. Indeed, the cost of sterling exchange rose to the point where it was cheaper to remit specie to Britain. By early 1837 a number of New York and Philadelphia banks were gathering specie with precisely this in mind, but before this happened the New Orleans cotton factors Herman, Briggs and Company failed in March 1837. That failure nearly brought down their primary creditor, the New York firm of J. L. and S. Joseph and Company. Panic then set in and credit in New York and other American financial centres tightened still further. Finally, on 10 May 1837 New York banking houses suspended specie payments, an action quickly followed in other American cities.

Thomas Wilson and Company had become hard pressed immediately upon the Bank of England's decision not to discount their bills. By early 1837 they found it increasingly difficult to collect outstanding debts in the United States and to remit funds needed to meet liabilities in England. Wilsons, together with Wiggin and Wildes and assisted by Barings, appealed to the Bank of England for a special credit to allow them to remain solvent. Although Horsley Palmer, the Governor of the Bank, believed all three were basically sound, he remained convinced that these companies had purchased too much commercial paper in the United States and now found "their engagements very much exceeding the command of their respective capitals."[32] Palmer offered to help but only on condition that these companies sought no new credit business. This they agreed to do; it proved too little, too late.

Wilson and Company immediately instructed their agent in New York, John Nicholas Gossler, to "reduce their engagements, as promptly as circusa will permit" and to enter into no new business. Melville Wilson, one of the firm's senior partners, journeyed to New York to supervise personally operations there. At the same time Wilsons informed Dunn of the problems faced by the company. Gabriel Shaw, another senior partner, warned that "[w]e may for a time be kept out of our funds in the United States; and we shall be glad if circumstances do not induce you to press too heavily on us."[33] The suspension of specie payments in New York a month later sealed Wilsons' fate: the company closed its doors in early June.

Dunn had been receiving warnings about a restriction of the London money market since late 1836. In November Barings had written that

> American securities of all descriptions are quite out of favor here, and nothing can be done except at ruinous prices. For the past two months there has been a heavy pressure on the money market, and we see no prospect of improvement for some time to come.

The same advice continued to be sent into 1837.[34] Yet Dunn, and in turn the Upper Canadian government, took little notice of the storm clouds gathering on the financial horizon. Despite continued reports of few prospects for sales in London, the government in March 1837 advertised for tenders for 23 separate loans worth a total of nearly £1 million. A few of these loans, such as the £10,000 for the Cobourg Railroad, were private issues with no provincial liability. A total of

£268,000, however, was secured exclusively by the provincial treasury, and nearly all the rest by various municipalities or districts and, thus, indirectly by the province.[35] Not until April 1837 did the first tender arrive;[36] by that time disquieting news about Wilsons' imminent demise had reached Dunn.

When Dunn received Gabriel Shaw's letter of 30 March 1837 requesting that the province issue no more drafts, the Receiver General proposed going immediately to London.[37] Before he left he urged the government to initiate restraint policies. He advised that no Bills of Exchange be issued, that expenditures on the St. Lawrence canals be reduced as much as possible, and that new projects be immediately suspended. Wilsons' failure, meanwhile, posed two immediate problems for the provincial government: the possible default on interest payments on the public debt due in July, and the maturation of a Bill of Exchange drawn on Wilsons for £10,000 stg.

The first problem was solved within days. Wilsons had closed their doors on 2 June 1837. On 4 June Barings notified the provincial government of the failure of seven houses, including Wilsons, Wildes, and Wiggin. Two days later, Barings offered to cover the July interest payments on all debentures, including those held by Wilsons. Barings also informed the government that the quotation for Canadian debentures had fallen to 98 and added that this was a nominal price as they were "without any demand."[38] Barings still had large numbers of debentures on hand, and they would suffer a substantial loss if the price collapsed, a sure result of a default. As long as a substantial portion of Barings' assets remained tied up in provincial debentures, that firm had little choice but to help maintain the provincial credit.

Wilsons also held a substantial number of provincial debentures; the government's priority in the short term was to retrieve them. Lord Glenelg lost little time in addressing the problem, sending Sir Francis Bond Head his views on 6 June, only four days after Wilsons' failure. Glenelg's despatch touched on a fundamental problem: the question of control over colonial finances. There was some irony in the situation since, according to Dunn, he had, at age 28 in 1820, received his life appointment as Receiver General through the influence of Lord Glenelg, then Charles Grant, Chief Secretary for Ireland and a relation of Dunn's brother-in-law.[39]

Although originally appointed by the Treasury in London, Dunn was a civil servant who functioned quite independently. Although not appointed to the Executive Council until early 1836, he had resigned, together with Robert Baldwin and John Rolph, a month later when Sir Francis Bond Head rejected their demand that the Council be consulted on all matters. Despite his brief tenure on the Executive

Council, Dunn often acted like a finance minister when advising Council.[40] Throughout his tenure he claimed as Receiver General exclusive control over the negotiation of all public loans and all matters connected with the management of the public debt.[41] Loans had to be approved by the Legislature, yet the initial contract with Wilsons had been undertaken by Dunn without prior legislative authority. In the case of the second £400,000 loan it was Dunn who advised the government, which in turn pushed through enabling legislation. Glenelg expressed surprise that these loans had been negotiated "without the consent or even the Knowledge of H.M. Gov't [sic]."[42] This, according to the Colonial Secretary, was the source of the province's troubles; had the Treasury supervised the loans the "irregularity of the whole proceeding" would have been avoided.[43] The primary irregularity, Glenelg argued, stemmed from the fact that Wilsons and Barings had been made the owners of the provincial debentures rather than depositors and agents. This was "an entire departure from the Principle upon which loans are negotiated for the public service in this Kingdom."[44] The province's debentures were the property of Wilsons, and all creditors had an equal claim on those assets.

There might still be a way to avoid a government crisis. Glenelg suggested that a Writ of Extent might be obtained since Wilsons remained, at least indirectly, a debtor to the Crown.[45] Such a Writ would "secure a priority of payment over other Creditors." The province might then still recover its money, but Glenelg warned that an Extent was a "difficult question of law" which the law officers of the Crown were already considering. In the meantime, Glenelg had already despatched a Colonial Office official to attend the meetings of Wilsons' creditors.[46]

Precisely what happened next is more difficult to trace. According to Dunn's later report — written after he had read Glenelg's subsequent critical comments, which he thought had censured his handling of these loans[47] — he contacted Barings immediately upon his arrival in London. At that meeting Barings reiterated their willingness to advance moneys to the province to meet the July interest payments. The following day Dunn met with Sir George Grey, Undersecretary of State at the Colonial Office. Grey informed Dunn that Glyn, Hallifax, Mills and Company had offered to pay the outstanding Bill of Exchange which Dunn had previously issued in Canada and which would fall due on 3 July.[48] Dunn immediately contacted Glyns, which agreed not only to honour the Bill of Exchange — for £10,000 stg — but to advance any money the province might require to meet the interest on debentures payable at Wilsons.[49] This they did; Glyns paid the £10,000 stg Bill of Exchange on 3 July and the interest on the public debt two days later.[50]

Glyns, according to Glenelg, had initiated this action; the arrangement had not been undertaken "at the suggestion of Her Majesty's Government."[51] While this first initiative from Glyns may have proved fortuitous for the province, their next initiative would prove beneficial to themselves. Glyn, Hallifax, Mills and Company were not disinterested parties; they were one of Wilsons' primary creditors. Glyns, together with Barings, sat on the committee of creditors charged with liquidating Wilsons' assets;[52] they had every interest in seeing that the province did not seek a Writ of Extent. The timing of Glyns' intervention would suggest that George Carr Glyn had been kept well abreast of developments at the Colonial Office. It was Grey, the Undersecretary, who first directed Dunn to the offices of Glyns.[53]

The problem became complicated because the Colonial Secretary received differing opinions. When Bond Head had heard of the problems at Wilsons, he had immediately despatched his Solicitor General, William Henry Draper, to England to investigate.[54] Head undoubtedly preferred Draper the Tory to Dunn the Reformer, although Glenelg was surprised that "any other person than Mr. Dunn should have been selected" whatever his political connections.[55] Dunn too requested and was granted leave to travel to England and while there worked at cross-purposes to Draper.

Draper, according to Glenelg, demanded that the Colonial Office seek an Extent on behalf of the province. Glenelg reported that "we have been compelled to pause before deciding on its adoption or rejection," because of the state of the "Commercial World."[56] By late July, however, both the law officers of the Treasury and the Attorney General ruled that an Extent could be secured, although it might not prove expedient for the province's credit. Draper had not changed his mind; at a final meeting with Glenelg before returning to Canada he insisted that an Extent be issued. The matter then went to the Cabinet, but before a final decision was reached, and after Draper had left town and was no longer available for consultation, Dunn informed Glenelg that he had come to an "irrevocable" agreement with Glyns. Glenelg reported that he "was not at all aware that such an agreement was contemplated until his [Dunn's] letter of 28 Ultimo [July] announced to me the completion of it." Glenelg expressed his surprise that the Canadian Receiver General could act "on his own single judgment, and without the control of any authority whatever," although he made no suggestion about altering the powers of the Receiver General.[57]

The agreement between Dunn and Glyns in late July marked a change in the Receiver General's previously adopted posture of deferring to the Colonial Office. Glenelg had involved the Colonial Office from the beginning of the crisis. George Grey and possibly James Stephens had been in contact with both Wilsons and Glyns even before

Dunn and the Upper Canadian government knew of Wilsons' failure. Indeed, when Gabriel Shaw informed Dunn that Wilsons had suspended payments, he reported that statements of the company's accounts had already been forwarded to the Colonial Office on Glenelg's insistence.[58] Dunn expected Wilsons to resume business, but when this had not happened by 19 June he demanded a complete and precise statement of the provincial account which he in turn forwarded to the Colonial Office. He commented at this point that he felt "unwilling to take upon [himself] the responsibility of deciding a matter of so much importance." Dunn preferred that Glenelg should adopt "such steps as His Lordship may deem necessary on behalf of the Government of Upper Canada."[59] Dunn also informed Glyns that he was "not disposed to take upon [himself] more responsibility than is necessary."[60] Yet after Draper demanded that an Extent be issued, Dunn reported that

> [a] few days previous to my leaving London, Messrs. Glyns [sic] called upon me as Receiver General to make them, as they were about to relieve the Province of its embarrassment with Messrs Wilson's, assignment of the Assets of that Firm, as well as appoint them agents to receive dividends from them.[61]

According to Dunn, he did not believe the Crown had the power to secure an Extent nor, apparently, did he doubt that Wilsons would eventually make good their debt to the province. As a result Dunn, at Glyns' suggestion, signed over the provincial claim on Wilsons' assets as security for advances made to the province. Far more importantly, Dunn signed an Indenture on behalf of the province giving Glyns, which sat on the committee of creditors charged with liquidating Wilsons' assets, power of attorney. In return Glyns agreed to act as "Bankers and Agents of the Province."[62] Glyns were not likely to initiate action leading to a Writ of Extent.

Dunn remained overly optimistic about Wilsons' prospects in spite of Gabriel Shaw's reports in December 1837 of his unsuccessful attempts to recover moneys owed in the United States. Shaw believed that Wilsons would eventually make good their debts to the province and other creditors, but he warned that it would take "much longer" than expected.[63] Not until October 1838 was there a first payment to creditors of 6s/8d on the pound. Based upon a total claim of £85,500 stg, Glyns credited the province with £28,500 stg which they charged against the outstanding advances made by their house.[64] A year and a half later this payment would lead to a row between the new Inspector General and the Lieutenant-Governor on the one hand and Dunn on the other. Ultimately it would lead to a complete alteration in the powers of the Receiver General.

Dunn had always exerted considerable influence, and he had functioned much like a minister of finance. He certainly believed he had exclusive administrative control over the negotiation of loans and the administration of the public debt. Politically, however, he was identified with the Reformers, and this led to some distrust among Tories. Much of the dislike expressed by Bond Head, Draper, John Macaulay, Arthur, Thomson, and others was clearly inspired by partisan rivalry. Reformers like Robert Baldwin and Francis Hincks had a more favourable view of the man. This seems the primary reason why Lieutenant-Governor Bond Head had despatched Draper rather than Dunn to London when he first heard of the financial problems at Wilsons. Draper, in turn, was incensed that Dunn, without his knowledge, had signed over power of attorney to Glyns rather than seeking a Writ of Extent.

Dunn's career did not suffer as much as one might imagine from such a twist of fate. Ironically the very characteristics that got him into trouble also kept him in office. His real problem was his weak personality. As Sir George Arthur once commented, "the Receiver General has neither nerve nor sense."[65] Despite his constant posturing[66] Dunn was easily manipulated. Charles Poulett Thomson understood this. Among Governors there existed a consensus on John Henry Dunn. In a confidential memo to his successor summarizing the strengths and weaknesses of members of the Executive Council, Sir Francis Bond Head had very little to say about the Receiver General: "Avoid Mr. Dunn" was his only comment.[67] Thomson, meanwhile, referred to him on occasion simply as "that ass." Sir George Arthur agreed: "Dunn is always an ass ... & either in the cellar or the garret on all."[68] Yet Dunn did have his uses. The civil servant had become very political; he ran in Reform circles and had become identified with the growing opposition in Toronto to the proposed move of the capital to Kingston. Thomson, meanwhile, was trying to construct a Reform/Tory coalition in Upper Canada to promote the Union. Dunn was just the thing — a Reformer who was weak enough to be controlled.[69]

In October 1839 the Colonial Office ended the practice of life tenure appointments in various colonial offices including the office of Receiver General,[70] yet Dunn kept his job. Indeed, to the degree that he was elevated to the Executive Council and provided with government support in his election to the Legislative Assembly, one might even conclude that he had been promoted. But Thomson had kept him in office not because he valued his opinions and advice, but because he provided a useful foil for potential opponents. Moreover, he had been brought in on the Governor's terms, and those terms effectively stripped the office of Receiver General of any effective independent decision-making power. Dunn survived but in an office with considerably reduced power.

The office of the Receiver General had never been intended as anything but a purely administrative position with no policy component. Dunn described his duties this way:

> Receiving into the different Funds and paying there from all public and provl. [sic] Revenues as well as those arising from the Casual and Territorial Revenue and Sales of Crown Lands to the Canada Co. and accounting for the same under their several and respective heads of Service. Negotiating all public Loans and transacting all matters relating thereto and generally superintending and managing all other business connected with the Department of Receiver General of this Province.[71]

Only on the question of negotiating public loans were wide discretionary powers claimed. It was precisely in this area that Dunn had acted independently in the past. Thomson intended that, in the future, he would no longer act with any discretionary power even within this narrowly defined area.

Thomson addressed the problem of financial control by upgrading the office of Inspector General. Thomson named John Macaulay, a strong personality and someone he trusted, as the new Inspector General.[72] Extremely conservative in his political views, Macaulay, an early advocate of the union of Upper and Lower Canada back in 1822, enjoyed a long-standing reputation as a well-informed expert on the economy in general and on public improvements in particular.[73] He had been appointed to the Legislative Council in 1835. In June 1838 he was named as Arthur's Civil and Private Secretary before being appointed Inspector General in September of the same year. Together Thomson and Macaulay transformed the office and made it "a kind of Finance Minister," although not until 1859 was the name changed.[74] Macaulay and Dunn did not get along, and it did not take long for Dunn to get testy. The issue was quickly resolved.

Dunn's agreement with Glyns stated that the provincial claim on Wilsons was £83,700, yet this figure was adjusted upward when the first payment was made to creditors in late 1838. Then, in early 1840, Macaulay questioned the accounts submitted to him by Dunn and argued that the balance owed the government by Wilsons was £90,000 stg. In May 1840 Glyns accepted Macaulay's claim and paid an additional £1,600 stg as a result, according to Glyns, of their earlier clerical error.[75] Dunn, meanwhile, complained bitterly about Macaulay's interference and at one point received a severe reprimand from the Lieutenant-Governor for his conduct. More importantly, in March 1840 the Lieutenant-Governor forced Dunn to withdraw two letters he had addressed to Barings and Glyns and to defer to the Inspector General, who was acting at the behest of the Lieutenant-Governor.[76] Primary responsibility for the finances of the province had clearly shifted from the Receiver General to the Inspector General despite Dunn's claim to exclusive jurisdiction.

Such changes involved more than the simple redefinition of administrative functions.[77] The failure of Wilson and Company demonstrated the pressing need to reform administrative structures and take control over money matters. Sydenham believed that the primary weakness of pre-Union colonial government resulted from the divorce of politics from administration. Too many unsupervised civil servants, like Dunn, had been running too many executive departments, while membership on the Executive Council often carried no clear administrative duties. Sydenham agreed with Arthur's comments that the demand for responsible government resulted primarily from the confused and disorganized state of colonial administration.[78] As regards financial control Arthur explained:

> The outcry, however, that has been made for "Responsible Government" does not surprise me; for, partly owing to the House of Assembly having into its own hands matters purely Executive, and, partly from other causes, there has been, in reality, in some transactions, no responsibility — a great intricacy exists, and a want of system in the manner in which the public Accounts have been kept, some of the Departments have worked most inconveniently to the Public, and there are, as it seems to me, no adequate checks over the receipts and disbursements of public money.[79]

Sydenham intended the Executive Council to be responsible for both the formation and the execution of government policy.

Political leaders who could work in "harmony" with the Legislature would henceforth hold seats on the Executive Council where each would assume specific administrative duties as heads of particular departments. Sydenham's restructured Executive Council provided the province with the equivalent of its first cabinet government.[80] When first outlining his views on reform to Russell, Thomson, not without reason, commented that "[t]he evils resulting from this defective organization of Govt [sic] are exemplified in the most striking manner in the present financial state of this Province."[81] As Sydenham explained,

> For the satisfactory conduct of public affairs, it has appeared to me absolutely necessary, that on the one hand, the Governor should be able to rely upon the zeal and attention of the Heads of Departments not merely to act under his immediate directions upon every minute point, but also to feel themselves really responsible for their conduct of their different offices, and on the other hand, their being members of one or

other House of Parliament, the public would possess a wholesome control over their acts, and the security would be obtained for the general administration of affairs being in accordance with the wishes of the legislature.[82]

This was not responsible government, but it was not far removed.

The adjustment in the initial payment to creditors in May 1841, meanwhile, was not the last payment received from Thomas Wilson and Company. In March 1841 the committee of creditors, which included John Cryder, Joshua Bates, a Barings associate, George Carr Glyn, and J. Horsley Palmer, Governor of the Bank of England, recommended a "final liquidation" of Wilsons' affairs. Shaw, too, felt the time had come for a formal bankruptcy.[83] In anticipation of a declaration of bankruptcy Dunn, at Wilsons' suggestion, again signed power of attorney over to Glyns.[84] But bankruptcy proceedings were not taken, and the committee of creditors continued to act as trustees while Wilsons continued to try to collect their outstanding debts. In March 1843 Glyns informed Dunn that the prospects of realizing any further payment out of Wilsons' assets were "most remote and uncertain." Two years later Glyns again informed the then Receiver General, William Morris, that nothing could be done at the time to get any payment from Wilsons as "their assets are locked up in the United States etc and much involved in Law Suits."[85] The Receiver General's records make no further mention of Thomas Wilson and Company until 16 years later when T. Douglas Harrington, the Deputy Receiver General, authorized Glyns to sign on behalf of the province a Deed of Release against the estate of Thomas Wilson and Company. The estate made a final payment of 7d on the pound; the provincial account at Glyns was credited with £2634.16/6 stg. Thus ended the Thomas Wilson and Company affair. The total loss to the province stood at over £57,500 stg.[86]

The failure of Thomas Wilson and Company was certainly inconvenient but in itself was not the source of Upper Canada's financial woes. Wilsons' suspension of payments should have produced a pause in the province's headlong rush into further debt, but it did not. In the short term the government had to scramble to raise new money to pursue its various projects, but new money proved surprisingly easy to find. Already overextended, the province continued to borrow large sums throughout 1837 and 1838. In the latter year, however, a rapid increase in expenditures combined with a decline in revenue to produce a huge budgetary deficit. In 1839 the government cut its public works spending to the bone, yet the deficit grew even larger. This inability to make ends meet in 1838 and 1839 rather than the Wilsons failure was at the heart of the problem.

During the mid-1830s the province of Upper Canada went on a spending binge trying to improve internal transportation. There were hundreds of local projects all encouraged and some supported by the provincial government. Successful negotiation of the 1834 and 1836 loans seems only to have encouraged proponents of such schemes. Then in early 1837, with a financial crisis already looming, Dunn circulated a notice calling for tenders for new loans of over £1 million stg. Most of these debentures were a combination of private and local issues supported by the provincial government. The sum of £268,000, however, was a direct provincial issue.[87]

When Dunn received word that Wilsons had suspended payments, he immediately advised that all public works projects be put on hold and that no drafts be issued on London. This was easier said than done as some work had already begun. While Dunn was in England, the Commission for the St. Lawrence Navigation began pressing for an immediate £10,000 stg to meet its needs.[88] The financial crisis in the United States had already restricted credit there, and this led to a substantial rise in discount rates which could prove very costly to the government. While sterling was selling in New York at 20 per cent premiums, few Canadian banks were willing to offer as much. In the end the province was able to get an acceptable price for only £10,000 stg. This was clearly insufficient to meet the various needs of the government.[89]

Dunn, meanwhile, was in England trying to enlist the help of the Colonial Office. He sent James Stephens a complete list of all authorized debentures, outlining the difficulties selling them domestically and in the United States. Dunn remained remarkably optimistic: "I propose, therefore, should his Lordship [Glenelg] approve it to offer and to use my exertions to dispose of those Loans in this City." To Barings he commented that the debentures were in the hands of the British government and asked for some "proposition on this subject."[90] Although there is no record of the response he received, there was clearly no market for Upper Canadian securities in London. These same securities, however, were much in demand domestically.

With the premium paid on sterling exchange reaching 20 per cent in New York, there existed considerable interest in purchasing sterling debentures payable in London at a somewhat lower rate.[91] In Dunn's absence B. Turquand, First Clerk at the Receiver General's Office, brought the matter to the attention of the Executive Council in July. Council in turn "ordered" that authorized debentures could be made payable either in London at 5 per cent interest or in the province at 6 per cent interest. Council further ordered that those payable in London "be issued payable at the Counting House of Messrs.

Baring Brothers and Co." Seven days later the Council accepted tenders for the first £65,000 stg worth of these debentures.[92] They were all issued in sterling and payable at Baring Brothers in London.

It is not clear whether Barings were fully aware of these arrangements; not until 11 August 1837 did Turquand forward copies of the appropriate legislation and Orders-in-Council. A month later Barings acknowledged receipt of this information, but made no comment other than "to call your particular attention to the importance ... of making timely provisions with us for the payment of the said dividends, when the funds still with us for account of the Government of Upper Canada shall have been absorbed by your drafts."[93]

Dunn was very much opposed to this policy, which had been adopted in his absence. In early October he argued that disposal of the debentures in Canada at premiums below that paid for sterling exchange was not to the advantage of the government[94] and he advised John Joseph that no more be sold. At that time he reported that £138,500 stg of an authorized £200,000 had been placed in the market. The remaining £61,500 he proposed sending to Barings for sale in London. This he proceeded to do on 23 October 1837.[95] Barings, meanwhile, were already having second thoughts about the whole business.

Barings had received notice of these new sales, but they had not actually seen the debentures themselves. Purchasers in Canada, meanwhile, were already forwarding these securities to their own varied agents in London for resale. One such agent, Bosauquet and Company, reported that they could not be sold because of inadequate signatures and wondered if Barings intended "to pay dividends as they become due." Barings responded that they would follow the instructions of the provincial government and would pay "if in funds."[96] Barings had already recognized the problem of the signatures on coupons but went further. They informed the government that

[i]t has heretofore been our custom to have the negotiation of Loans, when the dividends on which are made payable at our Counting House and as this is the system generally pursued in this Country, we must beg respectfully to decline paying the dividends on any future issues of debentures, unless they are passed thro' [sic] our hands in the usual way.[97]

What concerned Barings was the willingness of these various agents to unload Upper Canadian securities at substantial discounts of 5 per cent or more in anticipation of high profits on North American sales of sterling Bills of Exchange drawn on the proceeds. This would make it doubly difficult for Barings to market debentures in their hands at acceptable prices. Barings would get their way, but not before more sales were made in Canada.

Barings received £60,000 stg worth of the new debentures in December. By 1 January 1838 they reported that none had been sold and that it would be impossible to place any of these debentures at a "fair price" — not less than par — until there were "more favourable advices as to the state of things on your side."[98] Barings concluded that "under these circumstances we would beg to request that you will not issue any bills upon us in anticipation of the proceeds of said Stock." Dunn, however, had already issued such drafts. Moreover, most of the projects for which this money was needed were nearing completion and could not easily be abandoned except at great loss. Under the circumstances the government returned to its earlier policy of selling sterling debentures payable at Barings in Canada.[99] Whatever effect the rebellions had on the London money markets, they clearly did not inhibit sales in Canada. Between 1 May and 1 July 1838 a total of £66,000 stg payable at Barings sold in Canada.[100] Barings had every intention of putting a stop to these sales, although the difficulties of transatlantic communication prevented them from accomplishing this objective.

Not until June 1838 did Barings get their first indication that the provincial government intended to resume sales in Canada of debentures payable at their house. On this occasion Barings "again repeat[ed] our objections to that course." Barings objected "to having our names inserted on Stock, the issue of which has not had our previous knowledge and consent" and insisted that, if the government intended issuing any more sterling debentures, their name be removed as the agent for payment of interest.[101] Not until mid-August, after the final sales of Series BB had been completed, did Dunn acknowledge receipt of Barings' protest. On that occasion he commented only that "the Lieutent [sic] Governor has been as anxious to avoid the issue of Debentures as possible and to prevent the accumulation of the public Debt." The latest sales had only been sanctioned, according to the Receiver General, in order "to prevent the works in progress from sustaining injury."[102]

Dunn could not have been surprised by Barings' protest; he was already well aware of their objections. Dunn had forwarded Barings' note to Macaulay at the beginning of August,[103] and when Macaulay demanded more information Dunn reported that he had put a stop to domestic sales in late 1837 because of similar objections. Dunn recalled that he had earlier convinced Bond Head not to authorize such sales, but when Barings were unable to place the £60,000 stg debentures sent them, there was no alternative but to renew domestic sales if the public works were to be kept going.[104] It was now clear that these works could no longer be continued. In September 1838 Dunn informed Macaulay that

> it appears to me that the Government cannot issue any more until Messrs Baring's permission be obtained or arrangements can be made with some other House in London to act as agents in these transactions, which will require a full and complete investigation into the finances of the Province before I could expect to obtain the consent of any agent.

Dunn concluded his remarks with the lament that "I can see no way by which money can be procured for the public works."[105] The problem was that the finances of the province could not bear favourable scrutiny.

Even as these last debentures were being sold, the true state of the province's finances was becoming clear. With the economic depression Dunn had projected a possible deficit of £7,000 cy on the Consolidated Revenue Fund in 1838. In April Macaulay reported it was more likely to be "upwards of £20,000—." As Macaulay told C. A. Hagerman,

> We are indeed overtaken by the evils which I was sure should one day follow the incautious and uncalculating, I might almost say reckless legislation of recent Parliaments, and especially of the present Parliament, much sooner than anyone could have anticipated.[106]

In the end the deficit proved to be over £30,000 (see Table 1).

The problem was the burgeoning public debt which consumed a disproportionate share of government spending. In 1838 interest on the public debt and unsecured advances from various banks cost more than the total spent on government administration, the Legislature and the administration of justice. In 1839 interest cost 36 per cent more than these various branches of the civil government. By 1839 the deficit, excluding public works and the loans raised to support them,[107] still stood at over £38,000 cy. Put another way, interest charges represented 60 per cent and 70 per cent respectively of all revenue in 1838 and 1839. As long as the cost of servicing the public debt consumed such a high proportion of revenue, there could be little prospect of avoiding ever larger deficits; as long as deficits remained large and growing, there was little prospect for new loans. Upper Canada had clearly boxed itself into a financial corner.

Macaulay spelled out the options in April 1838; they were few. On the revenue side Macaulay wanted to get "our share of post-office surplus revenue." On the expenditure side he suggested making local districts, which could raise revenue through direct taxes, responsible for penitentiaries. Even if successful these two measures would

Table 1: **Income and Expenditures on the Consolidated Revenue
Fund, Upper Canada, 1838 and 1839 (£1,000 cy)**

	Income			Expenditure	
	1838	1839		1838	1839
Customs	£ 60	£ 84	Costs of		
Public Works	10	7	Collection	£ 4	£ 5
Other	11	15	Administration		
Loans*	151	11	and Justice	48	52
			Interest	48	71
			Public Works	148	25
			Other	16	16
	£232	£118		£264	£170
Balance	(£32)	(£52)			

* Prior to the appointment of a Board of Audit in 1855, the public accounts were kept, in the words of John Langton, in a "curiously complicated state." Cited in Wendy Cameron, "John Langton," *Dictionary of Canadian Biography*, Vol. XII, 1891–1900 (Toronto, 1990), 527. The listing of loans, here including the £28,000 payment on the Wilsons' account as well as the proceeds of debenture sales, as "income" illustrates just how "curious" and confused the public accounts submitted to the Legislature could be. See below, Chapter 5, 200–203.

Source: "Return of the Provincial Revenue and Expenditure for the years 1838, 1839 & 1840, Upper Canada," Appendix B, *Appendix to the Journals of the Legislative Assembly*, 4–5 Vic. 1841. All calculations are my own.

reduce the deficit by a mere £10,000. More would have to be done; specifically, the burden of servicing the public debt could be shared with others in a better position to pay. Macaulay observed that the St. Lawrence canals benefitted both Upper and Lower Canada. "It surely follows that, under all the circumstances, both should bear the burden."

> As the Constitution of Lower Canada has been suspended, our Parliament cannot negociate [sic] on the subject with the Lower Canada Parliament, & indeed during the virtual anarchy which has for years past reigned in that Colony negotiation must have been fruitless. But though Jean Baptiste cannot meet us through his favourite *Chambre*, and in no case, owing to his anti-commercial feelings, would be disposed to co-operate with us in the completion of the Saint Lawrence Canal from Lake Ontario to Lake Saint Peter, there is still a hope for us, since an eminent British Peer comes out to rule, with great powers, and in fact will be the Arbiter of our political destiny. Why should not an appeal be instantly made to the nobleman by the government of this Province? . . . Would

he not sympathize with the truly British spirit in which we embarked
in our career of navigable improvements, & be induced to do whatever
he might consider practicable to obtain relief for us?[108]

What Macaulay had in mind was a special fund created by an Act of
the British Parliament supported by an additional 2.5 per cent *ad
valorem* tariff on the imports of both Upper and Lower Canada. What
he got was a union of the two provinces, which effectively united their
debts and their financial resources, and an imperial guarantee for new
loans.

Notes

1. *The Arthur Papers*, ed. by Charles R. Sanderson, Vol. 1 (Toronto, 1939), John
Macaulay to C. A. Hagerman, 21 April 1838, 84–87.

2. *The Arthur Papers*, Vol. 3, Sir George Arthur to Lord Sydenham, 10 February 1841,
311.

3. Donald Creighton, *The Empire of the St. Lawrence* (Toronto, 1956), 210–223.
Creighton adds that "[t]he problem of cheap and rapid communications by land and water
could obviously not be solved by Upper Canada alone," *ibid.*, 220. Also see W. T. Easterbrook and Hugh G. J. Aitken, *Canadian Economic History* (Toronto, 1961), 253–254.
Other historians, meanwhile, suggest that the 1821-1822 proposal for union had more
to do with the fiscal crisis of Upper Canada and checking the political power of French
Canada than the commercial unity of the St. Lawrence. See, for example, Gerald M.
Craig, *Upper Canada: The Formative Years, 1784–1841* (Toronto, 1963), 101–102. Also
see Fernand Ouellet, *Le Bas Canada, 1791–1840* (Ottawa, 1976), 316–321.

4. "Our Kingston Correspondent, Monday, 14 June," *Montreal Gazette*, 17 June 1841.

5. "Our Kingston Correspondent, Tuesday, 15 June," *Montreal Gazette*, 18 June 1841.

6. *Debates of the Legislative Assembly*, ed. by E. Nish, Vol. 1, 15 June 1841, 14–16.

7. Of this total, £79,000 had been placed between 1830 and 1839 to cover Montreal
Harbour improvements. The remaining £35,000 went for the construction of the Chambly
Canal. See "Statement of the Public Debt of the Lower Part of Canada as authorized by
Acts or Ordinances of the late Province of Lower Canada," Appendix B, *Appendix to the
Journals of the Legislative Assembly*, 1841.

8. By comparison the Federal public debt in the United States stood at only
$3.5 million in 1840, although it rose to $5.3 million a year later. See Series Y368-379,
Public Debt of the Federal Government: 1791–1957, U.S. Bureau of the Census, *Historical Statistics of the United States, Colonial Times to 1957* (Washington, D.C., 1960),
721.

9. See John Ireland, "John H. Dunn and the Bankers," *Ontario History*, LXII (1970),
83–100. Dunn believed that in Britain the province could "get money at all times with
certainty and upon more reasonable terms." Metropolitan Toronto Library, *William Allan
Papers*, John H. Dunn to William Allan, 21 September 1834, cited in *The Bank of Upper
Canada: A Collection of Documents*, ed. by Peter Baskerville (Toronto, 1987), 91. Bas-

kerville suggests that opposition to this plan came from the Bank of Upper Canada which had profited handsomely from the old system of domestic borrowing. See *ibid.*, lxvi–lxviii.

10.   See National Archives of Canada (NAC), Department of Finance, R.G. 19, Vol. 1173, Dunn, Receiver General, to Baring Brothers and Company, 23 April 1833. The same letter was sent to Reid, Irving and Company, Thomas Wilson and Company, Edward Ellice and Company, and Gillespie, Moffat, Finlay and Company, all of London. The four loans were for (a) £70,000 cy for 20 years for the St. Lawrence navigation projects, (b) £58,300 cy for 20 years for war losses loans, (c) £20,000 cy for 20 years for various roads and bridges in the province, and (d) £84,300 cy for 15 years to redeem outstanding 6 per cent debentures. All loans were to pay 5 per cent interest. Also see Finance, R.G. 19, Vol. 1173, Dunn to Daniel Stoddard [a London broker], 24 April 1833.

11.   Finance, R.G. 19, Vol. 1173, Dunn to Lt.-Col. Rowan, Provincial Secretary, 15 May 1833, and Dunn to Messrs. Prime, Ward, and King [New York], 15 May 1833.

12.   See Finance, R.G. 19, Vol. 1136, Dunn to Wilsons, 6 February and 29 March 1834, Dunn to Jonas Jones, President of the Board of Commissioners, 6 November 1834, and Finance, R.G. 19, Vol. 1173, Receiver General's Office (RGO), "Notice," 30 December 1834. This notice called in 6 per cent debentures.

13.   Throughout the 1830s substantial premiums above the nominal exchange rate of £111.11 cy per £100 stg were charged for sterling Bills of Exchange. Large sterling deposits in London provided flexibility for the province, allowing the Receiver General to avoid purchases of sterling exchange if rates were unfavourable. For a discussion of exchange rates see A. B. McCullough, *Money and Exchange in Canada to 1900* (Toronto, 1984), 251–264, 270.

14.   See Finance, R.G. 19, Vol. 1173, Dunn to Jones, 29 July 1833, and Dunn to Rowan, 1 August 1833.

15.   Thomas Wilson and Company had extensive connections with British North America and were the London agents for the Bank of Montreal, City Bank, the Bank of Upper Canada, and the Commercial Bank of M.D. (Midland District). All of these banks later shifted their accounts before Wilsons' failure in 1837. See Ireland, "John H. Dunn and the Bankers," 95.

16.   Finance, R.G. 19, Vol. 1173, Dunn to Wilsons, 6 February and 8 March 1834. The time limit in the original agreement had already expired, and Dunn acted on the assumption that Wilsons would accept these debentures on the previously agreed terms. See Finance, R.G. 19, Vol. 1180, Dunn to Wilsons, 27 March, 8 April, and 2 May 1834. This Wilsons did.

17.   Finance, R.G. 19, Vol. 1136, Dunn to Wilsons, 29 March 1834.

18.   Finance, R.G. 19, Vol. 1180, Dunn to Wilsons, [?] May 1834.

19.   See Finance, R.G. 19, Vol. 1136, Wilsons to Dunn, 28 June, 14 August, and 19 August 1834; Vol. 1137, Wilsons to Dunn, 14 March 1835, and Thomas Mercer Jones to Dunn [April 1835].

20.   NAC, Governor General's Office (GGO), R.G. 7 G 1, Vol. 81, Despatch No. 186, Lord Glenelg to Sir Francis Bond Head, 6 June 1837.

21.   Finance, R.G. 19, Vol. 1137, Wilsons to Dunn, 22 January, 14 March, and 30 May 1835.

22.   Finance, R.G. 19, Vol. 1173, Dunn to Rowan, 25 April 1835.

23. *Ibid.*, and Dunn to Rowan, 13 May 1835.

24. Finance, R.G. 19, Vol. 1173, Dunn, "Circular," 4 May 1835, and Finance, R.G. 19, Vol. 1137, Gillespie, Moffat, Finlay and Company and Gould [Dorvant] and Company, London, to Dunn, 8 July 1835.

25. Finance, R.G. 19, Vol. 1173, Dunn to Rowan, 18 January 1836.

26. *Ibid.* Problems arose in 1835 when Baring inquired at the Colonial Office about the loan only to be told that "no official intelligence of the act in question has yet reached this Department" and, as a result, royal assent had not been given. This problem, however, was ironed out, royal assent granted, and the loan went through. See Finance, R.G. 19, Vol. 1137, Fletcher Wilson to Dunn, 22 July 1835, Wilsons to Dunn, 6 August 1835; Finance, R.G. 19, Vol. 1154, "Copy," George Grey, Colonial Office, to Barings, 14 August 1835, included in Barings to Dunn, 14 August 1835; Finance, R.G. 19, Vol. 1173, Dunn to Wilsons, 24 September 1835, and Dunn to Barings, 24 September 1835. For a general history of Barings see R. W. Hidy, *The House of Baring in American Trade and Finance, 1763–1861* (Cambridge, 1949).

27. Finance, R.G. 19, Vol. 1154, Barings to Dunn, 22 February 1836; Finance, R.G. 19, Vol. 1138, Wilsons to Dunn, 22 February 1836, and "Duplicate," Gabriel Shaw to Dunn, 22 February 1836.

28. See Finance, R.G. 19, Vol. 1173, Dunn to Barings, 13 April 1836, and Dunn to John Joseph, Civil Secretary, 22 April 1836. Also see the acknowledgement of receipt of the debentures in Finance, R.G. 19, Vol. 1138, Wilsons to Dunn, 14 June 1836, and Finance, R.G. 19, Vol. 1154, Barings to Dunn, 18 June 1836.

29. Finance, R.G. 19, Vol. 1138, Wilsons to Dunn, 14 April 1836, Wilsons to Dunn, 14 April 1836 [there are two separate letters with the same date in the Department of Finance records], Wilsons to Dunn, 6 August, 30 August, 6 September, 14 September, 14 October, 19 October, and 29 October 1836; Wilsons to Dunn, 14 January, 30 January, 6 February, 6 March, and 4 May 1837. The last letter, which acknowledged Dunn's issuance of a £20,000 stg exchange, came fully one month after Gabriel Shaw had informed Dunn of potential financial problems.

30. See Finance, R.G. 19, Vol. 1173, Dunn to Joseph, 27 January and 10 November 1836, and Dunn, "Statement," 9 January 1837.

31. For a good description of the Panic of 1837 see Peter Temin, *The Jacksonian Economy* (New York, 1969), 113–148.

32. Finance, R.G. 19, Vol. 1138, "Copy" [Mr. Horsley Palmer to the Liverpool Deputation], 23 March 1837, included in Shaw to Dunn, 30 March 1837.

33. Finance, R.G. 19, Vol. 1138, Shaw to Dunn, 30 March 1837, and "Copy," Wilsons to John Nicholas Gossler, New York Agent, 3 March 1837, and "Copy," [Mr. Horsley Palmer to the Liverpool Deputation], 23 March 1837, included in Shaw to Dunn, 30 March 1837.

34. Finance, R.G. 19, Vol. 1154, "Duplicate," Barings to Dunn, 9 November 1836, and Barings to Dunn, 30 January 1837.

35. See Finance, R.G. 19, Vol. 1173, RGO, "Notice," 11 March 1837. The largest of these loans were (1) £245,000 on account of the Welland canal secured by the province, (2) £200,000 on account of the London and Gore Railroad secured by the Gore, London, and Western Districts, (3) £100,000 on account of the Yonge Street Road secured by the Home District, (4) £100,000 on account of the Toronto and Lake Huron Railroad secured

by the company, the City of Toronto and the Home and other districts, and (5) £77,500 on account of the Trent River Navigation project secured by the tolls on the canals.

36.   Finance, R.G. 19, Vol. 1173, Dunn to Joseph, 11 April and 27 April 1837.

37.   *Ibid.*, 5 May 1837. When Dunn first requested leave to go to England, he was quite explicit about his "anxiety and apprehension for the safety of the House of Messrs Thomas Wilson and Co." and the need to make new arrangements to cover Bills of Exchange already issued. He also mentioned the need to retrieve all unsold debentures in Wilsons' hands and to arrange for another "agency" for their sale. See Finance, R.G. 19, Vol. 1173, Dunn to His Excellency Sir Fra's. [sic] B. Head, 25 April 1837. In the records of the RGO this letter is followed by another dated 26 April 1837, with the pencilled notation in the margin that "The above letter was substituted for the preceding one at the suggestion of His Excellency the Lieut. Governor." This second letter was shorter and less explicit. It simply requested leave to go to London on public business. Finance, R.G. 19, Vol. 1173, Dunn to Joseph, 28 April 1837.

38.   Finance, R.G. 19, Vol. 1154, Barings to Dunn, 4 June 1837, and "Duplicate," Barings to Dunn, 6 June 1837.

39.   Ken Cruikshank, "John Henry Dunn," *Dictionary of Canadian Biography*, Vol. VIII, 1851–1860 (Toronto, 1985), 251.

40.   See Ireland, "John H. Dunn and the Bankers," 84, and Cruikshank, "John Henry Dunn," 253.

41.   For a short description of the duties of the Receiver General according to Dunn see Finance, R.G. 19, Vol. 1175, Dunn, "Return of the Receiver General's Office," 12 January 1839.

42.   GGO, R.G. 7 G 1, Vol. 81, Despatch No. 186, Glenelg to Bond Head, 6 June 1837.

43.   Glenelg, James Stephens, and other officials at the Colonial Office usually preferred to keep all references to other departments, including the Treasury, to a minimum. See D. B. Swinfen, *Imperial Control of Colonial Legislation, 1813–1865: A Study of British Policy towards Colonial Legislature Powers* (London, 1970), 32–33.

44.   GGO, R.G. 7 G 1, Vol. 81, Despatch No. 186, Glenelg to Bond Head, 6 June 1837.

45.   See Ireland, "John H. Dunn and the Bankers," 96.

46.   GGO, R.G. 7 G 1, Vol. 81, Despatch No. 186, Glenelg to Bond Head, 6 June 1837.

47.   See Finance, R.G. 19, Vol. 1155, "Copy," Dunn to Glyns, 24 November 1837. Glyns in turn contacted the Colonial Office and then reassured Dunn that "there must be some misunderstanding." The whole arrangement, wrote Glyns, "has been fully and satisfactorily explained to the authorities here." Finance, R.G. 19, Vol. 1155, Glyns to Dunn, 6 February and 20 July 1838.

48.   For a general history of Glyns see Roger Fulford, *Glyn's: 1753–1953* (London, 1953).

49.   Finance, R.G. 19, Vol. 1173, Dunn to Joseph, 12 January 1838. Dunn would later claim Grey had arranged for Glyns to cover interest payments even before he arrived in London. See GGO, R. G. 7 G 1, Vol. 116, "Copy," John Dunn to Messrs. [F. A.] Harper and [Peter] Buchanan, 10 April 1847 [dated London], included in Despatch No. 59, Earl Grey to Lord Elgin, 19 April 1847. John Ireland supports this view and cites a letter from George Carr Glyn to Earl Grey in which Glyn asks to be appointed financial agent for the province. See Colonial Office, 42-442-422, George Carr Glyn to Earl Grey, 10 June 1837, cited in Ireland, "John H. Dunn and the Bankers," 97–98.

50. GGO, R.G. 7 G 1, Vol. 81, Despatch No. 202, Glenelg to Bond Head, 22 July 1837.

51. *Ibid.*

52. See Ireland, "John H. Dunn and the Bankers," 95.

53. Ken Cruikshank suggests that Robert Gillespie introduced Dunn to Glyns. See Cruikshank, "John Henry Dunn," 254.

54. GGO, R.G. 7 G 12, Vol. 28, Despatch No. 49, Bond Head to Glenelg, 29 April 1837. In his recent biographical essay on Draper, George Metcalf makes only a passing reference to his trip to London. See George Metcalf, "William Henry Draper," in *The Pre-Confederation Premiers: Ontario Government Leaders, 1841–1867*, ed. by J.M.S. Careless (Toronto, 1980), 36. Also see Cruikshank, "John Henry Dunn," 254.

55. GGO, R.G. 7 G 1, Vol. 81, Despatch No. 186, Glenelg to Bond Head, 6 June 1837.

56. *Ibid.*, Despatch No. 202, Glenelg to Bond Head, 22 July 1837.

57. *Ibid.*, Vol. 82, Despatch No. 216, Glenelg to Bond Head, 4 August 1837.

58. Finance, R.G. 19, Vol. 1138, Shaw to Dunn, 6 June 1837.

59. This information is based upon drafts of letters to Wilsons on 19 June 1837 and to James Stephens, Undersecretary of State for the Colonies, 24 June 1837. See Finance, R.G. 19, Vol. 1138.

60. Finance, R.G. 19, Vol. 1138, "Draft" [Dunn] to Glyns, 13 July 1837.

61. Finance, R.G. 19, Vol. 1173, Dunn to Joseph, 12 January 1838.

62. See NAC, *Glyn Mills Papers*, M.G. 24 D 36, "Indenture between J. H. Dunn, Receiver General Upper Canada and Glyn, Hallifax, Mills and Company," and GGO, R.G. 7 G 1, Vol. 82, "Copy," Dunn to Stephens, 28 July 1837, and "Copy," "Indenture, between John Henry Dunn and Glyn, n.d.," both included in Despatch No. 216, Glenelg to Bond Head, 4 August 1837. Dunn's letter of 28 July 1837 is the earliest mention of either security or repayment of advances made by Barings and Glyns.

63. Finance, R.G. 19, Vol. 1138, Shaw to Dunn, 8 December 1837.

64. Finance, R.G. 19, Vol. 1155, Glyns to Dunn, 11 September and 1 October 1838.

65. *The Arthur Papers*, Vol. 3, Arthur to Sydenham, 10 February 1841, 311.

66. Dunn later commented that Upper Canada had been saved "from bankruptcy by my own Personal exertions." Cited in Cruikshank, "John Henry Dunn," 256.

67. See *The Arthur Papers*, Vol. 1 [Bond Head], "Confidential," 432–433. This was an unsigned document in Bond Head's hand.

68. *Ibid.*, Vol. 3, Arthur to Sydenham, 15 February 1841, 320–322. Doubts as to Dunn's competence later led to the decision that the Treasury negotiate the new Guaranteed Loan on behalf of the province. See GGO, R.G. 7 G 12, Vol. 62, Despatch No. 3, Sir Charles Bagot to Lord Stanley, 14 January 1842, and "Confidential," Bagot to Stanley, 14 January 1842. See below, Chapter 2, 38.

69. When Sydenham offered the post of Receiver General in the new Union government to Dunn, he laid down his conditions. Arthur reported that "I saw Mr Dunn yesterday just after he had received your letter. He began, in his usual strain, to talk about the perfect indifference in which he held public office, and so forth — there is not a public man who regards his Office more — but it was easy to perceive that the gloom of the last few days had passed away — and the chances are that, before he reaches Montreal, he will have found some good reason why Kingston *ought* to be preferred to Toronto for

the meeting of the Legislature." *The Arthur Papers*, Vol. 3, Arthur to Sydenham, 17 February 1841, 324–325. Ten days later Sydenham reported his final discussions with Dunn. "Dunn is here arranging about his sureties and I shall appoint him and swear him into the Council today, if he comes into my terms about the Balances — but he cannot and shall not have the unlimited control as he wishes. He is ill, which makes him nervous more so even than usual — and renders it difficult to make him get on which I wish him to do in order that he may return to Toronto for his Elections." *The Arthur Papers*, Vol. 3, Sydenham to Arthur, 27 February 1841, 347–348.

70.   Cruikshank, "John Henry Dunn," 255.

71.   Finance, R.G. 19, Vol. 1175, "Return of the Receiver General's Department," 12 January 1839.

72.   See *The Arthur Papers*, Vol. 3, "Private," Sydenham to Arthur, 1 November 1840, 167-168. Also see *ibid.*, "Private and Confidential," Arthur to Sydenham, 7 November 1840, 172–174.

73.   Robert Lochiel Fraser, "John Macaulay," *Dictionary of Canadian Biography*, Vol. VIII, 1851–1860 (Toronto, 1985), 513–522.

74.   Cited in Fraser, "John Macaulay," 521. On the later creation of a Ministry of Finance, see Section 6, "An Act to amend the Act of 1858, to make more advantageous provision for the redemption of Provincial Debentures and the Consolidation of the Public Debt," 22 Vic., cap. 14, *Provincial Statutes of Canada*, 1859.

75.   Finance, R.G. 19, Vol. 1155, Glyns to Dunn, 15 May 1840.

76.   Finance, R.G. 19, Vol. 1140, Macaulay to Dunn, 19 March 1840, "Draft" [Dunn to Macaulay], 21 March 1840, "Draft," Dunn to Barings and Glyns, 20 March 1840, included in S. B. Harrison, Provincial Secretary, to Dunn, 25 March and 31 March 1840. Also see Finance, R.G. 19, Vol. 1175, Dunn, "Return of the Receiver General's Department," 12 January 1839, Dunn to Macaulay, 27 March and 30 March 1840, and Dunn to Harrison, 1 April 1840. A second struggle erupted over balances submitted to Macaulay and the physical location of government accounts. Charles Poulett Thomson believed "the war between the Receiver and Inspector Generals" would have to end. *The Arthur Papers*, Vol. 3, Charles Poulett Thomson to Arthur, 15 May 1840, 66–68. Arthur intervened on the side of the Inspector General to "put an end to any future contest between Messrs Macaulay & Dunn — the latter of whom is wayward enough." *The Arthur Papers*, Vol. 3, Arthur to Thomson, 8 June 1840, 77–78.

77.   Ian Radforth has suggested that the Canadas provided Thomson with an opportunity to apply Utilitarian reform ideas more broadly than would have been possible in Britain. Thomson turned down the Exchequer, which had previously been his "greatest ambition," in order to become Governor General. Part of the explanation involves the scope of the opportunity not only to impose a union but to determine the constitutional and administrative structures of the colony. See Ian Radforth, "Sydenham and Utilitarian Reform," in *Colonial Leviathan*, 71–75.

78.   Baskerville also notes the "decentralization of control" characteristic of the colonial administrative system, using the Receiver General to illustrate the point. See Baskerville, *The Bank of Upper Canada*, lxi–lxii. Also see Ian Radforth, "Sydenham and Utilitarian Reform," in *Colonial Leviathan*, 81–96.

79.   *The Arthur Papers*, Vol. 2, Arthur to Sydenham, 9 November 1839, 304.

80.   See Ian Radforth, "Sydenham and Utilitarian Reform," in *Colonial Leviathan*, 73. The real difference between this and "cabinet government" as usually understood

concerned lines of responsibility. Because Sydenham insisted each minister was respon-
sible to the Governor, his Council lacked a sense of collective responsibility. Carol Wilton-
Siegel, meanwhile, has argued that "Administrative reform . . . was the alternative to
Responsible Government that was endorsed by a majority of local officials." Carol Wilton-
Siegel, "Administrative Reform: A Conservative Alternative to Responsible Government," *Ontario History*, LXXVIII (1986), 120. Sydenham certainly saw his restructured
Executive Council in this light. Such reforms, however, created the essential preconditions for responsible government. "Administrative reforms meant to head it [respon-
sible government] off," as J.M.S. Careless observes, "all unintentionally, helped instead
to bring it on within the decade." J.M.S. Careless, "The Place, the Office, the Times, and
the Men," in *The Pre-Confederation Premiers*, 7. The Receiver General, meanwhile,
continued to be appointed under Warrant signed by the Treasury "because such instru-
ments are issued on their Lordships advice." GGO, R.G. 7 G 1, Vol. 97, "Copy," Trevelyan
to Stephens, 14 May 1841, included in Despatch No. 383, Russell to Sydenham, 25 May
1841. Macaulay, on the other hand, preferred the backrooms of power and always avoided
the more public role of electoral politics. Although he successfully resisted pressure from
both Arthur and Sydenham, Macaulay eventually resigned as Inspector General in early
1842 because he refused to run for a seat in the Legislative Assembly. See Fraser, "John
Macaulay," 521.

81.   *The Arthur Papers*, Vol. 2, "Confidential," Thomson to Lord John Russell, 15 December 1839, 347.

82.   NAC, R.G. 7 G 12, Vol. 57, 289–294, cited in J. E. Hodgetts, *Pioneer Public Service:
An Administrative History of the United Canadas, 1841–1867* (Toronto, 1955), 27.

83.   See Finance, R.G. 19, Vol. 1155, Joshua Bates, John Cryder, George Carr Glyn,
and J. Horsley Palmer, Creditors, "Statement of Assets," 25 March 1841, and [?] Wilson
to Dunn, 2 July 1841.

84.   *Ibid.*, Thomas Murdoch, Chief Secretary, Governor General's Office, to Dunn,
12 August 1841, Dunn to Wilsons, 16 August 1841, Dunn to Glyns, 18 August 1841,
Glyn Mills Papers, M.G. 24 D 36, "Warrant," 18 August 1841, and Dunn to Glyns,
18 August 1841. Also see Finance, R.G. 19, Vol. 1141, Wilsons to Dunn, 4 October 1841.

85.   Finance, R.G. 19, Vol. 1155, Glyns to Dunn, 3 March 1843, and Glyns to William
Morris, Receiver General, 19 May 1845.

86.   Finance, R.G. 19, Vol. 1165, T. Douglas Harrington, Deputy Receiver General, to
Glyns, 16 August and 6 September 1861. This final payment is not recorded in the Wilson
and Company account book in the Receiver General's records. See Finance, R.G. 19,
Vol. 1159, "The Hon. John H. Dunn, H.M. Receiver General of the Province of Upper
Canada in Account with Messrs. Thomas Wilson and Co," 6.

87.   See above, note 10.

88.   Finance, R.G. 19, Vol. 1173, B. Turquand, 1st Clerk, RGO, to Joseph, 18 May and
19 May 1837.

89.   See *ibid.*, Dunn to Joseph, 11 April and 27 April 1837, Turquand to Joseph,
13 May and 19 May 1837, Turquand to Thos. Ridout, Cashier, Bank of Upper Canada,
7 June 1837, Turquand to Joseph, 7 June, 26 June, and 27 June 1837, Turquand to
Benjamin Holmes, Cashier, Bank of Montreal, 27 June 1837, Turquand, RGO, "Circular,"
11 July 1837, and Turquand to Forsyth, Richardson and Co., 14 July 1837.

90.   Finance, R.G. 19, Vol. 1138, Dunn to Stephens, 22 June 1837, and Dunn to Barings,
30 June 1837, and NAC, *Baring Papers*, M.G. 24 D 21, Vol. 1, Dunn to Barings, 30 June

1837. Dunn commented that these new loans were for a series of projects in various towns and districts and were secured "by taxation upon the Inhabitants through the medium of the Magistrate in General Quarter Sessions." With time the creation of more appropriate local authorities with taxation powers and the shifting of responsibility for local public works would become a critical element in the new financial arrangements of the province. See below, Chapter 3, 75–76.

91.   See Finance, R.G. 19, Vol. 1173, B. Turquand to Joseph, 26 May and 15 June 1837, Turquand to Ridout, 17 June and 4 July 1837, Turquand to Joseph, 7 July 1837, Turquand to John S. Cartwright, President, Commercial Bank of the Midland District, 11 July 1837, Turquand to William Hamilton Merritt, 12 July 1837, Turquand to Cartwright, 18 July 1837, Turquand to Ridout, 27 July 1837.

92.   NAC, Executive Council Office (ECO), R.G. 1 E 1, State Book J, Vol. 54, Minutes, 21 July 1837, and 27 July 1837, 587–589. Turquand had circulated a notice for tenders on £117,500 stg worth of debentures.

93.   Finance, R.G. 19, Vol. 1154, Barings to Dunn, 19 September 1837, and Finance, R.G. 19, Vol. 1180, Turquand to Barings, 11 August 1837.

94.   Dunn believed far more money would be realized if the province sold the debentures in London and then sold sterling Bills of Exchange. He was optimistic that bonds could be sold at par or better, although the quotation in London at the time was closer to 94. See Finance, R.G. 19, Vol. 1173, Dunn to Macaulay, 19 June 1838.

95.   See *ibid.*, Dunn to Joseph, 2 October 1837, and Finance, R.G. 19, Vol. 1180, Dunn to Barings, 23 October 1837. Dunn later forwarded a complete list of all sterling debentures sold in Canada. See Finance, R.G. 19, Vol. 1173, Dunn to Joseph, 14 December 1837.

96.   Finance, R.G. 19, Vol. 1154, Bosauquet and Company to Barings, 18 October 1837, and Barings to Bosauquets, 19 October 1837.

97.   *Ibid.*, Barings to Dunn, 14 October and 19 October 1837.

98.   *Ibid.*, Barings to Dunn, 6 December 1837 and 1 January 1838.

99.   See Finance, R.G. 19, Vol. 1151 [Joseph] Government House to the Honble [sic] the Receiver General, 21 March 1838.

100. See "Schedule of Government Debentures redeemed and outstanding issued under Authority of Acts of the provincial Legislature [Upper Canada]," Public Accounts, Appendix B, *Appendix to the Journals of the Legislative Assembly*, 4–5 Vic. 1841. This brought the total amount of debentures sold in Series BB to £269,500 stg. Also see Finance, R.G. 19, Vol. 1173, Dunn, RGO, "Circular," to Bank of Upper Canada, Commercial Bank of the Midland District, and the Bank of British North America, 20 April 1838, Dunn to Joseph, 28 April 1838, Dunn to A. Stephen, Cashier, Gore Bank, 28 April 1838, Dunn to Joseph, 12 May, 25 May, and 29 May 1838, Dunn to Stephen, 31 May 1838, Dunn to Joseph, 6 June 1838, Dunn to Stephen, 8 June 1838, Dunn to Macaulay, 23 June 1838; Finance, R.G. 19, Vol. 1180, Dunn to Barings, 20 March, 3 April, 1 May, 15 June, 2 July, 9 July, and 10 July 1838.

101. Finance, R.G. 19, Vol. 1154, "Duplicate," Barings to Dunn, 14 June 1838.

102. Finance, R.G. 19, Vol. 1180, Dunn to Barings, 11 August 1838.

103. Finance, R.G. 19, Vol. 1175, Dunn to Macaulay, 1 August 1838. Also see Finance, R.G. 19, Vol. 1151, Joseph to the Receiver General, 6 August 1838.

104. Finance, R.G. 19, Vol. 1175, Dunn to Macaulay, 8 July 1838. This letter seems to be misdated. Its placement in the letterbooks of the Department as well as the logic of the events would indicate the date should be 8 August rather than July.

105. Finance, R.G. 19, Vol. 1175, Dunn to Macaulay, 28 September 1838. Also see Finance, R.G. 19, Vol. 1140, R. A. Tucker, Provincial Secretary, to Dunn, 16 March 1840, and "Draft," Dunn to Tucker, 17 March 1840.

106. *The Arthur Papers*, Vol. 1, Macaulay to Hagerman, 21 April 1838, 84–87.

107. Of the £10,000 cy loans raised in 1839, all had been authorized in 1837 and were placed in small amounts domestically, often to contractors in lieu of other payment.

108. *The Arthur Papers*, Vol. 1, Macaulay to Hagerman, 21 April 1838, 84–87.

Chapter 2
Financing the Union:
The Solution

With respect to the financial state of the
Province, Your Excellency [Thomson] is
aware that it is under the greatest
embarrassment, and that, without some
support from England, there is no prospect
of a better state of things.
Yet, depressing as the fiscal condition of
the Province now is, the debt would be
nothing if the resources were fully
brought into action.
— Sir George Arthur, 1839[1]

There is considerable truth to W. A. Mackintosh's observation that "[p]ioneers are by necessity and selection sanguine people. They are prone to take over-optimistic views of the effects of such community investment in future income and to assume that government guarantees may be obtained at no cost."[2] Still pioneers in 1841, British North Americans refused to allow the financial travail of Upper Canada to dampen their optimism. They continued to believe that canals were not only necessary but would with time be self-financing. Only occasionally could cynics like R. B. Sullivan be found suggesting that

> [t]he period when the Welland Canal and Saint Lawrence Canal will yield a revenue equal to the annual interest of the money expended on their construction is itself sufficiently remote. I do not conceive that for generations to come they will also restore the principal much less produce a surplus fund.[3]

More typical were the sanguine views contained in the 1841 estimates submitted to the Legislative Assembly by Hamilton Killaly, the newly appointed head of the Board of Works. Killaly grouped projects into three classes. The first class consisted of those works of purely a national character, and which are indispensable to the advancement of the Commercial and Agricultural interests of the Country at large and from which the prospective revenue may be calculated upon, with certainty, to pay the interest of the necessary expenditure.[4]

Such works included the Welland and St. Lawrence canals. If British North Americans supported union for a variety of reasons, in the minds of many one was paramount. Union provided a means for pursuing public works programmes.

Although all British North Americans wanted internal improvements, they were never unanimous in their support for each individual project.[5] On occasion some observers even recognized duplication in the system of transportation improvements. R. B. Sullivan, for example, considered the St. Lawrence canals extravagant and wasteful. Millions would be spent completing a work that "merely established a rival canal to the Rideau."[6] Visions of future wealth, however, could sway the most cynical. Killaly, for example, counted himself among those who "doubted the prudence" of the St. Lawrence canals, but by 1841 he had become a consistent supporter of the project. "The vastly increasing trade, doubling almost annually," he suggested, combined with "the productiveness of the Western Countries," would undoubtedly "increase still further this Trade to an almost inconceivable extent." This, he concluded, "convinced me that a second and more facile outlet is called for."[7] Perhaps being appointed as head of the Board of Works, charged with supervising the work, also helped convince Killaly of the wisdom of the programme.

The Province of Canada in 1841 was a sparsely populated string of settlements stretching the entire length of the St. Lawrence/ Great Lakes water system. In Upper Canada in particular, settlers were just beginning to penetrate inland townships behind those fronting the shores of the lower lakes and major rivers. Here was a vast territory which businessmen, colonial politicians, and imperial authorities wanted to open up for settlement, trade, and profit. If the current population could not generate sufficient traffic to justify large expenditures on canals, surely the future population would. "These works," as Charles Poulett Thomson assured Lord John Russell, "cannot fail to produce a Return when completed."[8]

The increase in trade was not expected to come from domestic sources alone. There was an even larger population settling on the south side of the lower lakes. Dreams of capturing the American trade had always lain behind commercial demands for canal projects, as they would later lead to demands for railway systems.[9] Such expectations consistently moved Legislative Assemblies. They could also sway Governors, who in turn willingly lobbied the Colonial Office. Imperial authorities were also interested in facilitating trade if it meant, as Sir George Arthur believed it would, expanding markets for British manufactured exports as well as trade for Canada.[10]

The Colonial Office would also listen to military arguments for the canals. Military concerns in the aftermath of the 1812 conflict convinced the imperial government to bear the cost of the Rideau Canal.[11] Border disturbances in 1838 convinced some that a military threat still existed. Without improvements to the Welland Canal, John Macaulay argued, British forces would be unable "to command both Lakes Erie and Ontario." Macaulay believed the Americans were already laying plans to attack the Welland, itself proof of the military importance of that canal.[12] Acknowledging particular vulnerability in Lake Erie, Lieutenant-Governor Arthur recognized the importance of the Welland, as well as the inability of Upper Canada to complete this work on its own. Arthur went so far as to suggest to Sir John Colborne that the work be undertaken "as part of the Military defence of the Province, & defrayed by H. M. Govt. [sic]."[13]

The military argument was not pressed, perhaps because it would not bear scrutiny. The central requirement underlying Macaulay's muddled military thinking was a system of canals that allowed ocean-going steamers — both commercial and military — to sail into both Lake Erie and Lake Ontario. With this in mind, proposals to refurbish the Welland called for reconstructed locks with at least 10-foot draughts. Even 10-foot draughts, as Killaly observed, would not accommodate ocean steamers and were "unnecessary for those well suited to the Lakes, and to the commerce of the Country." From a military point of view, Killaly conceded, larger locks would be a great advantage, but one "quite beyond the means of the Province."[14] When completed, the system would not accommodate military vessels beyond Montreal.

Other more important advantages, however, would accrue from canal construction. Post-Napoleonic Britain had a "surplus" population. The enclosure movement was entering its final intense stage, coincident with a capital-intensive stage of industrialization that eliminated jobs for countless thousands of hand-loom weavers and other artisans. As Captains Ludd and Swing disturbed the towns and countryside, authorities looked to emigration to the colonies to provide a critical social safety valve. Lord Durham was sent to investigate the rebellions, but it was no accident that he spent a considerable part of his time and no small portion of his report talking about the problems of land disposal and emigration.[15] Emigration and public works were intimately related.

Lord Sydenham would make the linkage explicit in his 1841 Speech from the Throne. On that occasion he announced his intention to pursue a vigorous public works programme and to seek an imperial guarantee for a new Canadian loan.

> In immediate connexion with the outlay of capital upon public works is the subject of Emigration, and the disposal and settlement of public land. There exist within the Province no means so certain of producing a healthy flow of Immigration from the Mother Country, and of ultimately establishing the Immigrant as a settler and proprietor within the colony, as the power of affording sure employment for his labor on his first arrival. The assistance of [the imperial] Parliament, for the Public Works which may be undertaken here, will in a great measure provide for this.[16]

Lord John Russell also believed the greatest block to emigration remained "the difficulty in finding employment for Emigrants on their arrival in British North America."[17] Public works spending would, Bagot suggested in 1842, provide "employment for almost any number of Emigrants" for several years to come.[18]

Public works projects certainly promoted immigration during the 1840s, although it is not clear if the result was the kind of agricultural settlement Sydenham and others had in mind. His successor, Sir Charles Bagot, was more circumspect and pointed to the difficulties faced by "Emigrants who come here merely as Labourers without any previous knowledge of agriculture or any Mechanical Trade." Bagot was "disposed to dissuade rather than encourage the emigration of this class,"[19] and experience, he believed, confirmed his views. He argued that "[l]ittle good has arisen from giving employment upon the public works to the laborers or to the country." Rather than promoting agricultural settlement, the work on the canals attracted only "persons ... committed to an unsettled and wandering life."[20]

In spite of Bagot's more critical views and the very real problems faced by the immigrants themselves, the Colonial Office remained favourably disposed to public works projects which claimed to promote immigration and agricultural settlement. As late as 1847 Earl Grey commented that, if railways, canals, and other public works could be devised in order to provide employment for immigrant labour,

> Her Majesty's Servants will not be slow to propose nor judging from the opinions generally expressed would Parliament be slow to sanction the employment of the pecuniary resources of the Country [Britain] in furtherance of such an object.[21]

Such considerations led to a British promise to guarantee new Canadian loans in 1839 but very little support after that date, despite Earl Grey's comments.

By 1839 Upper Canadians saw only one way out of their financial troubles: assistance from the Colonial Office. They could find many reasons why the imperial government should come to their aid and had no difficulty convincing Governor Generals. Yet the Colonial Office resisted. As late as July 1839 J. B. Robinson, for one, began to despair of any help from the mother country. Lord Normanby seemed willing, but, according to Robinson, "he met with no disposition whatever on the part of his Colleagues to second his suggestions either as regards the imposition of duties to be levied at Quebec, or to contract a loan, in order to relieve us from the present pressure of our debt."[22] Robinson's pessimism proved unwarranted; within the month the Cabinet would commit itself to aid the colonial government.

The Colonial Office sympathized, but was not moved by arguments for trade, for emigration, or even for military protection. It had, however, already decided that a political union — or "re-union," as Thomson insisted — of Upper and Lower Canada would help solve many of the political problems that had lately provoked rebellion in the colonies. In 1838 a Bill to accomplish this had been introduced into the British Parliament, but had been withdrawn when the Upper Canadian Assembly protested vehemently against being joined to the Lower province. Arthur would later comment that the initial defeat resulted from the combination of factions "of the most opposite views and of the most adverse intentions." He was convinced that a proposal for union could be carried in the Assembly, although not as originally framed.[23] Upper Canada would need some incentive.[24]

Lord Melbourne chaired a Cabinet meeting in August 1839, one attended by Charles Poulett Thomson, at which it was agreed to submit

> to Parliament a proposal to guarantee a Loan to Upper Canada or to the United Provinces for the purpose of diminishing the Interest on the Debt and of continuing the Public Works, of a sum not exceeding £1,500,000 (One million and a half sterling).[25]

Thomson was being sent to North America to achieve a legislative union of the two Canadian colonies,[26] and the promised assistance would be "discretionary on the part of the Governor-General and only to be used in order to obtain the consent of the Provinces to what may be deemed by him a final and satisfactory settlement."[27] As expected the proposal for an imperial guarantee on new loans proved its worth in winning Upper Canadian consent for the union. Nearly everyone would get what they sought: the British would get a union, Thomson would get his peerage, and Upper Canada would get its loan. Lower Canada, meanwhile, would be saddled with the Upper Canadian debt, a point raised by John Nielson in the debate over Sydenham's loan bill.[28]

When Sir George Arthur recommended that assistance be extended to Upper Canada, he did not specify whether it should be used to liquidate the existing debt or to promote new public works. He did, however, stress that the province must be freed from "that pecuniary pressure, which, without assistance, must terminate in Colonial bankruptcy."[29] After his arrival in Canada, Thomson also became convinced that the loan was indeed "absolutely necessary," although he made no specific proposal until February 1841.[30] Thomson, now Lord Sydenham, suggested that a cash grant to the colony "would be a wise economy," yet it is clear he did not expect the imperial government to go this far. He estimated the existing debt at more than £1.2 million stg, which had been accumulated almost entirely on public works projects. Like so many others, Sydenham believed these canals would eventually pay for themselves, but additional expenditures to expand and update the system would be required. New money could be raised only at exorbitant interest rates of 8 or 10 per cent or by selling debentures at substantial discounts. Between April 1839 and August 1840 Barings had been able to sell only £10,200 stg worth of Canadian 5 per cent debentures at prices ranging from 87 to 91.[31] An attempt to market a large issue would undoubtedly drive the price down further.

Sydenham proposed that the Treasury issue £1.5 million stg colonial debentures, the interest on which would be guaranteed by the imperial government. The proceeds would then be used "first to the liquidation at par of the Canadian Debt and the residue for the completion of such public works as might be deemed expedient."[32] Since the new debentures would pay 4 per cent interest as opposed to 5 and 6 per cent on the outstanding bonds, the cost of servicing the debt and thus the expenditures of the provincial government would be substantially reduced. The effective rate of interest would be even less since the imperial guarantee would likely ensure that the new debentures would sell at premiums. Under this scheme holders of old Canadian securities would "be compelled to receive their money at par or new stock at a price proportionate to it." Those who accepted new debentures with their lower interest rates would be more than compensated by receiving full par value for 5 per cent debentures quoted in the market at 75 to 80 and 6 per cents quoted at 85 to 90. Sydenham doubted if these debentures were "salable at all," or that their value would ever rise to par without the new guaranteed loan.[33]

Sydenham knew that additional expenditures would be required if the dream of a revenue-generating transportation system along the St. Lawrence were ever to be realized. With the guaranteed loan used to redeem old debentures, the province would still be required to raise money to complete its canal system. Sydenham believed that the balance between the existing debt and the new £1.5 million stg loan should be used to promote additional construction. For the rest, he put his faith in the beneficial effects his scheme would have upon Canadian credit in general. Redemption of the outstanding debt at par would, he believed, restore investor confidence in the province and allow it to raise new loans as needed at lower rates of interest.[34] Although the question of these additional loans later proved critical, for the moment all signs pointed to the quick acceptance of Sydenham's proposals.

In May 1841 Russell, in anticipation of the opening of the Canadian parliamentary session, informed Sydenham that the British government was

> ready to propose to Parliament to guarantee a Loan which may be required for public works, (under the restrictions suggested by you) for the repayment of the debt as may be now redeemable, or may be held by creditors who declare themselves willing to accept reasonable terms.[35]

Russell clearly had endorsed Sydenham's financial plans.

In his Speech from the Throne in June 1841 Sydenham announced that the British government would guarantee a £1.5 million stg loan for the province "for the double purpose of diminishing the pressure of the interest on the Public Debt, and of enabling it to proceed with those great public undertakings."[36] In September, when the Assembly debated Sydenham's Bill, the question of whether or not the money should be used to refinance the debt or finance new construction did not arise; members debated only — and that very briefly — the justice of having Lower Canadians charged for the Upper Canadian debt.[37] The Act, 4–5 Vic. cap. 33, which was sent to London for Colonial Office approval, accurately reflected Sydenham's proposals outlined to Russell in February. Fate then intervened to alter governments and their policies. Sydenham first resigned and then died, while a change in government in Britain delayed approval of the Act. The Treasury, meanwhile, had decided to re-evaluate the entire scheme.

When Sir Charles Bagot assumed his post as Governor General in Canada, one of the first problems he confronted was the as yet unfulfilled promise to guarantee the interest on Canada's new loan. With apparently little reflection, but basing his opinion on political rather than economic considerations, Bagot urged immediate action by the imperial government. The delay occasioned by Lord Stanley's rise at the Colonial Office had created, according to Bagot, considerable anxiety in the colony. Sydenham's Act authorized the Governor to name agents to handle the loan, and, although it was not the usual procedure, Bagot suggested the Lords Commissioners of the Treasury should immediately negotiate the loan.[38] He was more explicit in his confidential despatches, observing that even the hint of a British government decision to renege on its pledge of assistance would prove "fatal to our hopes of governing them [the Canadians] successfully." He believed that prompt action would allow him to defeat the opposition in the Assembly in the coming struggle over the civil list.[39] Bagot also explained his reasons for wanting the Treasury to handle the loan:

> If an Officer is to be selected here it would be impossible to pass over the Receiver General Mr. Dunn, yet from all I have seen and from what I can learn of him I could not conscientiously entrust to his discretion so important a task.

Bagot added rhetorically, "how is it possible for me to find any one here known on the London money market, or who might be a match for the persons with whom he would have to deal [?]"[40]

On the following day Bagot addressed a second confidential despatch to the Colonial Office, suggesting that the government itself begin speculating in Canadian debentures. He believed it might

> be very advantageous before any public steps are taken in the market that an attempt should be made quickly to purchase up to half of the Government of Canada Debentures now for sale in the London Market.

The announcement of the imperial guarantee would undoubtedly lead to a rise in the quotations for Canadian securities from the current quotations of 78 to perhaps par. Bagot was sure that "the expediency of this proceeding would have occurred to Your Lordship and the Lords of the Treasury," yet he felt it his duty to mention the plan.[41] The potential for speculative profit which Bagot saw in Sydenham's proposals had indeed occurred to Stanley and the Lords Commissioners of the Treasury; it was precisely on these grounds that the Treasury would recommend against acceptance of Sydenham's legislation.

Although the imperial government waited until April 1842 to inform Bagot officially of its intention to review its loan policy, it had briefed him on the Treasury's objections in a secret despatch earlier in February.[42] The Treasury raised two problems: the redemption of the old debt at par, and, more importantly, the loans needed to pursue new public works. This second concern was the more important because 4–5 Vic. cap. 33, Sydenham's legislation, arrived at the Colonial Office accompanied by 4–5 Vic. cap. 28, which authorized new loans for more than £1.6 million to be raised over the next several years for canal construction. Bagot estimated public works expenditures in 1842 would be between £150,000 and £180,000 and a similar amount would be required in 1843. Under Sydenham's scheme this money would come initially from the estimated surplus of £274,000 stg which remained from the £1.5 million stg guaranteed loan once the old debt had been redeemed at par. C. E. Trevelyan at the Treasury, and eventually Lord Stanley, believed that it would be far better to use the new guaranteed loan for the projected new public works rather than for the redemption of old debts, only to generate new debts.[43]

Stanley, in an interesting bit of sophistry, reviewed the various exchanges between Sydenham and the Colonial Office and concluded that what the Canadian government was now proposing was very different from what Sydenham had intended. Together the two Acts — 4–5 Vic. cap. 28 for new canal construction and 4–5 Vic. cap. 33 for the guaranteed loan — would require loans totalling £3.2 million stg, considerably more than contemplated by previous British governments. Stanley believed that Sydenham originally intended to reduce this amount through one of his other proposals, the "Issue of Paper payable on demand," a policy he later abandoned, and by his changes in the customs duties. Stanley also observed that, if the province had had trouble raising money at 6 to 8 per cent in the past, he could see no reason to expect a lower rate of interest in the future. In addition, he questioned the wisdom of redeeming at par debentures that had a nominal market value of 75 to 80.

On the advice of the Treasury, Stanley rejected the Canadian proposals:

> Her Majesty's Government are of opinion that it would be inexpedient to interpose the credit of [the Mother] Country between the Province and the creditors under the existing Debt, and that it is more for the advantage of the Province that the aid to be rendered should be applied exclusively to the promotion of the [intended Public] Works than to effecting any reduction in the interest of the Debt as it stands at present.[44]

Stanley advised that the province pass new legislation to this effect which would include a provision for the creation of a sinking fund "at the rate of not less than 5 per cent per annum of the principal."[45] Bagot initially felt this new policy to be less advantageous to both the province and the British government, but upon reflection he quickly changed his mind.[46] This change of heart proved short-lived as Bagot faced political pressures in the colony which favoured the original Sydenham proposal. As a result he again changed his mind and reverted to his original opinion that the Sydenham Acts "should not be interfered with."[47]

This was not a dispute between the Colonial Office and its Governor General; rather, it was between the Colonial Office and the provincial government. Sydenham had been sent to ensure the success of the Union. In so doing he had run roughshod over a number of local interests,[48] not the least of which were those of the majority party from French Canada. As Bagot explained,

> The means which Lord Sydenham had resorted to, in order to carry and complete the measure [Union], may have been absolutely necessary — but they involved a public, and something very like a private quarrel on his part with the whole mass of the French inhabitants . . . and it would have been totally impossible for *him* ever again to conciliate them, or indeed ever again to have met, with any prospect of success, another Parliament in this country.[49]

Bagot inherited a legacy of ill-feeling and political turmoil, much of it centring around the call for responsible government so popular among many MLAs from Canada West as well as with the opposition from Canada East. A change of policy on the guaranteed loan threatened the government's support from Upper Canada and might conceivably lead to the government's defeat in the Assembly. Bagot wanted desperately to avoid a conflict over the loan. In order to keep his political options open, he became the voice of the Executive Council at the Colonial Office rather than the voice of the Colonial Office in the colony. Although the Colonial Office would eventually get its way, the Executive Council was not without ways and means of its own to pressure London.

The Treasury's hesitations over the loan created other problems. Legislation authorizing construction on the canals had been approved on the assumption that the guaranteed loan would be negotiated without delay. As Bagot observed, contracts had been signed and work begun with money advanced by domestic banks "on the faith of the Acts passed during the last session." By August 1842 a total of £112,000 cy had been borrowed, of which only £15,000 had been repaid. The outstanding debt — all of it at 6 per cent secured only by the promissory note of the Receiver General — stood at £97,000 cy.[50] Delay now would produce financial embarrassment, the closing of construction sites, and extensive unemployment. Bagot believed that the Treasury would have to make a special advance to the province.[51] Stanley's response was as diplomatic as it was ambiguous, if not contradictory. He announced the Colonial Office's acceptance of 4–5 Vic. cap. 28 and suggested that there was no reason why work should not proceed on the canals. At the same time he reserved 4–5 Vic. cap. 33 and warned against any expectation that the British government would support a loan above the promised £1.5 million stg. He also repeated his belief that the £1.5 million guaranteed loan should be used only for public works construction. Stanley seemed to concede ground when he suggested that the British government was "not prepared to press them [its views on the loan] further than to direct you to bring the question before the Canadian Legislature, and to invite their deliberate consideration of the whole subject,"[52] but few could miss his intention to see the Treasury's proposals adopted.

There can be little doubt that the Executive Council preferred Sydenham's original legislation, yet the changes proposed by the Treasury and the Colonial Office were minor. In both 1834 and 1836 loans intended to refinance existing debts had in the end been redirected to new canal construction without the interference of the imperial government. Having proceeded thus in the past, there was little reason to believe that anyone could be terribly upset about the changes being introduced in 1842. Moreover, the underlying issue was the province's financial needs which could not be solved without the imperial guarantee. If the province wanted both solvency and canals, any resistance to such minor changes would have been both foolish and foolhardy.

The Colonial Office had prevaricated and delayed the granting of the imperial guarantee; it had then forced a minor change of policy on the province. The province would accept the change. It also took some unconventional measures of its own to ensure the imperial government delayed no longer. The Assembly had passed its original legislation in September 1841, and in 1842 work began on the canals. With the delay in London, contractors could not be paid. Facing default in August 1842 the provincial government issued drafts on the Treasury. Bagot was "not blind to the objections to this course" but felt he had no other option but to sign the unauthorized drafts. In explaining his reasons he noted that advances from Canadian banks hurt commerce by reducing available capital and restricting "their accommodation to the public."[53] In a "private" despatch Bagot also noted his political difficulties. He would be "exposed to great embarrassment," when the Legislature opened on 8 September, "if I were not able to shew [sic] that I had adopted some measure to relieve the Banks and the public from the difficulties in which I have been the means of placing them."[54]

Against these unauthorized drafts the Receiver General would sell Bills of Exchange to domestic banks "so as to discharge the debts due each of them."[55] This did not in itself solve the problem. By October only £7,000 was left in the government's hands against which there remained a debt of £10,000 owed the City Bank. More importantly, funds for public works were again exhausted and, unless the guaranteed loan was negotiated, the government would again have to solicit unsecured loans from domestic banks.[56] The government negotiated the first of a series of such short-term loans — £20,000 each from the Banks of Montreal and Upper Canada at 90 days — in October. By November it was anticipating borrowing another £85,000. By December its newly acquired debts totalled £120,000.[57] These advances would be repaid in January 1843.[58]

The unauthorized draft on the Treasury, meanwhile, produced a sharp reprimand. Despite the rebuke the Treasury observed that new legislation providing the guarantee, 5–6 Vic. cap. 118, had recently passed the imperial parliament which, C. E. Trevelyan observed, should allay any doubts as to the intentions of the imperial government. Despite its rebuke the Treasury paid the unauthorized draft in anticipation of provincial legislation.[59] The Treasury had little choice as it could ill afford to default on a draft signed by the Governor. After spending thousands of pounds of as yet unauthorized funds, there would be little delay in getting royal assent for new legislation covering the guaranteed loan. That new legislation moved swiftly through the Canadian Legislature. The Executive Council discussed the question in late September 1842; Council was, according to Bagot, "unanimous in agreeing with me that it would be expedient to adopt the views of Her Majesty's Government." On 30 September Bagot sent an Address to the Assembly; by 10 October he was able to forward a Bill to London for imperial approval. He also "ordered" the Treasury to raise immediately £200,000, the first £107,000 of which was to cover already issued drafts. By November the province decided to issue a first instalment of £300,000 stg debentures.[60]

The imperial government's quick acceptance of new legislation had a positive effect on Canada's credit in London. By mid-November 1842 the quotation for Canadian 5 per cent debentures rose to 94–96, and Glyns reported that "these are real prices and obtainable." One month later Glyns reported the first sales of the guaranteed 4 per cent debentures at 108. The quotation for Canadian fives, meanwhile, had reached par.[61]

Between January 1843 and December 1845 the balance of the guaranteed loan was sold in London. All debentures sold for substantial premiums ranging from 108 in December 1842 to a high of 112 in December 1844.[62] The government made additional profits by selling Bills of Exchange at premiums in the province. The money was all used to pay for public works construction; outstanding debentures would run to maturity. Finally, in July 1846 the Colonial Office notified the province that it should draw the £128.1/6 stg which remained as the final instalment on the loan.[63] There would, however, be one more draw.

There remained one problem yet to be solved. The provincial government, "in compliance with the wishes of Her Majesty's Government," had passed new legislation making the proceeds of the new guaranteed loan "applicable to the Public Works."[64] The proceeds of the first sales could be used to repay unsecured advances from domestic banks which had been used to pay contracts in 1842, but proceeds could not be used to settle other accounts. Indeed, the loans as well as expenditures connected with the canals were not included within the Consolidated Revenue Fund in the Public Accounts. This left the province with no obvious way to settle its other outstanding, unsecured liabilities. Debentures would not have to be redeemed until maturity; this was far enough in the future as to cause no particular concern in the short term. Advances from Glyn, Hallifax, Mills and Company and Baring Brothers and Company were another matter. Both Glyns and Barings had advanced money in July 1837 and January 1838 to pay interest on the public debt in Britain. Some money had been remitted during 1838, but the province was still very much in arrears.

In January 1839 interest fell due again, and again Barings had to advance £10,500 to pay it. On this occasion Barings attempted to reimburse themselves by selling debentures in their hands. This raised very little money as they were able to make only two sales in January and March for a total of £2,400. They had also made these sales at substantial discounts of 91 and 92 respectively. These sales posed an interesting problem since, in the opinion of Dunn, the relevant legislation forbad sales under par. Dunn informed Macaulay and the Lieutenant-Governor that he considered these sales to be a "violation of the Law," but the matter was not pursued.[65]

The surviving records of the Inspector General's and Receiver General's Offices would suggest that, prior to the Union, the government did its best to avoid confronting all questions related to the public debt, and in June 1839 Dunn was denied permission to go to England in order to negotiate a new loan.[66] Barings, meanwhile, were becoming concerned. In July they reminded the government of their previous warning that interest payments could not be made by debenture sales. Barings had received no instructions or remittances and had now had to pay the July interest out of their own funds. As a result "our advance to your government has been considerably increased." Barings wanted information as to the government's financial plans. By October Barings remained "without any official information on the subject of the finances of the Province, and are ignorant whether any or what plans are in contemplation for the restoration of its credit." At this point the unsecured provincial debt to Barings stood at £17,000 stg. Barings reminded Dunn that they were liable as agents only for the interest on the £200,000 stg loan, and their names on other debentures had been inserted without their permission.[67] They warned that, unless adequate information arrived, "[w]e shall experience deepest regret to be unable to pay" interest on debentures when it fell due in January.[68]

The matter could be put off no longer. Dunn recommended that "all disposable Public funds in my hands should be without delay transmitted half [to] Messrs Baring Brothers and Co., and half to Messrs Hallifax, Glyn & Co. who are also greatly in advance for this government." He also recommended that both be ordered to avoid all sales below par. By the end of November Dunn sent a bill for £10,000 stg to Barings, drawn on Glyns. Two weeks later he scraped together enough money to purchase a £10,000 stg Bill of Exchange to be forwarded to Glyns. To Barings Dunn commented that "I have no doubt that your affairs will be fully [brought] before the Legislature at its next session and I hope for such results as will satisfy you and the friends of Upper Canada." To the Chief Secretary he was more pessimistic:

> I have my serious apprehensions that unless some provision is made by the Legislature beyond the ordinary Revenues of the Province to meet this interest that those houses will be left without the means of doing so perhaps this year.[69]

The £10,000 stg remitted would cover most of the January interest payment, but the Barings account remained in deficit for over £17,000 stg. Glyns, meanwhile, were owed an even larger amount. After crediting the provincial account for £28,500 received from Wilson and Company, the province still owed over £31,600 stg.[70]

With a budgetary deficit of over £50,000 cy on total revenues excluding loans of less than £110,000 cy in 1839, the province had few options. With little cash in hand it could only hope to raise money through debenture sales. To achieve this a new Act in January 1840 made previously authorized but unsold debentures worth a total of £105,000 cy payable in London. In February a second Act authorized the sale of up to £70,000 cy worth of debentures in order to repay advances to Barings and Glyns.[71] Barings claimed to be very positive and optimistic when they received information on this new legislation, but then added, "[I]t is far from desirable and must be very prejudicial to the credit of your Government, that the periodic payments in this country for the interest of its debt, should be provided by sales of its debentures, thereby cancelling one debt by the creation of another." More to the point, Barings saw "no likelihood" of being able to sell any of these debentures. Glyns reported the same thing and commented that "[i]t is surprising the apathy which exists in this market towards the securities of the Province of U.C."[72] Dunn could not have been surprised by this response since he saw little prospect of satisfactory sales. He pointed out to the Executive Council that the quotation for Canadian 5 per cent debentures then stood at only 83 and that Barings already had over £44,000 worth of unsold debentures in their hands.[73]

Thomson tried a different tack. He suggested that the Treasury advance the province £50,000 for which it would take as security the £60,000 claim on Wilson and Company.[74] The Colonial Office was not interested. Dunn had still another plan. He proposed selling the stock of the Bank of Upper Canada owned by the government. By June 1840, 1,900 shares had been sold for £24,000 cy. This allowed the government to remit £20,000 stg to cover the July 1840 interest payments,[75] but that only postponed the problem.

Of the two banking houses, Barings were the more impatient. To try to keep the provincial account at Barings from falling further in arrears when the July 1840 interest payments fell due, Dunn, as he had done the previous November, remitted a Bill of Exchange for £10,000 stg drawn on Glyns. Despite this remittance the debt still stood at £13,000 stg in October, and Barings could see no prospects for debenture sales.[76] Barings, however, did make occasional sales which produced much consternation in Toronto.

At the beginning of August 1840 Barings notified Dunn of the sale of £2,000 stg debentures at discount. Dunn had always believed that such sales were illegal and he worried that Barings would continue the practice unless specifically instructed not to do so. Earlier, in March 1840, he had penned a letter to Barings demanding to know upon what authority they had previously sold debentures under par, but on that occasion he had been overruled and the letter was never sent. The Executive Council took the matter under consideration on 3 September and instructed Dunn to inform Barings that they were not to sell debentures in their hands under par.[77] Dunn, however, declined:

> I feel unwilling to take upon myself the responsibility of communicating or transmitting the Order-in-Council for the information and guidance of these Gentlemen without authority so to do, from the circumstances that this Province is largely indebted for advances made to sustain the credit of Upper Canada without the means of paying that debt off and fearful that Messrs Baring & Co. might feel from the observation made, a desire to relinquish their agency which would embarrass the Government in its present situation and produce difficulty without the means of meeting the same.

Dunn would only act on the "express direction" of the Lieutenant-Governor.[78]

Sydenham, meanwhile, was no more willing to confront the issue. He believed that the sales were legal as the various Acts had not specified a sale price. He added that "after all 88 for 5 pct. stock, in our condition ... is no such bad affair." Later, when Sullivan submitted a legal opinion that such sales were indeed illegal, Arthur commented to Sydenham that "still, it may be as well, under all circumstances not to interfere, and, perhaps it may be more convenient to withdraw my reference to you upon the subject." He also noted that, since Barings and Glyns reported they were unable to make any further sales, the matter was not worth pressing.[79] Here the matter stood until March 1841. After the declaration of the Union of Upper and Lower Canada Dunn recommended that Barings suspend further sales of Upper Canadian debentures. On this occasion Dunn commented that

> I am not authorized to make this communication to you but I have been aware for a long time past that the Debentures ought not, according to law to have been disposed of under par, but as I invariably reported the sales from time to time to the government and not having had any direction on the subject, I did not consider myself authorized to write you thereon.[80]

The issue, as Arthur had observed, did not justify a confrontation with Barings since the amounts involved were so minor.

As the date for union approached, the debt to Glyns had been reduced somewhat but that to Barings had increased marginally. The financial situation had been spelled out in mid-October 1840. Cash in hand, plus probable income to 31 December, less probable expenditures on both the Consolidated Revenue and Crown Funds, gave the Receiver General £49,000 cy. Against this stood £14,500 stg due Barings, £22,000 stg due Glyns and £21,000 stg interest on the public debt, due on 1 January 1841. At 12.5 per cent exchange rate this added up to £71,800 cy. There remained the £60,000 stg claim on Wilsons, but no one expected relief from that quarter except, apparently, Dunn.[81] Thus, despite the improvement in revenues in 1840, the financial picture had not substantially improved.

Neither Barings nor Glyns, however, were yet ready to foreclose. Both remained surprisingly patient because both well understood that the Union would improve the financial prospects of the colony and that the imperial government had already committed itself to guaranteeing a new loan. As Dunn explained in February 1840,

> You are aware no doubt that a Union of the two provinces of Upper and Lower Canada is contemplated and should it take place, both provinces will share the Debt of this, and in Lower Canada there is no Debt at all.

I cannot conceive of any better security and which should afford ample and sufficient confidence to the holders of Upper Canada Debentures.[82]

Barings later commented that they were willing to advance money on the assurance that "the finances of the Province will shortly be placed on a proper footing."[83] Glyns, too, were glad that the finances of the new Union would soon "come under discussion" so "as to relieve us of our present advance, which has acquired an amount and permanency certainly beyond what we had anticipated."[84] They were also more patient because throughout 1841 the province had been able to regularly remit enough funds so that the outstanding balance did not substantially increase.[85] The province, meanwhile, was as anxious to clear these debts as Barings and Glyns.

As originally intended, the proceeds of the guaranteed loan would have been used for this purpose, but with the new legislation in late 1842 this was not possible. Despite the improved financial conditions of the Union, little cash remained to clear these debts. The new Inspector General, Francis Hincks, had another option.[86] Without cash and unable to use the proceeds of the guaranteed loan, Hincks ordered Barings and Glyns to sell at not less than par £30,000 stg worth of the debentures in their hands and to use the proceeds to settle the provincial account.[87] He then used government funds to create a market for these debentures. Hincks ordered the Bank of England to sell Consols[88] held on account of the Clergy Reserve Fund and to use the proceeds to buy £57,800 stg worth of provincial debentures.[89] The province thus became its own creditor.

The proposed operation would not proceed without difficulty for the Clergy Reserve Fund and its use had become a matter of dispute before Hincks became Inspector General. In 1840 Upper Canada had questioned Britain's policy of investing proceeds from land sales intended for the Military Chest in imperial rather than provincial securities.[90] Most of the moneys in the Clergy Reserve Fund, the Crown Reserve Fund, and the Indian Fund held at the Bank of England had been invested in imperial securities, usually Consols. In 1842 the Executive Council ordered the Receiver General to invest funds held at the Bank of England in provincial securities. Although accepting in principle that the province controlled these funds, the Treasury refused to act, arguing that the instructions and despatches in their hands could not be considered Orders-in-Council. More was involved than a legal technicality, for the Treasury advised that no action be taken "until the important questions now pending respecting the Finances of Canada shall have been settled."[91]

In late 1842 the government again ordered the transfer of funds from Consols to provincial debentures; again Stanley reported his agreement with the Canadian position, but again the Treasury delayed acting. According to the Treasury, the contemplated purchase of provincial 5 per cent debentures was unwise since the speculation about the use of the imperial guaranteed loan had led to a recent rise in quotations for 5 per cent debentures from 92 to 95.[92] Indeed, it was this speculation that forced a change in policy for the guaranteed loan.[93] Only after the province passed new legislation covering the guaranteed loan did the Treasury begin selling Consols and buying Canadian debentures. The first transactions involved the debentures held by Barings and Glyns as security for their advances to the province.[94]

A similar debate unfolded with regard to the Indian Fund, but here Stanley suggested that the Indians must be consulted before the funds could be shifted from Consols to provincial securities.[95] Not until late 1845 did the Treasury approve the transfer of the Indian Fund to provincial debentures.[96]

Despite the delay, the province's absolute control over these funds had been firmly established. During the 1840s and beyond, the provincial government continued to use its control over various trust accounts to help facilitate financial operations by periodically investing such funds, including moneys held in the Sinking Fund, in provincial rather than imperial securities.[97] In the process the province had first taken direct responsibility for moneys under its control and then designed a financial policy to maximize the return to the province.

By 1843, then, the various financial problems which had plagued Upper Canada since 1837 appeared to have been solved. Administrative reforms had lodged control of financial administration in the hands of the Executive Council. During the first years of the Union, the Executive Council began defining financial and economic policies with a view to ensuring maximum return to the province. Part of this process allowed the government to pay off outstanding advances to Barings and Glyns with investment funds controlled by the government. The Union, together with the return of economic prosperity, also ensured that healthy surpluses began to accumulate in the Consolidated Revenue Fund. Its stronger fiscal position allowed the government to meet its various obligations without resort to further advances from its financial agents in Britain. Questions about the use of the guaranteed loan produced short-term difficulties, but the final resolution of this problem ensured that canal construction proceeded rapidly. This in turn stimulated immigration and economic growth. Despite the government's improved fiscal circumstances, however, the province was rushing headlong towards a new crisis.

Notes

1.   *The Arthur Papers*, Vol. 2, Arthur to Thomson, 9 November 1838, 304.

2.   W. A. Mackintosh, *The Economic Background of Dominion–Provincial Relations: A Study Prepared for the Royal Commission on Dominion–Provincial Relations* (Toronto, 1964), 14.

3.   *The Arthur Papers*, Vol. 2 [Macaulay] to [Arthur], [c.15 September 1839], 262. Arthur had asked R. B. Sullivan to draft a despatch to the Colonial Office on the proposed union. He then asked C. A. Hagerman and John Macaulay to review and comment upon Sullivan's very long draft. Either Arthur or Macaulay deleted the paragraph quoted here and substituted a much more innocuous comment on the prospects for revenue from the canals. In the end, however, the despatch was never sent. See *The Arthur Papers*, Vol. 2, footnotes 1 and 2, 238–239.

4.   Hamilton H. Killaly, Board of Works, "Memoranda: Respecting various Public Works heretofore in progress, or projected in the Province of Canada; shewing [sic] the ultimate cost of their completion, and the amount of the appropriations proposed to be apportioned thereto, for the several years respectively," 12 August 1841, Appendix CC, *Appendix to the Journals of the Legislative Assembly*, 4–5 Vic. 1841.

5.   By lumping all projects together, legislative approval was virtually guaranteed. In September 1841, for example, the Legislative Assembly voted 55–1 to spend nearly £1 million on various projects, including the Welland, the St. Lawrence, the Richelieu, the Ottawa, Burlington Bay, the "Waters of the Newcastle District, and various harbours and light houses." See *Debates of the Legislative Assembly*, Vol. 1, 7 September 1841, 845.

6.   *The Arthur Papers*, Vol. 1, Sullivan to the Lieutenant-Governor [Arthur], [?] May 1838, 93.

7.   Killaly, Board of Works, "Memoranda," 1841.

8.   GGO, R.G. 7 G 12, Vol. 54, Despatch No. 67, Thomson to Russell, 11 March 1840.

9.   See, for example, "Duplicate," Arthur to R. Hon. Marquess of Normanby, 25 September 1839, "Duplicate," Capt. George Philpotts, Royal Engineers, to S. B. Harrison, 12 September 1839, and extracts from C. J. Burckle [an Oswago merchant], and Benjamin Wright [an American civil engineer], included in GGO, R.G. 1 G 1, Vol. 44, Despatch No. 31, Russell to Thomson, 31 October 1839. In his discussions of railway development, G. P. de T. Glazebrook commented that the pursuit of the "will-o'-the-wisp" of American traffic lay behind transportation projects. "The traffic of the railways, therefore, was not calculated on a basis of local business." See G. P. de T. Glazebrook, *A History of Transportation in Canada* (Toronto, 1938), 151.

10.   "Duplicate," Arthur to Normanby, 25 September 1838, included in GGO, R.G. 7 G 1, Vol. 44, Despatch No. 31, Russell to Thomson, 31 October 1839.

11.   See Craig, *Upper Canada: The Formative Years, 1784–1841*, 84, 152–153, Glazebrook, *A History of Transportation in Canada*, 80–83, and Robert F. Leggett, *Rideau Waterway*, Second Edition (Toronto, 1986), 21–33.

12.   *The Arthur Papers*, Vol. 1, Macaulay to Arthur, 2 April 1838, 69.

13.   *Ibid.*, Vol. 2, Arthur to Sir John Colborne, 16 March 1839, 85–86. Sydenham also saw these canals as contributing "to the military defense of the country." See GGO, R.G. 7 G 12, Vol. 56, Despatch No. 224, Sydenham to Russell, 26 January 1841.

14. Killaly, Board of Works, "Memoranda," 1841.

15. See *Lord Durham's Report*, ed. by Gerald M. Craig (Toronto/Montreal, 1963), 110–126, passim.

16. *Debates of the Legislative Assembly*, Vol. 1, 15 June 1841, 15. Also see GGO, R.G. 7 G 12, Vol. 56, Despatch No. 224, Sydenham to Russell, 26 January 1841.

17. GGO, R.G. 7 G 1, Vol. 48, "Separate," Russell to Thomson, 19 June 1840.

18. GGO, R.G. 7 G 12, Vol. 62, "Confidential," Bagot to Stanley, 23 February 1842.

19. *Ibid.*, Despatch No. 34, Bagot to Stanley, 17 February 1842.

20. GGO, R.G. 7 G 12, Vol. 63, Despatch No. 28, Bagot to Stanley, 22 February 1843. For a discussion of labour on the canals see H. C. Pentland, "The Development of a Capitalist Labour Market in Canada," *Canadian Journal of Economics and Political Science*, XXV (1959), 450–461, and "Labour and the Development of Industrial Capitalism in Canada," unpublished Ph.D. thesis, University of Toronto, 1960; Léon Pouliot, "Un conflit ouvrier au Canal de Beauharnois en 1843," *Bulletin des recherches historiques*, LXII (1956), 149–155, and Ruth Bleasdale, "Class Conflict on the Canals of Upper Canada in the 1840s," *Labour/Le Travailleur*, VII (1981), 9–40.

21. GGO, R.G. 7 G 1, Vol. 116, Despatch No. 47, Grey to Elgin, 1 April 1847.

22. *The Arthur Papers*, Vol. 2, J. B. Robinson to Arthur, 7 July 1839, 190–192.

23. *Ibid.*, Arthur to Thomson, 9 November 1839, 300–306. Thomson had just arrived in Canada. In this letter Arthur submitted his views on a wide range of problems.

24. See Craig, *Upper Canada: The Formative Years, 1784–1841*, 270–271, and J.M.S. Careless, *The Union of the Canadas: The Growth of Canadian Institutions, 1841–1857* (Toronto, 1967), 9.

25. "Memorandum," cited in *Letters from Lord Sydenham, Governor-General of Canada, 1839–1841 to Lord John Russell*, ed. by Paul Knaplund (Clifton, New Jersey, 1973), 25, footnote 6.

26. Thomson's instructions clearly spelled out the commitment to the union. See Despatch No. 1, Russell to Thomson, 7 September 1839, in *Debates of the Legislative Assembly*, 20 August 1841, 642ff.

27. "Memorandum," cited in *Letters from Sydenham to Russell*, 25, footnote 6. Also see D. McArthur, "History of Public Finance, 1840–1867," in *Canada and its Provinces*, ed. by Adam Shortt and Arthur G. Doughty, Vol. V (Toronto, 1914), 167.

28. *Debates of the Legislative Assembly*, Vol. 1, 7 September 1841, 843. After proposing an amendment to send the whole question of the guaranteed loan back to committee, Nielson observed that Lower Canadians could not in justice be expected to pay for past Upper Canadian debts. Nielson won some Upper Canadian support as both Robert Baldwin and Sir Allan MacNab agreed, at least in part. His amendment, however, was defeated by a vote of 18–38. Reformers divided on this issue as Baldwin voted yes, but Francis Hincks voted no. Later, when the Sydenham Bill was read for the third time, Nielson introduced a similar amendment which was again defeated. The guaranteed loan eventually passed 39–9. Baldwin again joined the Lower Canadian Reformers in voting against the measure. See *ibid.*, 11 September 1841, 926–927.

29. "Duplicate," Arthur to Normanby, 25 September 1839, included in GGO, R.G. 7 G 1, Vol. 44, Despatch No. 31, Russell to Thomson, 31 October 1839.

30. GGO, R.G. 7 G 12, Vol. 54, Despatch No. 129, Thomson to Russell, 27 June 1840. In mid-1840 Thomson asked for an immediate loan of £50,000 stg. In referring the

question of the imperial loan to the Treasury Russell categorically rejected a loan to Upper Canada but reminded the Treasury of the government's previous commitment. Since Thomson had not "announced" the promised guarantee, the imperial government was "unpledged and uncommitted." Despite this, Russell continued to believe that it was "imperative on the Government" to act and concluded that he intended to introduce "such a guarantee of the actual debt of Canada as may enable the Legislature to reduce the interest now payable to a lower rate." Russell added, however, that the Governor General "was left at liberty to announce it if he thought it necessary in Canada." See GGO, R.G. 7 G 1, Vol. 51, "Copy," Russell to the Lords Commissioners of H. M. Treasury, included in Despatch No. 282, Russell to Sydenham, 11 January 1841.

31. Finance, R.G. 19, Vol. 1154, Barings to Dunn, 30 March, 30 April, 6 May, 6 June, 18 July, and 18 October 1839, and 3 August 1840.

32. GGO, R.G. 7 G 12, Vol. 56, "Confidential," Sydenham to Russell, 22 February 1841.

33. *Ibid.*

34. *Ibid.* and "Confidential," Sydenham to Russell, 25 February 1841.

35. GGO, R.G. 7 G 1, Vol. 97, Despatch No. 369, Russell to Sydenham, 3 May 1841. The most important of those restrictions was that public moneys would be spent only on projects that were "wholly and absolutely" controlled by the government. See GGO, R.G. 7 G 12, Vol. 56, "Confidential," Sydenham to Russell, 22 February 1841.

36. *Debates of the Legislative Assembly*, Vol. 1, 7 September 1841, 15.

37. *Ibid.*, 843. Although Lower Canada would now share the debt, most observers pointed out that it would also share the benefits of improved transportation facilities. It would share, too, in the revenue all expected the canals to generate. See, for example, GGO, R.G. 7 G 12, Vol. 54, Despatch No. 67, Thomson to Russell, 11 March 1840.

38. GGO, R.G. 7 G 12, Vol. 62, Despatch No. 3, Bagot to Stanley, 14 January 1842.

39. Good general accounts of the political struggles that greeted Bagot can be found in Careless, *The Union of the Canadas*, 58–74, and Jacques Monet, *The Last Cannon Shot: A Study of French-Canadian Nationalism, 1837–1850* (Toronto, 1969), 91–123.

40. GGO, R.G. 7 G 12, Vol. 62, "Confidential," Bagot to Stanley, 14 January 1842.

41. *Ibid.*, 15 January 1842. After the Treasury questioned the wisdom of redeeming depreciated debentures at par, Bagot observed that since "those Debentures were originally sold, none of them below par, and some of them at a premium, the Government has no right to expect to make a profit in their redemption." See GGO, R.G. 7 G 12, Vol. 62, Despatch No. 101, Bagot to Stanley, 6 May 1842. Buying and selling in the open market, however, was a different matter.

42. On 4 April 1842 Bagot responded to a "secret" communication from Stanley of 28 February 1842. Although I have been unable to find a copy of that "secret" despatch in the records of the Governor General's Office, it is clear from Bagot's response that Stanley had included a copy of a special report from C. E. Trevelyan at the Treasury which voiced serious reservations about the Sydenham proposals. Bagot, for his part, rejected Trevelyan's alternate suggestions, preferring the original Sydenham plan. Trevelyan's proposals, however, would become the basis of the Colonial Office's new policy. See GGO, R.G. 7 G 12, Vol. 62, "Private," Bagot to Stanley, 4 April 1842.

43. *Ibid.*

44. See GGO, R.G. 7 G 1, Vol. 101, Despatch No. 112, Stanley to Bagot, 2 April 1842.

45. *Ibid.*

46. GGO, R.G. 7 G 12, Vol. 62, Despatch No. 90, Bagot to Stanley, 28 April 1842, and Despatch No. 101, Bagot to Stanley, 6 May 1842.

47. *Ibid.* R. S. Longley suggested that Hincks was an enthusiastic supporter of Stanley's position but seems to base this conclusion on little more than Hincks' introduction of new legislation in October 1842. See R. S. Longley, "Francis Hincks and Canadian Public Finance," Canadian Historical Association, *Annual Report*, 1935, 35.

48. As Ian Radforth comments, Sydenham had prepared for elections to the first Legislative Assembly with a "sweeping gerrymander and intimidation at the polls on a scale that far outstripped even the standards of that era." Radforth, "Sydenham and Utilitarian Reform," in *Colonial Leviathan*, 74. Also see Irving Martin Abella, "The 'Sydenham Election' of 1841," *The Canadian Historical Review*, XLVII (1966), 326–341.

49. NAC, *Bagot Papers*, Bagot to Stanley, 12 June 1842, cited in Careless, *The Union of the Canadas*, 65.

50. A summary of these loans can be found in Finance, R.G. 19, Vol. 1174, Turquand to R. Rawson, Provincial Secretary, 26 August 1842. £26,000 cy of this total had been borrowed in July and September 1840, and another £21,000 in April 1841. Also see Vol. 1140, Ridout to Dunn, 22 June 1840, Vol. 1141, A. Steven, Cashier, Gore Bank, to Dunn, 15 September 1840, Ridout to Dunn, 9 September 1841, Vol. 1142, C. H. Castle, Cashier, City Bank, to Dunn, 16 June 1842, Castle to Dunn, 1 August 1842, John Frothingham, President, City Bank, to Dunn, 20 September 1842, Castle to Dunn, 31 October 1842, Finance, R.G. 19, Vol. 1175, Dunn to W. Proudfoot, President of Bank of Upper Canada, 20 June 1840, Dunn to Harrison, 22 June and 25 June 1840, and 7 April 1841, Dunn to Ridout, 4 June 1841, Dunn, "Circular" to Cashier, Montreal Bank, 15 October 1841, and Vol. 1174, Dunn to F. A. Harper, Cashier, Commercial Bank of M.D., 12 April 1842, Dunn to Sullivan, 18 April 1842, Dunn to Harrison, 5 May 1842, Dunn to Benjamin Holmes, Cashier, Bank of Montreal, 14 May and 21 May 1842, Dunn to Castle, 14 June and 20 June 1842, Dunn to Steven, 18 July 1842, Turquand to Steven, 26 July 1842, and Dunn to Holmes, 3 September 1842.

51. GGO, R.G. 7 G 12, Vol. 62, Despatch No. 101, Bagot to Stanley, 6 May 1842.

52. GGO, R.G. 7 G 1, Vol. 102, Despatch No. 190, Stanley to Bagot, 2 July 1842. As Bagot pointed out, Stanley had approved work continuing on the canals but had provided no means for paying contractors. See GGO, R.G. 7 G 12, Vol. 63, Despatch No. 162, Bagot to Stanley, 26 July 1842.

53. GGO, R.G. 7 G 12, Vol. 63, Despatch No. 183, Bagot to Stanley, 26 August 1842. Also see Vol. 63, Despatch No. 211, Bagot to Stanley, 10 October 1842. Also see Finance, R.G. 19, Vol. 1174, Dunn to Rawson, 5 October 1842, and Baskerville, *The Bank of Upper Canada*, xcvii.

54. See GGO, R.G. 7 G 12, Vol. 63, "Private," Bagot to Stanley, 26 August 1842. Longley mentions this episode but does not link it to problems encountered with the guaranteed loan. See Longley, "Francis Hincks and Canadian Public Finance," 33.

55. ECO, R.G. 1 E 1, State Book A, Vol. 61, Minute, 16 September 1842, 448.

56. See Finance, R.G. 19, Vol. 1174, Dunn to Rawson, 5 October and 7 October 1842.

57. *Ibid.*, Dunn to Holmes, 22 October 1842, Dunn to Ridout, 22 October 1842, Dunn to Holmes, 2 November 1842, Dunn to Castle, 5 November 1842, Dunn to Harper, 9 November 1842, Turquand to Holmes, 9 November 1842, Dunn to Ridout, 17 November 1842, and Dunn to Harrison, 12 December 1842. Also see ECO, R.G. 1 E 1, State Book

A, Vol. 61, Minute, 10 October 1842, 461–462, and State Book B, Vol. 62, Minutes, 22 December 1842 and 10 January 1843, 54, 87–88.

58.   See ECO, R.G. 1 E 1, State Book A, Vol. 61, Minute, 16 September 1842, 448, and State Book B, Vol. 62, Minutes, 10 January, 13 January, and 24 January 1843, 87–88, 140, 147–148. Also see Finance, R.G. 19, Vol. 1173, Dunn to Holmes, 13 January 1843, Dunn to Harrison, 17 January 1843, Dunn to Holmes, 21 January 1843, Dunn to Harrison, 26 January 1843, Dunn to Holmes, 26 January 1843, Finance, R.G. 19, Vol. 1174, Dunn to Harrison, 10 January 1843, Dunn to Ridout, 10 January and 11 January 1843, Dunn to Castle, 13 January 1843, and Dunn to Hincks, 13 January 1843.

59.   See "Copy," G. W. Hope to Trevelyan, 15 August 1842, and "Copy," Trevelyan to Hope, 23 August 1842, included in GGO, R.G. 7 G 1, Vol. 103, Despatch No. 240, Stanley to Bagot, 1 September 1842, and "Copy," Trevelyan to Stephens, 2 November 1842, included in Despatch No. 269, Stanley to Bagot, 3 November 1842. In a "Private" despatch, Stanley warned that he would not officially authorize any advances but believed there would be no problems with further drafts. See GGO, R.G. 7 G 1, Vol. 103, "Private," Stanley to Bagot, 3 November 1842. Also see GGO, R.G. 7 G 12, Vol. 63, Despatch No. 187, Bagot to Stanley, 12 September 1842. Dunn, meanwhile, had drawn £107,000 against this draft for which he received a sharp rebuke. Dunn was reminded that "the whole transaction was, as you are aware, unauthorized by the Secretary of State, and there was, therefore, a more stringent necessity for adhering to every customary form." See Finance, R.G. 19, Vol. 1151, Rawson to the Receiver General, 4 October 1842, and GGO, R.G. 7 G 12, Vol. 63, Despatch No. 196, Bagot to Stanley, 27 September 1842, and Despatch No. 210, Bagot to Stanley, 10 October 1842. Also see "Copy," Dunn to [Governor General], 5 October 1842, "Copy," Order-in-Council, 16 September 1842 and "Copy," Order-in-Council, 10 October 1842 included in Despatch No. 210, Bagot to Stanley, 10 October 1842.

60.   See GGO, R.G. 7 G 12, Vol. 63, Despatch No. 196, Bagot to Stanley, 27 September 1842, Despatch No. 211, Bagot to Stanley, 10 October 1842, Despatch No. 230, Bagot to Stanley, 8 November 1842. Much of the proceeds of this first £300,000 went to repay advances from domestic banks. See Finance, R.G. 19, Vol. 2753, Hincks to Rawson, 13 May 1843.

61.   See Finance, R.G. 19, Vol. 1155, Glyns to Dunn, 18 November and 17 December 1842. Also see GGO, R.G. 7 G 1, Vol. 103, Despatch No. 295, Stanley to Bagot, 3 December 1842. This despatch was submitted to the Executive Council in January 1843. ECO, R.G. 1 E 1, State Book B, Vol. 62, Minute, 10 January 1843, 99, 114–115, and State Book C, Vol. 63, Minute, 9 August 1843, 37.

62.   See ECO, R.G. 1 E 1, State Book B, Vol. 62, Minutes, 16 March, 24 March, and 9 May 1843, 263, 297, 428, State Book C, Vol. 63, Minute, 9 August 1843, 37, ECO, Despatches and Reports, 1841–1845, Vol. 65, Stanley to Sir Charles Metcalfe, 15 July 1843, 3 May and 27 December 1844, 135, 240–241, 356, State Book D, Vol. 64, Minute, 9 May 1845, 310, and State Book E, Vol. 66, Minute, 23 December 1845, 137.

63.   ECO, R.G. 1 E 1, State Book E, Vol. 66, Minute, 20 July 1846, 541, and GGO, R.G. 7 G 1, Vol. 113, Despatch No. 104, William E. Gladstone to Earl Cathcart, 3 July 1846.

64.   ECO, R.G. 1 E 1, State Book B, Vol. 62, Minute, 9 May 1843, 423.

65.   Finance, R.G. 19, Vol. 1154, Barings to Dunn, 12 January, 19 January, and 22 March 1839, and Finance, R.G. 19, Vol. 1175, Dunn to Macaulay, Civil Secretary, 28 February 1839. Dunn observed that a price of 91 in Britain brought more money to

the Consolidated Revenue Fund than par in Canada because of the premium on sterling exchange.

66.   When he was refused, Dunn immediately requested a six-month leave of absence to travel to England because of a death in the family. Although travelling on private matters, Dunn took the opportunity to meet with Colonial Office officials. Finance, R.G. 19, Vol. 1175, Dunn to Macaulay, 8 June and 13 June 1839, Dunn to Harrison, 24 June and 23 November 1839.

67.   See above, Chapter 1, 18.

68.   Finance, R.G. 19, Vol. 1154, Barings to Dunn, 5 July 1839 and Barings to the Receiver General, 18 October 1839.

69.   See *Ibid.*, Vol. 1175, Dunn to Harrison, 12 October 1839. It would appear that this letter is misdated in the letterbooks and should read 12 November. Also see Dunn to Barings, 16 November 1839, Dunn to Glyns, 16 November 1839, Dunn to Wilsons, 16 November 1839, Dunn to Barings, 26 November 1839, Dunn to Forsyth, Richardson and Company, 19 December 1839, and Dunn to Thomas Murdock, Chief Secretary, 8 January 1840.

70.   Finance, R.G. 19, Vol. 1155, Glyns to Dunn, 31 December 1839. In January Dunn remitted £8,000 stg but by then January interest had already fallen due. See Glyns to Dunn, 24 January and 30 January 1840.

71.   4–5 Vic. cap. 72, and 4–5 Vic. cap. 78, *Statutes of Her Majesty's Province of Upper Canada*.

72.   Finance, R.G. 19, Vol. 1154, Barings to Dunn, 30 April 1840, Vol. 1155, Glyns to Dunn, 31 March and 30 April 1840.

73.   See *Ibid.*, Vol. 1175, Dunn to William H. Lee, Acting Clerk of the Executive Council, 5 June 1840. Also see Vol. 1140, Dunn to Harrison, 21 May 1840.

74.   GGO, R.G. 7 G 12, Vol. 54, Despatch No. 129, Thomson to Russell, 27 June 1840.

75.   See Finance, R.G. 19, Vol. 1175, Dunn to Harrison, 24 March 1840, Dunn to Ridout, 3 April 1840, Dunn "Notice of Tender," 12 April 1840, Dunn to Harrison, 21 May 1840, Dunn, "Circular," 22 May 1840, and Dunn to Macaulay, 2 June 1840. Also see Baskerville, *The Bank of Upper Canada*, lxxxviii. Later in 1842 the government reduced their advances by shipping to Glyns for disposal over 2,000 French crowns and 27,000 half-crowns which could no longer be accepted on government accounts. See Finance, R.G. 19, Vol. 1155, Glyns to Dunn, 3 June, 4 July, and 3 August 1842, Vol. 1174, Dunn to D. Daly, 5 February 1842, Dunn to Forsyth, Richardson, 30 May 1842, Dunn to Rawson, 26 August 1842.

76.   Finance, R.G. 19, Vol. 1154, Barings to Dunn, 3 July and 31 October 1840.

77.   See *ibid.*, Vol. 1175, Dunn to Harrison, 27 August 1840, and Dunn, "Receiver General's Report upon a Minute of Council dated 3rd September 1840 relating to the sale of Government Debentures by Messrs Baring Brothers and Co.," n.d., ECO, R.G. 1 E 1, State Book M, Vol. 57, Minute, 3 September 1840, and Finance, R.G. 19, Vol. 1180, Dunn to Barings, 20 March 1840. At the bottom of this draft there is a note signed "B.T." stating that the letter had, at the insistence of "His Excellency," been substituted for letters written by Macaulay. There is no indication, however, that, as Dunn later claimed, the letter was withdrawn.

78.   Finance, R.G. 19, Vol. 1175, Dunn to Harrison, 4 November 1840.

79. *The Arthur Papers*, Vol. 3, "Private and Confidential," Sydenham to [Arthur], 16 November 1840, 180–181, and "Private and Confidential," Arthur to Sydenham, 26 November 1840, 189–191.

80. Finance, R.G. 19, Vol. 1180, Dunn to Barings, 12 March 1841.

81. *Ibid.*, Vol. 1175, Receiver General's Office, "Balances in the Receiver General's Hands in Provincial Funds," 15 October 1840, and *The Arthur Papers*, Vol. 3, Arthur to Sydenham, 29 October 1840, 164–165.

82. Finance, R.G. 19, Vol. 1180, Dunn to Barings and Glyns, 14 February 1840.

83. *Ibid.*, Vol. 1154, Barings to Dunn, 18 June 1841.

84. See Vol. 1141, Glyns to Dunn, 3 July 1841. Also see Vol. 1155, Glyns to Dunn, 3 July, 18 August, 18 September, and 4 October 1841.

85. See Finance, R.G. 19, Vol. 1154, Barings to Dunn, 3 March, 18 May, 18 June, 18 September, 4 October, and 3 November 1841, 3 January, 18 May, 3 June, 4 July, and 3 December 1842. Also see Vol. 1141, Barings to Dunn, 19 July 1841, Dunn to F.W.C. Murdoch, Chief Secretary, 11 August 1841, Vol. 1175, Dunn to Harrison, 17 November and 25 November 1840, Dunn to Forsyth, Richardson, 6 December 1840, Dunn to Harrison, 18 December 1840, Dunn to Macaulay, 18 January 1841, Dunn to Murdoch, 11 August 1841, Dunn to Forsyth, Richardson, 16 August 1841, and Dunn to Glyns and Barings, 16 August 1841. Advances from Glyns increased to £34,500 by July 1841.

86. William Ormsby, in his recent biographical essay, does not discuss the financial policies pursued by Hincks during his first term as Inspector General. See William Ormsby, "Sir Francis Hincks," *The Pre-Confederation Premiers*, 148–196.

87. By early 1843 the provincial government owed Glyns £20,000 stg and Barings another £13,000 stg. See Finance, R.G. 19, Vol. 2753, Hincks to Harrison, 22 March 1843 and ECO, R.G. 1 E 1, State Book B, Vol. 62, Minute, 9 May 1843, 420–424.

88. Consols were non-redeemable securities paying 3 per cent interest. Originally introduced in 1759, they remained a favoured investment for over 200 years and provided a bench mark for British interest rates. In the 1840s they sold in the low 90s, making the effective average annual rate of interest 3.26 per cent. See Sidney Homer, *A History of Interest Rates*, Second Edition (New Brunswick, New Jersey, 1977), 159–163, 196.

89. ECO, R.G. 1 E 1, State Book C, Vol. 63, Minutes, 4 July, 25 July, 4 September, 12 October, 22 December, and 29 December 1843, 31 January 1844, 3, 19, 59, 169, 218, 233, 302, and Despatches and Reports, Vol. 65, 109, 121, 144, 150, 178, 180, and 184.

90. GGO, R.G. 7 G 1, Vol. 49, "Copy," Trevelyan to Stephens, 6 June 1840, and "Copy," Dunn to William Sargent, 18 April 1840, included in Despatch No. 241, Russell to Sydenham, 19 October 1840.

91. GGO, R.G. 7 G 1, Vol. 101, "Copy," Stephens to Trevelyan, 8 March 1842, included in Despatch No. 93, Stanley to Bagot, 8 March 1842, and Vol. 100, "Copy," Trevelyan to Stephens, 23 March 1842, included in Despatch No. 119, Stanley to Bagot, 4 April 1842. The "questions" referred to the guaranteed loan then under discussion.

92. GGO, R.G. 7 G 1, Vol. 102, "Private and Confidential," Stanley to Bagot, 2 July 1842, and Despatch No. 190, Stanley to Bagot, 2 July 1842.

93. *Ibid.*, Vol. 105, Despatch No. 28, Stanley to Metcalfe, 12 May 1843, Despatch No. 53, Stanley to Metcalfe, 3 July 1843, and "Copy," Trevelyan to Stephens, 30 July 1843, included in Despatch No. 53.

94. *Ibid.*, Vol. 105, Despatch No. 53, Stanley to Metcalfe, 3 July 1843, GGO, R.G. 7 G 12, Vol. 63, Despatch No. 25, Metcalfe to Stanley, 18 May 1843, and Despatch No. 32, Metcalfe to Stanley, 24 May 1843. Also see Finance, R.G. 19, Vol. 1154, Barings to Dunn, 3 June 1843. In April 1843 Dunn had suggested that, since the government's Order-in-Council had not yet been carried out, moneys due the Clergy Reserve Fund should not be sent to England but instead invested in provincial securities in Canada. See Finance, R.G. 19, Vol. 1174, Dunn to Harrison, 5 April 1843.

95. GGO, R.G. 1 G 12, Vol. 62, "Copy," R. B. Sullivan, Chairman, "Report of the Council," 18 January 1842, included in Despatch No. 14, Bagot to Stanley, 22 January 1842, and Vol. 63, Despatch No. 176, Bagot to Stanley, 20 August 1842, Despatch No. 177, Bagot to Stanley, 20 August 1842.

96. See GGO, R.G. 7 G 1, Vol. 110, Despatch No. 469, Stanley to Metcalfe, 3 December 1845, and Vol. 111, Despatch No. 39, Gladstone to Cathcart, 23 March 1846.

97. In June 1846 the Executive Council approved a recommendation from the Deputy Inspector General that all funds, including those in special accounts, be invested in provincial securities. Council then authorized the issue of £100,000 worth of 5 per cent debentures for this purpose. See ECO, R.G. 1 E 1, State Book E, Vol. 66, Minute, 22 June 1846, 467–468, 482.

Chapter 3
From Canals to Railways

*[O]ur Chest this evening shows £17,000 cy
cash on hand, but you must bear in mind
that £19,500 we hold on loan from the two
banks and the renewal of which we are
not yet quite sure of, in fact the Bank
of Montreal has made some objections
which however I hope to overcome.*
— Louis-Michel Viger, 1849[1]

The Province of Canada inherited more than the Upper Canadian debt; it inherited a set of attitudes and assumptions which ensured that the financial difficulties of the old colony would be replicated in the new. The first of these was the continued belief that large-scale internal transportation improvements guaranteed rapid economic growth. The second was the belief that such projects could be self-financing. The central economic motive of the Union had been the completion of the St. Lawrence–Great Lakes canal system. The Board of Works threw itself into the task during the decade and in turn became unquestionably the single largest spender of public moneys and the engine of debt. The assumption that such projects would be self-financing ensured no one became alarmed by the province's mushrooming liabilities.

Upper Canada had clearly overextended itself on its public works programme. Sydenham believed that this resulted from two factors: the absence of close political control and supervision and the tendency to treat all local projects as provincial schemes backed by provincial credit. To solve the latter problem he created a system of District Councils with power to initiate and oversee local projects as well as the power to tax residents for their support. To solve the former problem he reordered the political and administrative structures of colonial government and then created a new and powerful government department, the Board of Works, whose administrative head sat on the Executive Council. But in the short term Sydenham's administrative initiatives failed to provide effective control of spending.

The Executive Council did not as yet act collectively; each member may have been both a political and an administrative head of a government department, but each in turn was made to feel responsible to the Governor rather than to his colleagues. Effective and coordinated control was possible as long as the Governor General involved himself in the affairs of the province as directly as Lord Sydenham. Under someone less autocratic, ambitious heads of department could and often did attempt to establish their own independence. Sir Charles Bagot was very much the head of the government in a political sense, but he clearly exercised less control over the administration of individual departments than his more aggressive predecessor. This opened the door to the ambitions of people like Hamilton Killaly and his Board of Works.

Killaly was not much interested in politics; he was interested in public works. Although a member of the Executive Council, he took the first opportunity to resign his seat in both the Council and the Legislature, but not his office. Under his direction the Board had by 1843 established a remarkable independence from effective legislative or executive control.[2]

Killaly's vision was grand but myopic. He shared all of the dreams of commercial greatness predicted for the new canal system he was charged with constructing. He threw himself into the task with drive and enthusiasm. The problem was that he could see only the works themselves. He wanted these canals built and built to his own standards. He felt perfectly free to alter specifications or expand projects as he saw fit. He based all such decisions on engineering considerations alone. Certainly he seemed utterly unconcerned with costs. An independent Board dominated by such a character put the province on the fast track to financial trouble.

Everyone knew the canals were going to be expensive, but with the guaranteed loan the money would be available. Although the Board was charged with a number of public works including roads and small canals, its major efforts focused on six key projects: improvements to the Welland Canal; a series of improvements on the St. Lawrence from Prescott to Dickenson Landing; the Cornwall and Beauharnois canals; improvements to the Lachine Canal; and navigation improvements in Lac St-Pierre. By September 1843 the Board had already spent over £300,000 on these works and estimated that £1.25 million would be required for their completion.[3] Lord Stanley worried that the province was moving too fast with its construction; Killaly admitted as much but explained that contracts had been let faster than anticipated to take advantage of the favourable terms available in London capital markets, the favourable labour markets that resulted from the cessation of a number of projects in neighbouring

American states, and in anticipation of a rapid increase in trade. He suggested that the spring of 1845 was a suitable target date for the opening of the completed system.[4] Killaly's spending habits were not modified; throughout 1844 he remained overdrawn, forcing the Receiver General to seek new drafts to cover these expenditures.[5] Moreover, Killaly and the Board, without legislative authority, also adopted a number of changes to the plans for these projects which, he was convinced, would improve the quality of the works. They also increased the cost. By 1845–1846 appropriations had already been spent, and the works were still not complete. This prompted a highly critical inquiry into the affairs of the Board, and eventually to its abolition and replacement by a Department of Public Works.[6]

The Legislature which investigated and condemned the extravagance of the Board of Works was no less committed to the completion of the St. Lawrence navigation system. The government restricted the independence of the Board of Works, but this did not modify its spending habits. By the end of 1847 projects on the St. Lawrence system from Lac St-Pierre to the Welland had cost £1.7 million. Other projects had cost another £700,000.[7] The canals, however, remained uncompleted, and money to finish the work was becoming increasingly hard to find.

Some new money was available under the terms of the guaranteed loan. The British legislation provided a guarantee for the interest on a Canadian loan of £1.5 million stg; the provincial legislation, meanwhile, provided that a *sum* of £1.5 million stg be raised, the interest on which would be guaranteed by the imperial government. A problem emerged because debentures issued under the guarantee sold at a premium. The Treasury suggested that the wording of the provincial legislation limited the amount of the loan since the "sum raised" would include both principal and premium. Lord Stanley, on the advice of the Treasury, suggested the colonial government amend its Act to conform to the imperial legislation. The provincial government, in a surprisingly querulous response, suggested the Treasury had misinterpreted the Canadian Act and refused to amend it.[8]

It is difficult to understand why the Canadian government adopted this attitude other than to assert its autonomy. With time, however, necessity required adjustments in the Canadian position. By 1846 the original debentures had all been sold, and the proceeds spent. The province then passed two new Acts in 1846, the first to authorize £140,000 stg under the original imperial guarantee and the other to extend that guarantee to cover another £250,000 stg loan.

From Canada's perspective several reasons justified the extension of the guarantee, not the least of which was the deteriorating economic position of the colony. Lord Cathcart observed that prices for wheat, flour, and lumber were falling, and the continuation of public works would help relieve "a great and general stagnation of business."[9] As Cathcart explained, the expenditure of public funds drawn on Britain

> will be of most material advantage, and by affording employment for labour and consumption for produce, will tend to alleviate the pressure which I anticipate as inevitable, tho' [sic] I trust it will be only temporary.

Cathcart was quick to add that Canadians would likely blame an economic depression on changes in British commercial policy, and that "relief" from the imperial government on this occasion would "materially strengthen me in the administration of this government." Unimpressed, Earl Grey rejected any suggestion that the imperial government should guarantee interest on any loan beyond the £1.5 million stipulated in the 1842 legislation. He saw no reason, however, why the province should not benefit from that guarantee to the full amount. Grey authorized the issue of a final £140,000 stg worth of debentures under that Act.[10] This represented the amount that would have been available had the colonial government accepted Lord Stanley's advice back in 1844.

Earl Grey used this opportunity to raise a second problem with the guaranteed loan. When changes had been introduced to the provincial legislation back in 1842, the imperial government had insisted that a sinking fund be created. Measures for the future repayment of loans at maturity had never been included in previous legislation authorizing debenture issues; the sanguine assumption that transportation projects would generate revenue made other arrangements for repayment unnecessary. The more prudent imperial government, however, insisted on hedging its bets. As Francis Hincks, then serving his first term as Inspector General, assured the Legislative Assembly, "the only terms upon which the loan could be granted was to pay by a Sinking fund five per cent. [sic] on the consolidated fund of the Country."[11]

Although the province was bound to provide an annual payment, remittances were not forthcoming. In April 1843 the Treasury had agreed to defer the question of the Sinking Fund until precise estimates of the works to be undertaken allowed a clearer idea of when the money would be required. The Treasury, meanwhile, was quick to find fault with Canadian policy. It warned the province against proceeding too quickly and suggested that greater attention be given to supervision of the works. It also warned against the possibility of "distress which, if an undue and extravagant demand for labor were created, would probably ensue, on its sudden discontinuance." The

Executive Council in response ordered the Inspector General to report on the question of the Sinking Fund and the Commissioner of Public Works to provide estimates.[12]

Killaly drafted a reply to the Treasury which clearly indicated that the Canadians had defined their own agenda. Killaly admitted that contracts had been let much faster than originally anticipated in order to take advantage of the favourable labour market, and then repeated the now standard argument about the self-financing nature of the work. The situation demanded haste, he asserted, since the revenue necessary to service the debt would not be available until the entire system was complete.[13] The colony would set its own pace, although the Colonial Office continued to believe it was too fast.

With expected revenues still in the future, the Receiver General suggested as early as July 1843 that interest payments on the loan should be paid out of debenture sales. This was rejected outright by both the Treasury and the Colonial Office, both of whom reiterated that it was "extremely desirable that punctual and timely remittances should be made by the Receiver General for the payment of the interest."[14] Although interest payments could be met, no remittances could be made to the Sinking Fund. The prolonged political crisis provoked by the Lafontaine-Baldwin government's resignation in late 1843 further complicated financial concerns. This prompted a reminder from Stanley in June 1844. When no remittance arrived Stanley again raised the issue, and the Executive Council ordered the Inspector General to report on the situation.[15]

Joseph Cary, the Deputy Inspector General, reported in late 1844 that remittances were impossible. He pointed to the "depressed state of Trade of last year and the consequent reduction of the Provl [sic] Revenues" which, he argued, "precluded the possibility of applying any part of the Revenue of 1843 to that purpose." Cary added that fluctuating trade combined with changes to revenue laws made estimating future revenue impossible. For the time being he suggested that all revenue from public works not already appropriated be committed to the Sinking Fund until some future date when the canals became "sufficiently productive to reach the full annual amount of 5 per cent on the Loan."[16]

In early 1845 the government was able to remit £44,000 stg to cover arrears, but then made no payment for 1845 itself. The Treasury, in turn, decided not

to press for Remittance of any Instalment for Investment in the Fund on account of the past year, but they consider it to be incumbent on the Governor General and Council, on completion of the Loan to its full amount, not to delay the adoption of some conclusive arrangement for insuring for the future the regular periodical Remittance of a settled Rate of contribution.[17]

The Colonial Office regularly reminded the Canadian government of the need to remit funds; the Canadian government equivocated.[18] Failure to remit funds undoubtedly influenced the Colonial Office's decision in 1846 and 1847 not to guarantee further provincial loans. Certainly Earl Grey used the occasion of the £140,000 stg "extension" in 1846 to call the province's "particular attention" to the need for prompt payments to the Sinking Fund.[19]

The province got an extra £140,000 stg from the guaranteed loan, but there would be no further assistance from the British government. William Gladstone had made the British position quite clear in early 1846 when he rejected a proposal to assist the Halifax to Quebec Railway. Although he was "disposed to view with great favor" such a project, Gladstone added that

> I must distinctly observe to you, that a very strong and also a very peculiar case must be made out to justify those provinces in the expectation that Her Majesty's government would take upon themselves the responsibility of recommending the promotion of any such undertaking.

British North Americans would have to rely upon "private enterprise and capital."[20] Although hope for such assistance died slowly, all subsequent issues of Canadian debentures would stand on their own in London. In the short term the province would be completely frustrated in its efforts to raise new money.

In late 1846 Glyn Mills agreed to negotiate on behalf of the province a new £50,000 stg issue. By the time the debentures arrived, however, quotations for Canadian securities had slipped below par; by April 1847 nominal quotations stood at 97–98. At that point interest rates at the Bank of England rose to 6 per cent which, according to Glyns, made it impossible to sell Canadian 5 per cent debentures.[21] During the summer a few sales were made at 95, but by the fall the nominal price had slipped to 90–92. A full-scale business recession gripped financial markets by the fall of 1847, and Glyns reported that "the extreme commercial failures ... have had a very adverse effect on the market for Canadian Securities, so much so that it is utterly impracticable to obtain purchasers for the new Bonds." Still confident, Glyns offered to advance £20,000 stg to the province on security of the debentures in their hands.[22] Rather than avail itself of this offer immediately, the province opted instead to withdraw its 5 per cent debentures and substitute instead debentures paying 6 per cent interest. The increased interest rate did little to promote sales. By January 1848 quotations for Canadian fives had slipped to 83, and there were no sales of the new sixes.[23] With few other options the province accepted in February 1848 the £20,000 stg advance offered by Glyns.[24] Having exhausted the guaranteed loan and being unable to raise money on its own credit, the government also had to confront a wholly unexpected increase in expenses occasioned by the Irish famine immigration. The resulting financial embarrassment produced a serious squabble between the Colonial Office and the provincial government.

Throughout the 1830s and 1840s the British government had been concerned with programmes to encourage emigration to its colonies. Arguments that linked public works spending to jobs for immigrants had as a result always been advanced to win imperial support for Canadian projects. There were other issues as well, not the least of which was the question of who should bear the cost of immigrant reception programmes. Prior to the Union Lord John Russell suggested that the care of newly arrived immigrants, together with the contingent expenses, was the responsibility of the colonial administration. Lord Sydenham, however, argued that the colony could not afford this expense. Bowing to the opinions of his Governor General, Russell arranged a "temporary" advance in 1840 of £5,000 from the Military Chest to cover such expenditures, but he expected to be "repaid out of the Provincial Revenue as soon as the Legislative Union shall have taken place."[25]

Like many temporary measures this one became more permanent when Russell announced a new imperial policy in 1841. The Commissary General would pay a new five shilling head tax and the imperial Parliament would annually provide a special grant — Russell suggested £8,000 for 1841, although considerably less was actually given — to cover emigration expenses. According to Russell, Britain "ought to pledge itself indefinitely to the expenses of maintaining the Emigrants in Canada till they are able to obtain employment."[26] The imperial government had apparently abandoned any notion that the colony should contribute to the cost of caring for newly arrived British immigrants. Under this system introduced by the Colonial Office the province made the initial payments and supervised services rendered at reception centres. The imperial government then reimbursed the province through the Commissariat. This was the situation in 1847 when thousands of destitute immigrants suddenly overwhelmed the reception centres at Quebec and along the St. Lawrence.

To some extent the problems had been anticipated. In December 1846 Earl Grey warned of the large numbers of emigrants expected to leave the United Kingdom during the coming season.[27] In addition Grey increased the parliamentary grant for 1847 to £10,000, more than double, the Colonial Secretary pointed out, the grant for any previous year. Yet it remained clear that the nature of the crisis about to strike had not been fully appreciated by either imperial or provincial authorities.

Grey observed that £10,000 was more than would likely be needed, and it had been voted only as a precaution against possible financial complications.[28] He remained magnanimous even after receiving the first reports on the "wretched condition" of emigrants arriving at Quebec. "I hasten to instruct your Lordship," Grey told Lord Elgin, the newly appointed Governor General,

> to adopt all measures which may appear to you best calculated to mitigate their suffering, whether by increasing the number of medical attendants at the Quarantine Station, or providing a greater extent of accommodation, even if for that purpose it should unfortunately be necessary to exceed the amount of the vote which has been obtained from Parliament for these services.[29]

As the summer wore on more and more destitute immigrants arrived, the problems multiplied, the costs skyrocketed, and Earl Grey changed his tune. By July he expressed his view that the colony should enforce "the strictest economy" in providing only "absolutely necessary" assistance. The earlier sympathy for the emigrants had been replaced by the more usual fear that "the grant of such assistance, if not rigidly guarded, may have the effect of inducing the Emigrants to relax in their exertions to provide for themselves."[30] The generosity of the Colonial Office had been spent.

More significant from the provincial perspective, Grey suddenly suggested that the added expenditures would not be paid by the imperial government alone, although he recognized the difficulty in determining the proportion which "properly" fell to Britain. Grey asserted that, since the province benefitted from immigration, it was not unreasonable to expect Canada to shoulder "a fair share of the burthen," particularly since local authorities were better able "to limit the expenditure by enforcement of a rigid economy."[31] The Executive Council, supported by their Governor, rejected this position. Grey in turn authorized the Commissariat to advance another £20,000, but this again proved insufficient.[32] The province, meanwhile, faced the possibility of default on interest payments on the public debt due in January 1848.

The Executive Council, not without means of its own for exerting pressure on the Colonial Office, denied any responsibility for immigration expenses incurred in 1847. The imperial government had, according to Grey's calculations, already paid £49,000 of the estimated £65,000 total cost. Grey believed the province should pay the balance, a small sum considering "the benefit, direct and indirect, which the trade and Revenue of the province has derived from the resort of Emigrants to the Saint Lawrence." At the same time Grey warned of the consequences that would follow any delay in remitting funds due on the public debt.[33]

Elgin, for his part, outlined the provincial case. Disbursements had already absorbed moneys previously set aside for interest payments and had as well crippled the public works construction programme at a time when Canadian securities could not be sold in London.[34] In late November Elgin forwarded a Minute of the Executive Council together with a report from William Cayley, the Inspector General, outlining the difficulty in meeting the January interest payments. Those reports produced the desired result: Grey ordered the Treasury to make arrangements for the payment of interest due on the guaranteed loan and opened a special provincial account at the Bank of England for £25,000 stg "as an advance in aid of the Expenses incurred by the Canadian Government for the relief of distressed Emigrants during the past year."[35]

Although clearly emigration expenses were not the only factor contributing to the crisis of 1847–1848, Elgin observed that many in the colony blamed them for the government's financial woes. The Governor reminded the Colonial Secretary that additional expenditures had been authorized on the clear understanding that the imperial government alone was responsible. The change in government in early 1848 did not alter the attitude of the province. Hincks insisted, like Cayley before him, that Britain alone must pay. Like Cayley, Hincks threatened default on future interest payments due on the public debt unless funds were remitted.[36]

In the end Grey relented; he had little choice since the imperial guarantee made Britain liable for interest payments on nearly half of the provincial debt. The problems of 1847, Grey wrote, were "the result of a calamity in the United Kingdom" not likely to be repeated and "the Province should not suffer pecuniary loss in consequence of the distress which reached it from this Kingdom." Parliament would foot the entire bill. Grey added, however, that "in future all the expenses incurred on account of Immigrants arriving in Canada should be provided for by the Provincial Government, to which the entire management of this service should be entrusted." The Executive Council accepted this change in policy on the understanding that the imperial government clearly recognize its jurisdiction over all aspects of immigration policy.[37] It now remained to settle accounts.

Some money had already been made available to the provincial government in 1847. The Treasury had also paid the interest on the guaranteed loan for the province. The province, meanwhile, had been forced to arrange an advance from Glyns in February 1848, secured by provincial debentures, to pay the interest on that portion of the public debt not guaranteed by the British. In May Hincks forwarded a statement which estimated emigration expenses for 1847 at £83,000 cy. Later in June he increased this estimate to £157,300 cy, a sum disputed by the Treasury. Glyns, meanwhile, were unable to sell debentures held as security for their advance, and Hincks ordered the Treasury to settle that account — £20,000 stg — out of funds due the province. This was arranged in May 1848.[38] The accounts for 1847 could now be closed, but the province was still not out of the woods. Hincks continued to spend the better part of the next year and a half juggling accounts in an effort to make ends meet.

By the time the dispute over immigration expenses was settled, the province faced severe financial pressures. Commodity prices had begun to fall in 1846; by 1847–1848 a commercial depression gripped the province. As trade declined, revenue from customs duties fell from £419,000 cy in 1845 to £381,100 cy in 1847 (see Appendix I). Revenues from customs fell even more sharply in 1848 to £304,400 cy. The collapse of customs revenue brought total revenues to the Consolidated Revenue Fund down from £506,900 to only £379,700 cy between 1847 and 1848. Expenditures on the Consolidated Revenue Fund also fell, although not nearly as rapidly as revenue. Total expenditures dropped from £523,000 cy in 1845 to £474,500 in 1848. As the province tried to complete its canal system, interest on the public debt increased from £148,300 cy to £169,200 cy between 1846 and 1848. In 1848 interest payments accounted for fully 36 per cent of total expenditures on the Consolidated Revenue Fund. Canada's budget deficit of £94,800 cy in 1848 increased the debt still further. This ensured interest in 1849 would consume fully 38.3 per cent of expenditures on the Consolidated Revenue Fund.

This, then, was the immediate situation facing the new Reform government which took office in February 1848. Many Canadians blamed the depression of 1848 on Britain's repeal of mercantilist legislation such as the timber duties and the corn laws.[39] The St. Lawrence canals, instead of generating great riches, produced insufficient revenue to pay interest on the loans negotiated for their construction. After 1847 Canadian credit in London had collapsed; sales of new debentures were impossible given discount rates of up to 10 per cent on 6 per cent bonds. There was little room for manoeuvre since the British government had already refused to guarantee further Canadian loans. Unable to negotiate a regular loan in London, the government had been forced to arrange short-term cash advances from both domestic and British banks to meet the interest due on the public debt. Yet Canadians remained convinced that economic growth and prosperity — perhaps even economic survival — demanded more, not less, public works expenditure. More public works required additional capital. The financially troubled years 1848–1849 demanded a strong self-assured hand; the Reform Cabinet expected its Inspector General to provide economic solutions.

The LaFontaine–Baldwin government had come to power in late February 1848. The legislative session that year lasted only long enough to confirm the Reform victory and was then prorogued. As J.M.S. Careless points out, the new government needed "time to develop a broad programme of reform for the 1849 session."[40] That session would prove one of the busiest in the Union period. Yet despite all the changes associated with the triumph of responsible government, very little changed in terms of financial and economic policy. Looked at from the perspective of the financial history of the Union, one would hardly know that a major shift in power had occurred. The most significant change came not with political shifts but with technological innovations. During the 1840s canals constituted the major public works projects pursued by the province; at the end of the decade the enthusiasm for canals gave way to an equally strong enthusiasm for railways.

Thomas Coltrin Keefer caught the new mood in his *Philosophy of Railroads*, first published in 1849.[41] His father, George Keefer, had been a close associate of William Hamilton Merritt as well as the first president of the Welland Canal Company. The young Keefer not only followed his father's profession of engineering, but shared his vision of the commercial potential of the St. Lawrence–Great Lakes system.

Keefer's first essay on railways in 1847 predicted the failure of the portage road from Montreal to the head of the Lachine Rapids because it was too short. Like canal promoters Keefer looked further afield: up river was the trade of a continent. When discussions began on a possible intercolonial railway to Halifax, several Montreal merchants turned to Keefer to prepare a manifesto designed to convince sceptics of the need for rails to the West. A firm believer in Montreal's commercial vision, he threw himself into the task using most of the arguments that had sustained canal construction for decades. *Philosophy of Railroads* epitomized the new railway fever that would sweep the province. Railways, like canals, required government assistance; the new Reform government would deliver that assistance just as soon as it completed the canals and sorted out the financial difficulties.

The LaFontaine–Baldwin government left financial and economic policy in the deft and experienced hands of Francis Hincks. Born in Cork, Ireland, Hincks had trained in the counting houses of Belfast before emigrating to Canada. In Upper Canada he opened an import-wholesale business in York and later became Cashier of the People's Bank.[42] He had a well-established reputation as an economic and financial expert. At the time of his first appointment as Inspector General back in 1842, Bagot commented that "[i]n matters connected with finance Mr. Hincks is I believe admitted to be the ablest man now in the Legislature."[43] Although his financial reputation influenced Bagot's decision, it is doubtful if Hincks would have been appointed had he not previously broken with Baldwin and supported many of Sydenham's economic initiatives, including the guaranteed loan, the creation of a bank of issue and the District Council scheme for Upper Canada. Hincks' reputation as a financial expert, meanwhile, proved far more durable than his very temporary quarrel with Baldwin. A dominant player in Reform politics, he would again assume control of government finance as Inspector General in 1848. With his firm hands on the till, a case could be made that Hincks exerted a far greater influence on the formation of government policy than Baldwin. In terms of his economic policies and programmes, he proved in the end Lord Sydenham's rather than Robert Baldwin's true heir.

Hincks spent most of 1848 juggling accounts, trying to pay all the bills. By the end of the year, however, he submitted the broad outlines of his economic strategy to the Executive Council. Little record remains of the discussion that ensued; the Minutes of 20 December 1848 record only that the Executive Council "concurs with the opinion expressed in the Report of the Inspector General."[44] Fortunately, the accompanying Memorandum is unusually long and detailed. Despite the absence of any record of debate and discussion in the minutes of the Executive Council, this document had gone through a number of drafts and had circulated widely within government circles. Clearly one object of Hincks' Memorandum was to build a consensus on economic and financial issues around a set of ideas and assumptions that already enjoyed wide currency. In addition to the familiar assumptions and arguments, however, one finds a coherent strategy for economic development which linked all of the major policy initiatives soon to be enacted by the provincial government.

Hincks intended to change little. He certainly had no thought of trying to alter the nature of the Canadian economy, nor would he attempt to reorient the patterns of Canadian trade. Hincks believed that he could maintain and foster the old colonial economy in spite of free trade. Using arguments and ideas which had been current for more than a decade he based his programme on the assumption that Britain's surplus population could be "removed to a country where under a system of free commercial intercourse the products of the soil will be exchanged for British manufactures." He believed that Canada was a suitable destination for the "immigration of an industrious population" provided "that it is possible to procure English capital to promote Colonization through the instrumentality of the Imperial Government or of Associations of individuals in England."[45] Immigration could be promoted, according to the Inspector General, through public works projects which would provide jobs for newcomers but which would also require British capital to finance them. Hincks accepted the repeal of the corn laws and the timber duties, and he looked forward to the repeal of the Navigation Acts. Yet he expected continued imperial aid for emigration programmes because Britain, too, should be concerned "not only in getting rid of a redundant population, but in securing a more extensive market for her manufactures."[46] Emigration could best be promoted by providing financial assistance to the province's public works programmes.

The link between British financial assistance, public works projects, and immigration policy did not, as we have seen, originate with Hincks. Arguments suggesting that employment opportunities on public works projects were essential to the successful settlement of newly arrived immigrants had been used by Lord Sydenham and repeated by Lord John Russell in their justification for Britain's loan guarantees. As late as 1847 Earl Grey commented that if railways, canals, and other public works could be devised in order to provide employment for immigrant labour,

> Her Majesty's Servants will not be slow to propose nor judging from the opinions generally expressed would Parliament be slow to sanction the employment of the pecuniary resources of the Country [Britain] in furtherance of such an object.[47]

Hincks cited this despatch in his Memorandum to Council as evidence that the imperial government might yet extend further loan guarantees to Canada.

Private railways also applied for imperial assistance on the grounds that construction promoted emigration. In March and April 1847 Elgin forwarded separate Memorials from the Toronto and Lake Huron and Great Western railways each requesting government aid "for the employment and settlement of Emigrants from the United Kingdom."[48] Grey refused to support either request. Financial aid to private railways was not a "proper object for the interference of the Imperial Parliament." The provincial government alone, in the opinion of the Colonial Office, had authority to decide such questions.[49] The railways, in turn, wasted little time appealing to the Legislative Assembly for help.

Setbacks during the decade did nothing to undermine Hincks' belief that continued immigration was in both the imperial and the Canadian interest. He believed, as we shall shortly see, that only land sales could provide the necessary income to repay past and future loans. Immigrants needed jobs if they were to earn and save enough money to buy crown land and become agricultural settlers. More importantly, public works opened new areas for settlement and at the same time increased land values. Immigration and settlement would also increase trade in general and in turn government revenue from customs duties. Public works construction was central to Hincks' immigration plan.

If Hincks intended to pursue an active public works policy to build railways he needed to promote an influx of British capital. Unlike the United States, Canada suffered from a "want of the capital required to construct those Public Works which have become almost indispensable as auxiliaries to the canals in securing the Western Trade." Capital on a colonial frontier, Hincks argued, tended to accumulate in land and other forms of fixed property.[50] The most important consequence of colonialism in Canada, then, was the already large public debt contracted to build canals. Hincks was less sanguine about the financial prospects of those canals than many of his contemporaries. He reminded the Cabinet that canal revenues would probably not increase in the foreseeable future. This meant that the debt

> which though not by any means so large as to afford ground for serious embarrassment, is nonetheless sufficient so to render it inexpedient that it should embark at present in any further speculation.[51]

Hincks' problem, then, was clear: he must improve Canada's credit in order to attract more capital investment for public works.

Although rapidly increasing immigration expenses and declining customs revenue certainly complicated the government's fiscal situation, Hincks assured Barings and Glyns that the real source of "embarrassment" resulted from the inability to negotiate new loans following the final £140,000 on the guaranteed loan in 1846. Unable to sell new debentures, the government had been forced to use current revenue to pay public works contracts. Hincks commented that £400,000 in "surplus" revenues over the past several years had been used to support construction rather than to reduce outstanding liabilities. Hincks considered it an "absolute necessity" that the government discontinue the practice of using current revenue for large capital projects.[52] To prevent any further drain on the Consolidated Revenue Fund, in early 1848 he asked J. H. Dunn, the ex-Receiver General then living in Britain,[53] to negotiate a new £200,000 stg loan with Barings.

Although only a few debentures could be marketed in Britain,[54] Hincks refused to be dispirited and in 1849 went himself to Britain to seek a £500,000 stg loan which would pay 6 rather than 5 per cent interest.[55] With this money the province could complete its canals and meet other obligations. As long as the government required such large loans to cover existing commitments, there could be no further public borrowing to pursue new projects.

A number of other problems confronted Hincks during 1848. When the guaranteed loan was altered in 1842, the "whole of the new loan," according to a later Cabinet Minute, "was made applicable to the Public Works."[56] Using the proceeds from the guaranteed loan exclusively for new construction meant that the old debentures of Upper and Lower Canada remained outstanding. By the end of the decade some were maturing, and Hincks was hard pressed to redeem them.[57] Hincks preferred to renew rather than redeem these maturing debentures, and this in turn required a more flexible system of issuing securities. Each issue under current practice required specific legislative sanction. At the same time the government lacked the necessary financial flexibility to respond to short-term budgetary deficits because of the earlier failure to establish a provincial bank of issue as advocated by Sydenham. These various problems ensured that before Hincks could address the question of new public works he had first to turn his attention to reassuring Canada's creditors. When the legislative session opened in 1849 he had his proposals ready.

His Act for the Better Management of the Public Debt was intended to correct all of these problems.[58] To mollify the imperial government and restore faith in Canadian securities, the Act promised a minimum contribution of £73,000 cy annually to the Sinking Fund. In addition, all revenue from public works in excess of £20,000 cy and all unappropriated revenue at the credit of the Consolidated Revenue Fund could be placed at the credit of the Sinking Fund. The Act also allowed the government to issue by Order-in-Council new debentures to redeem maturing securities. The total debt of the province, however, could not be increased by such operations.

Equally importantly the Act provided permanent legislation covering two measures Hincks had already introduced by Order-in-Council. In 1847 the government ran its first budgetary deficit which forced it to negotiate short-term cash advances from the Banks of British North America and Montreal. In December 1848 £15,000 on loan from the banks would fall due. Hincks recommended that these loans be repaid, but at the same time asked for and received authority to borrow £20,000 to £25,000 if necessary to meet future exigencies.[59] Rather than repay these loans the government sought an extension.

After considerable hesitation the Bank of Montreal agreed to extend the government's credit from £7,500 to £12,000 cy for three months. The Bank of British North America refused to extend the government's credit to £12,000 but did agree to renew the original £7,500 cy loan for another three months. The government asked for and received several further renewals; not until September 1849 did it repay these loans.[60] At the same time both banks equivocated when requested to advance another £20,000 stg exchange to cover interest payments on the public debt due in Britain. As a result of this failure "to meet the views of the Government and facilitate the public business," Hincks shifted the government account to the Bank of Upper Canada.[61] The Act for the Better Management of the Public Debt, meanwhile, authorized all such loans provided they did not exceed "the amount of the deficiencies in the said Consolidated Revenue Fund."

The Act dealt with a second problem plaguing the government. Since the last of the £140,000 stg on the guaranteed loan had been spent, the government had been unable to sell debentures in Britain. The canals were not yet completed, and the Consolidated Revenue Fund was already in deficit. Somehow contractors would have to be paid. In early 1848 Hincks proposed paying contractors with special short-term small denomination debentures — no more than £2 10/0 or $10 face value. These debentures, according to the Inspector General, would in turn be received by the government for all "payments of public dues," including customs, and re-issued "if necessary, in payment of public expenditures" including the Civil List. They were to circulate, as Hincks said, "in lieu of money."[62]

Although opposition to this proposal emerged within the Executive Council, Hincks had won the debate on the principle of using small denomination debentures as money. The Council, however, reduced the amount authorized from £125,000 cy to only £40,000 cy, a restriction that proved temporary. When the original issue ran out and still there were no sales of regular long-term debentures in London, the Council subsequently and repeatedly extended the limit. By November 1848 additional Orders-in-Council brought the total authorized to £182,000 cy, of which £177,000 cy had already been placed in circulation. As Lord Elgin commented, "not a shilling can be raised on the credit of the Province. We are actually reduced to the disagreeable necessity of paying all Public officers, from the Gov'r Gen'l [sic] downwards, in debentures, which are not exchangeable at par."[63]

The extensive use of such debentures proved too much for the market to bear. In December 1848 a combination of improved cash reserves — an improvement that proved temporary — and substantial discounts on these debentures forced Hincks to restrict their use. He recommended that such debentures be issued only in payment of public works contracts. The government would pay all other accounts with cash.[64] This too proved a short-lived restriction.

Although such issues were used extensively throughout 1848, legislative authority for them did not come until 1849. The Act for the Better Management of the Public Debt raised the maximum face value for these short-term debentures from £2 10/0 to £10.[65] Under the provisions of the Act such debentures would be payable "on demand or at any time after date [of issue]" and would be "receivable in payment of monies payable to the Provincial Government."

Rather than risk a collapse in the market for such debentures, Hincks had restricted their use to public works contracts. The financial situation, however, continued to be bleak into 1849. Although short-term loans negotiated in 1848 could be renewed, servicing the public debt remained a more pressing problem. When the government approached the Banks of Montreal and British North America for sterling advances in early 1849, both prevaricated. These banks held the government account and both knew the true state of the province's financial situation. As Receiver General Louis-Michel Viger explained to Hincks, then in London personally supervising negotiations for a new provincial loan,

> I am fully of opinion that ... we cannot depend upon any further accommodation from the Banking Institutions here; and this may also in some degree be attributed to the knowledge the Banks possess of the state of our Chest.[66]

Viger managed to scrape together the £20,000 stg due in Britain, but money remained in short supply. In early June Viger commented that

> [m]oney does not continue to come in as [fast] as I could desire and should you not succeed in affecting a loan I plainly see that we [shall] be much pinched for Cash during the next 3 to 4 months, and it will be a source of much uneasiness should we not be in funds to redeem in Cash the [illegible] Debentures as they fall due.[67]

The nadir of the financial crisis came at the end of the month when Viger informed Hincks that the government had literally run out of money. Viger reported he had only £17,000 cy cash on hand, and added that advances from domestic banks totalling £19,500 would fall due the following morning. Arrangements for renewal of those loans had not yet been finalized, and "[i]n fact," Viger explained, "the Bank of Montreal has made some objections which however I hope to overcome."[68] These loans were renewed, but when military pensions came due one week later Viger informed Thomas Ridout at the Bank of Upper

Canada that "owing to circumstances it is not deemed expedient for
the time being to pay these pensions or any other *in Cash*. . . . It is the
intention of the Government for the present to pay the above in Prov.
[sic] Debentures."[69] By September the government again extended its
policy of paying accounts in short-term, small-denomination debentures rather than cash to cover the Civil List. Although the Act for the
Better Management of the Public Debt set the limit for such issues at
£250,000 cy, the Council by the end of February 1850 had authorized
a total of £662,445 cy, of which £630,820 had been placed in circulation.[70] These debentures served their purpose by providing short-term
credit until a more conventional loan could be negotiated. Upon completion of the £500,000 stg loan in May 1850, the government called
in and redeemed all of these debentures.

The final element of the Act for the Better Management of
the Public Debt was the transfer to municipal jurisdiction of some
provincially owned public works.[71] The clause, although of marginal
significance if taken in isolation, anticipated another piece of legislation
of far greater importance: the Municipal Corporations Act.[72]

Previous public works spending had nearly bankrupted the
province and had also created local, sectional rivalry and jealousy. The
Act for the Better Management of the Public Debt and a new loan
would improve the financial situation, but even if they were successful
the province was in no position to borrow more than the £500,000 stg
then being negotiated. If new projects were to be promoted — and
Hincks believed they must be promoted — other agencies and institutions would have to shoulder much of the financial burden. One
option might involve the establishment of local institutions capable of
borrowing on their own credit to finance local works. Alternatively
private companies might be encouraged to build "public works" through
measures such as guarantees for bonded debts. In both cases the object
would be the same: to provide enough public assistance to ensure the
projects were implemented without directly increasing the provincial
debt.

Local public works had always created political headaches
for the government. If they were undertaken by the provincial government, all inhabitants would be taxed to service the provincial debt
while only some of them benefitted. Political alliances, meanwhile,
depended upon patronage, trade-offs, and logrolling. Various localities
could also be counted on continually to demand provincial assistance
for any number of new projects. Hincks reacted bluntly: "[A]n end
must be made to these local grants."[73] He believed local projects should
be undertaken but not by the provincial government. Local authorities
would have to be created with the power to tax and borrow.

The problem was as old as the British North American colonies, and Hincks' policy, as in so many areas, demonstrated the influence of Lord Sydenham. When he arrived in Canada in 1839, Charles Poulett Thomson became convinced that the political situation demanded the creation of local governments with taxing powers of their own. When the imperial government failed to include such provisions in its Bill for union, Thomson reacted strongly. He asserted that the "Absence of Local Government" ensured that there would be only a "simple Legislative Re-Union of the two Provinces without providing any machinery by which they can be satisfactorily governed when united." Without institutions for local government

> the Executive Government will be called upon to propose every grant of five or ten pounds for a road or a bridge for 700 miles from the seat of Government and of which it can learn nothing except through representations which it has no opportunity of testing.[74]

The suspension of the constitution in 1838 allowed Thomson to impose his District Councils on Lower Canada prior to union. He had to wait, however, until the new parliament met in 1841 before his proposals for Upper Canada could be enacted. On this issue Hincks broke with his Reform colleagues and supported the Governor,[75] although he believed these proposals did not go far enough.[76] The Municipal Corporations Act in 1849 would better ensure that local public works would be dealt with by local governments. Hincks would later explain to Barings that "the policy of the Canadian Government adopted by your advice and your concurrence is to throw what may be considered as *Local improvements* on the several localities." This, according to Hincks, had been the purpose of the Municipal Corporations Act, and, although there was no similar legislation for Lower Canada, the largest cities already held special charters which achieved the same objective.[77]

The Municipal Corporations Act did not immediately lead to the initiation of local projects as anticipated. Later Hincks would reconsider the problem and propose new initiatives with the Consolidated Municipal Loan Fund. In the meantime he turned his attention to a second problem — provincial public works schemes. He had several worthy projects in mind: the St. Lawrence and Atlantic Railway, Quebec harbour improvements, the Quebec–Sherbrooke Railway, the St. Lawrence and Champlain Canal, the Great Western Railway, and the Toronto and Lake Huron Railway. These "public works" would cost an estimated £3.5 million stg and, more importantly from Hincks' point of view, would provide thousands of jobs for immigrants.[78] The question, as always, was money.

All of the government's revenue "for the foreseeable future" was, according to Hincks, committed to meeting "the normal expenses of civil government, to paying interest charges on the already large debt, and for the creation of the Sinking Fund."[79] In the context of late 1848 the provincial government was in no position to borrow the necessary funds to build any of these projects. Nor were they likely to be assisted by the imperial government, although Hincks remained optimistic that his requests for imperial guarantees might yet receive a favourable hearing at the Colonial Office. Hincks had raised the issue of new guarantees for railways in March 1848; Grey's positive response on that occasion undoubtedly encouraged him to pursue this line of argument. Hincks clearly tailored many of the arguments in his December Memorandum to a British audience, and Elgin wasted little time in forwarding that Memorandum to the Colonial Office the same day it had been approved by Council.[80]

If this document was intended to help secure a new imperial guarantee for railway construction, it failed to achieve its objective. Although Grey assured the Canadians of "the earnest desire of Her Majesty's Government to promote the success of any measures which may be adopted for the improvement of Canada and the development of its great resources," the measures proposed by Hincks were "such as the local Government and Legislature have alone the authority to carry into effect." Grey insisted that capital would have to come from the private sector, not from the imperial government.[81] The projects, however, might still be undertaken if proper and judicious encouragement could be given to private companies. Anticipating the Guarantee Act, Hincks suggested in late 1848 that the government could raise half of the costs of construction on its own credit provided private enterprise first completed half of the proposed projects out of their own resources.[82]

An important point to note here is Hincks's constant reference to projects such as the St. Lawrence and Atlantic Railway as *public works* which, unfortunately, the government lacked the financial resources to build on its own account. This helps explain Hincks' willingness to provide financial aid to privately owned and operated companies in ever larger amounts. Only the inability of the province to raise money in London would limit the assistance Hincks would provide.

The idea of a provincial guarantee for private railway borrowing did not originate with Hincks.[83] The St. Lawrence and Atlantic Railway had made its first request for provincial assistance in March 1845, the same month in which it incorporated. The Viger–Draper government rejected that appeal.[84] After a number of unsuccessful attempts to raise capital in London the railway — now headed by the prominent Reformer A. N. Morin who had replaced the Tory George Moffat after the Reform electoral victory in 1848 — again asked for assistance. The Great Western Railway also sought financial assistance after an equally unsuccessful attempt to tap Lombard Street.[85] The idea of a guarantee for private railways, meanwhile, enjoyed wide support from both sections of the province. A series of resolutions recommending the adoption of the guarantee passed in the Legislative Assembly by a vote of 62-4. Only Louis Joseph Papineau spoke at considerable length against granting the guarantee. He suggested such a guarantee "would bind the credit of the Province to an indefinate [sic] amount" and that "the government ought to have made more accurate calculations." Papineau also questioned the wisdom of aiding railways which would run parallel to and compete with government-owned canals.[86]

In late 1848 Hincks suggested to Cabinet that the province raise half of the capital needed for the construction of various railways. Yet the Bill presented to the Assembly in 1849 proved far more restrictive. The Guarantee Act provided only a provincial guarantee up to 6 per cent for "the interest on loans to be raised by any Company chartered by the Legislature of this Province for the construction of a Line of Rail-way not less than seventy-five miles in extent."[87] The guarantee would come into effect as soon as half of the proposed line had been completed. To protect its interests, the government insisted that, in the event of any payments being made out of the provincial treasury as a consequence of the guarantee, the province would "be the first charge upon the Tolls and profits of the Company," and no dividend could be paid until the company settled the government account. The province also assumed a first mortgage.

The financial crisis of 1848–1849 explains Hincks's retreat from a proposal to guarantee half of the capital raised to a guarantee of only the interest payments on half of that capital. The government, as we have seen, was critically short of cash in 1848, and the situation continued bleak throughout 1849 in spite of the use of small denomination debentures for paying accounts. In early 1849 Hincks had decided to seek a £500,000 stg loan in Britain to cover current revenue needs and in anticipation of the large debenture issues due to mature over the course of the early 1850s. That loan would prove difficult to raise even without the added burden that might arise if the province attempted to guarantee principal as well as interest on private railway bonds. Both Thomas Baring and George Carr Glyn made this clear when they expressed their concern about the Guarantee Act. Baring, like Papineau, feared that an unlimited commitment to use provincial credit to support private borrowing might increase the public debt to unacceptable levels. He demanded a clarification of the government's intentions as well as assurances that the province would not allow the public debt to increase beyond the projected £500,000 stg loan. Thomas Baring wanted the Guarantee Act repealed.

In an effort to reassure Baring, the Executive Council passed a special Minute for his benefit. The Council would not repeal the Act, but reiterated that

> should any of the Railroad Companies put themselves in a position to call for such a guarantee, the Debentures will not be Debentures of the Province, but those of the respective Companies, and that the Guarantee will not be a Guarantee of the Capital but of the interest only.[88]

The government also reminded Barings of its power to add by Order-in-Council "ten per cent to the Customs as a means of securing the necessary funds to meet" any payments that might result from a default by any railway. This satisfied Barings and Glyns and efforts continued on the £500,000 stg loan. Not until May 1850, however, was that loan finally negotiated; Barings took the opportunity to remind the province again of its commitment not to increase the public debt any further.[89]

As with the Municipal Corporations Act, the Guarantee Act did not immediately provide the boon to railway construction anticipated by Hincks. In the longer term he would return to the question and modify the Act to make it work better. In the context of 1849, however, he remained convinced that together the Act for the Better Management of the Public Debt, the Municipal Corporations Act and the Guarantee Act, combined with a new £500,000 stg loan, would end the short-term financial embarrassments of the government while promoting both local and provincial public works projects.

One final element of his economic strategy remains to be discussed: land policy. In his Memorandum of 1848 Hincks commented that many British observers favoured charging high prices for land and using the revenue to improve internal communications. Hincks thought this impossible because of Canada's proximity to the United States where land sold "at very moderate prices." Although rejecting high prices as impractical, he had no intention of adopting a policy of free grants except in limited and tightly controlled circumstances, as had been done during the early 1840s. Sir George Arthur had originally suggested using free grants of 50 acres to encourage settlement along the Garafaxa Road. Sydenham had later made two similar proposals to promote settlement along the Kennebec Road and through the townships of Langton and Forsyth in Lower Canada.[90] Access to land, meanwhile, was critically important to promote settlement; it was also important for Hincks because land represented a valuable asset which offset the province's growing liabilities. While others looked to increasing revenue generated by canals to repay debts, Hincks looked as well to increased revenue from the sale of public lands. Hincks suggested the government could, as Arthur and Sydenham had done, provide free grants of up to 50 acres if in so doing settlement could be promoted in specific areas of the province, thus increasing the value of the crown lands that remained available for sale. It was important that the value of crown lands be increased because Hincks intended that they and the public domain should be "a good security for borrowed capital."[91]

There was nothing new in linking crown land to debt payments. At the time of union, to cite but one example, a group of British "memorialists," including the Canada Company and the British North American Land Company, had suggested that land revenue be separated from the Consolidated Revenue Fund and committed to the payment of loans raised to construct public works. First Lord John Russell and then Sydenham and his Executive Council had rejected any suggestion to separate land revenue from the Consolidated Revenue Fund, yet the door was left open for a more practical plan.[92] Interestingly, in Australia Britain had placed revenue from land sales in a special fund to assist emigration, but Bagot did not believe the situation in Canada warranted a similar programme as the revenue was needed to meet existing charges on the Consolidated Revenue Fund.[93] Hincks, in turn, proposed using the revenue not only from crown lands but also from the Clergy Reserves and other special funds controlled by the government to buy back the Canadian debt in the open market. Although the origin of this idea is ambiguous, Hincks, as we have seen, during his first term as Inspector General in 1842–1843 had made good use of the Clergy Reserve Fund to facilitate the government's various financial operations.

Hincks intended "to capitalize the funds arising from the Sales of Crown Lands as has been done with regard to the Clergy Reserves."[94] He pointed out that £600,000, "all of which is now bearing interest," had been raised by the sale of just a third of the 2.4 million acres of Clergy Reserve lands. The public domain constituted, according to Hincks, another 200 million acres.[95] For the purposes of his calculations Hincks confined himself to land within 15 miles of seigneuries or townships in Canada East and the Huron Tract and the Ottawa Valley in Canada West. Here lay 16 million acres, "a million of which is valuable land," estimated to be worth 2s/6d per acre. Under existing circumstances Hincks believed the province could expect an income of at least £2 million. Moreover, the value of public lands available for sale "would be increased materially by the construction of the public

works in the Province." Money generated by land sales would be more
than enough to create an "efficient Sinking Fund for the repayment of
any loan raised by the Imperial Government."[96] If the imperial government refused to guarantee new loans, the provincial government
could still borrow now and pay later with the proceeds of its land sales.
The Clergy Reserve Fund, the Sinking Fund, and the Indian Fund
provided additional funds for investment "that will ultimately in all
probability very nearly absorb our entire debt." Hincks suggested the
government would become "purchasers of its own Securities to the
extent of at least £120,000 Sterling per annum."[97]

    The link between the immigration, railway, and settlement
policies outlined by Hincks came with the proposed capitalization of
crown lands as security for the public debt. From Hincks' perspective
immigration was in both the British and the Canadian interest. Emigration would ease Britain's population problems while at the same
time expanding export markets for its manufactured goods. Immigration would increase trade and bring vacant land into production. Both
of these objectives required improved internal transportation and communication in the colony, and this necessitated increasing the public
debt in order to build canals, railways, and other public works. The
construction in turn would promote immigration and settlement by
providing jobs. Jobs would permit immigrants to earn and save enough
money to buy crown lands, which in turn would provide the government
with the necessary income to enable it to acquire its own public debt
through the repurchase of its outstanding debentures.

    The immediate task, then, was the promotion of public works
projects. Hincks proposed to handle this problem in a variety of ways.
The public debt was already substantial and could not, in the short
term, be increased further. The financial crisis of 1848–1849 demanded
that the direct debt not be increased beyond the proposed £500,000 stg
loan then being negotiated. In order to promote public works and avoid
any increase in the *direct* public debt, Hincks proposed the creation of
local municipal institutions with the power to tax and borrow. Local
authorities would then be in a position to promote local projects. Larger
provincial projects, such as trunk railways, would be encouraged by
provincial guarantees to private companies.

    This was a policy designed to maintain the existing com-
mercial relations between colony and empire. Britain — either the
imperial government or private capitalists — would provide capital for
development, which in turn would promote immigration and trade.
Britain would thereby solve its population problem and at the same
time expand its own export markets. Canada would increase its population and trade, develop its infrastructure, and, most importantly,

enhance the value of its primary resource, land. The potential wealth that existed in a frontier society could be realized and then used to repay any debts incurred in the process of development. Canada, meanwhile, would remain an exporter of the primary products of forest and soil and an importer of British manufactured goods. This was a strategy that in its details built upon the experiences of the 1840s. In the course of the late 1840s and early 1850s, Hincks implemented his plans piece by piece. Each piece was part of a coherent development strategy which remained virtually unchanged for the rest of the Union period and beyond. Neither free trade nor responsible government altered Canadian economic policy.

There was another, less explicit, implication in Hincks' programme: the partially articulated notion that the public debt would become essentially permanent. The Act for the Better Management of the Public Debt allowed government at its discretion to issue by Order-in-Council new debentures to redeem maturing issues; at the same time Hincks intended "investing" moneys owed the Clergy, Sinking and Indian Funds in provincial debentures. When explaining his plans to Barings, Hincks commented that this process — "investing" in your own liabilities — would create "perpetual Annuities"[98] for beneficiaries of those investments. These were clearly not "annuities" since benefits would continue to be paid only so long as the government chose to use tax revenues to pay interest on liabilities which it owned and chose to renew indefinitely. Beneficiaries of the Clery, Indian or other funds had none of the guarantees usually associated with "annuities," yet Hincks's use of the term clearly suggests that in his mind the public debt would be permanent.

Notes

1.   See Finance, R.G. 19, Vol. 1160, Louis-Michel Viger, Receiver General, to Hincks, 29 June 1849. Emphasis in the original.

2.   See Doug Owram, "'Management by Enthusiasm': The First Board of Works of the Province of Canada, 1841–1846," *Ontario History*, LXX (1970), 171–188.

3.   "Report of the Board of Works," 1843, Appendix Q, *Appendix to the Journals of the Legislative Assembly*, 1843.

4.   See Hamilton H. Killaly, President of the Board of Works, "Report," 30 May 1843, ECO, R.G. 1 E 1, Vol. 65, Despatches and Reports, 91–95, and State Book B, Vol. 62, Minute, 9 May 1843, 424–428.

5.   See Finance, R.G. 19, Vol. 2753, Joseph Cary, Deputy Inspector General, to D. Daly, Provincial Secretary, 24 February 1844, Vol. 2754, Cary to Daly, 15 July 1844, and Cary to J. M. Higginson, Civil Secretary, 21 September 1844.

6.   For a more complete discussion of these problems see Owram, "Management by Enthusiasm," especially 181–186.

7.   "Return," 14 July 1847, Appendix SS, *Appendix to the Journals of the Legislative Assembly*, 1847.

8.   See ECO, R.G. 1 E 1, Vol. 65, Despatches and Reports, Stanley to Metcalfe, 29 July 1844, 297–302. The Canadians argued that the £1.5 million stg covered interest and principal as well as a 1 per cent payment — the theoretical minimum — to the Sinking Fund. The interest rather than the premium limited the total amount of debentures issued. ECO, R.G. 1 E 1, State Book D, Vol. 64, Minute, 10 December 1844, 41–43. Metcalfe, meanwhile, explained that there was no need to change the provincial legislation since "the larger sum will not be required for the Works in progress." GGO, R.G. 7 G 12, Vol. 64, Despatch No. 186, Metcalfe to Stanley, 23 December 1844. Also see Finance, R.G. 19, Vol. 2754, Cary to E. Parent, Clerk of the Executive Council, 26 September 1844.

9.   GGO, R.G. 7 G 12, Vol. 65, Despatch No. 84, Cathcart to W. E. Gladstone, 27 June 1846. Inspector General William Cayley proceeded to London to supervise personally arrangements for the new loans, while the government sought temporary loans from domestic banks. Although eventually successful, Cathcart noted the difficulty negotiating such loans and the "extreme embarrassment" to the provincial credit which would result from a failure to negotiate a new guaranteed loan. See GGO, R.G. 7 G 12, Vol. 65, Despatch No. 103, Cathcart to Earl Grey, 8 August 1846, Despatch No. 111, Cathcart to Grey, 12 August 1846, and Despatch No. 118, Cathcart to Grey, 27 August 1846. To help promote sales of its debentures, the government "authorized the investment of certain special funds, the interest where of is expended in the Province, in the new debentures authorized, and trust that in this way a sum of £100,000 under the second act [to extend the imperial guarantee beyond £1.5 million] may be realized."

10.   See ECO, R.G. 1 E 1, State Book E, Vol. 66, Minutes, 21 August, 7 September, and 21 September 1846, 66, 650, 687, 727, and State Book F, Vol. 67, Minute, 10 November 1846, 117. Also see GGO, R.G. 7 G 1, Vol. 113, "Copy," C. E. Trevelyan, the Treasury, to James Stephens, Undersecretary, Colonial Office, 15 August 1846, included in Despatch No. 20, Earl Grey to Lord Cathcart, 18 August 1846, Despatch No. 23, Grey to Cathcart, 29 August 1846, Vol. 114, Despatch No. 45, Grey to Cathcart, 29 October 1846, GGO, R.G. 7 G 12, Vol. 65, Despatch No. 125, Cathcart to Grey, 11 September 1846, Despatch No. 132, Cathcart to Grey, 25 September 1846, Despatch No. 133, Cathcart to Grey, 26 September 1846, Despatch No. 144, Cathcart to Grey, 28 October 1846, Finance, R.G. 19, Vol. 3365, Charles Wood, Chancellor of the Exchequer, to William Cayley, Inspector General, 14 August and 26 August 1846, "Copy," J. B. Heath, Governor, Bank of England, and W. R. Robinson, Deputy Governor, Bank of England, to Wood, 1 September 1846, and Cayley to Wood, 2 September 1846. As part of the deal, the Bank of England agreed to advance £140,000 stg immediately for nine months. As security it would take provincial debentures under the guaranteed loan. Although the debentures were delivered in October 1846, authorization for their sale did not arrive until the end of May 1848. These debentures were not, however, issued. In early 1849 new debentures arrived which the Treasury placed on the market, the proceeds being used to liquidate the 1846 advance to the Canadian government. See ECO, R.G. 1 E 1, State Book H, Vol. 70, Minute, 1 July 1848, 614–615, and GGO, R.G. 7 G 1, Vol. 121, "Copy," Trevelyan to Governor and Deputy Governor of the Bank, 6 December 1848, and Trevelyan to H. Merivale, 22 January 1849, included in Despatch No. 316, Grey to Lord Elgin, 22 January 1849, GGO, R.G. 7 G 12, Vol. 65, "Extract," Mr. [William] Marshall, Chief Cashier, Bank of England, to F. P. Bruneau, Receiver General, 25 February 1848, and

"Copy," F. Hincks, Inspector General, to Marshall, 27 March 1848, included in Despatch No. 36, Elgin to Grey, 27 March 1848, Despatch No. 91, Elgin to Grey, 6 July 1848, and Finance, R.G. 19, Vol. 2755, [Hincks] to Marshall, 28 March 1848.

11. *Debates of the Legislative Assembly*, Vol. II, 30 September and 4 October 1842, 218–220, 317.

12. ECO, R.G. 1 E 1, State Book B, Vol. 62, Minute, 9 May 1843, 424–429.

13. ECO, R.G. 1 E 1, Vol. 65, Despatches and Reports, 1841–1845, Killaly, President, Board of Works, 91–95.

14. *Ibid.*, "Copy," Trevelyan to Stanley, 30 June 1843, included in Stanley to Metcalfe, 3 July 1843, 124–125.

15. *Ibid.*, Stanley to Metcalfe, 3 June 1844, 248–249, ECO, R.G. 1 E 1, State Book D, Vol. 64, Minute, 23 December 1844, 61–63.

16. *Ibid.*, [J. Cary], Report of the Inspector General, 10 October 1844, 317–318, and Finance, R.G. 19, Vol. 2754, Cary to Higginson, 10 October 1844.

17. See GGO, R.G. 7 G 1, Vol. 113, "Copy," Trevelyan to Stephens, 15 August 1846, in Despatch No. 20, Grey to Cathcart, 18 August 1846.

18. ECO, R.G. 1 E 1, State Book D, Vol. 64, Minutes, 3 March 1845, 191, Vol. 65, Despatches and Reports, 359, ECO, R.G. 1 E 1, State Book E, Vol. 66, Minutes, 20 July and 7 September 1846, 541, 687, and GGO, R.G. 7 G 1, Vol. 113, Despatch No. 104, Gladstone to Cathcart, 3 July 1846.

19. GGO, R.G. 7 G 1, Vol. 113, Despatch No. 20, Grey to Cathcart, 18 August 1846.

20. *Ibid.*, Vol. 111, "Copy," Despatch No. 4, Gladstone to Sir William Colebrooke, Lt. Governor, New Brunswick, 2 February 1846, included in Despatch No. 13, Gladstone to Cathcart, 3 February 1846.

21. Finance, R.G. 19, Vol. 1146, James Hopkirk, Provincial Secretary to William Morris, Receiver General, 27 October 1846, and Vol. 1155, Glyns to Morris, 18 November and 3 December 1846, 3 February, 3 March, and 19 April 1847. The Colonial Office voiced its surprise and concern when it found out about this new loan in late 1846, but it did not interfere. See GGO, R.G. 7 G 1, Vol. 115, "Copy," Stephens to Trevelyan, 15 December 1846, and "Copy," Trevelyan to Stephens, 26 December 1846, included in Despatch No. 13, Grey to Elgin, 4 January 1847, GGO, R.G. 7 G 12, Vol. 65, Despatch No. 148, Cathcart to Grey, 11 November 1846, and Despatch No. 159, Cathcart to Grey, 28 December 1846.

22. See Finance, R.G. 19, Vol. 1155, Glyns to Morris, 3 June, 18 June, 3 July, 3 September, and 18 September 1847.

23. *Ibid.*, Glyns to Morris, 18 October, 3 November, 18 November, 17 December 1847, and 14 January 1848. By July 1848 the quotation had slipped to 78. See Glyns to Viger, 7 July 1848.

24. See Finance, R.G. 19, Vol. 1155, Bruneau to Glyns, 17 February 1848, Glyns to Bruneau, 4 March 1848, and Bruneau to Glyns, 25 February 1848. In June 1848 this advance was paid out of funds transferred to Glyns from the Treasury, part of the settlement of the emigration expenses owed the province. See Glyns to Viger, 9 June 1848.

25. GGO, R.G. 7 G 1, Vol. 47, Despatch No. 145, Russell to Thomson, 30 May 1840, and Despatch No. 151, Russell to Thomson, 12 June 1840. Also see GGO, R.G. 7 G 1, Vol. 44, Despatch No. 22, Russell to Thomson, 18 October 1839.

26.   GGO, R.G. 7 G 1, Vol. 97, Despatch No. 369, Russell to Sydenham, 3 May 1841, and Despatch No. 431, Russell to Sydenham, 26 August 1841. Stanley introduced some slight administrative changes in the policy in 1842. GGO, R.G. 7 G 1, Vol. 100, Despatch No. 62, Stanley to Bagot, 3 February 1842. A dispute over payment came in 1844 when, rather than remit funds to the province, the Treasury observed that advances from the Commissariat for Indian and other government services had not been paid by the province. The Treasury credited the provincial account at the Commissariat for the amount of emigration expenses, thus reducing the balance owed by the province. The Executive Council immediately protested these arrangements. See GGO, R.G. 7 G 1, Vol. 108, Despatch No. 325, Stanley to Metcalfe, 31 December 1844, and GGO, R.G. 7 G 12, Vol. 64, Despatch No. 5, Cathcart to Gladstone, 26 January 1845.

27.   GGO, R.G. 7 G 1, Vol. 114, Despatch No. 11, Grey to Elgin, 31 December 1846.

28.   *Ibid.*, Vol. 116, Despatch No. 48, Grey to Elgin, 1 April 1847. Elgin used the occasion to try to get an extension of the imperial guarantee for new loans. He observed that "money cannot be raised on Provincial Debentures under existing circumstances without a considerable sacrifice. It is to be feared that this may tend to diminish the means of employing the large Immigrant population who are expected during the summer unless indeed the guarantee of the British Treasury could be somewhat extended." GGO, R.G. 7 G 12, Vol. 65, Despatch No. 8, Elgin to Grey, 25 February 1847.

29.   GGO, R.G. 7 G 1, Vol. 116, Despatch No. 87, Grey to Elgin, 18 June 1847.

30.   *Ibid.*, Vol. 117, Despatch No. 102, Grey to Elgin, 3 July 1847, and Despatch No. 109, Grey to Elgin, 19 July 1847.

31.   *Ibid.*, Vol. 117, Despatch No. 109, Grey to Elgin, 19 July 1847.

32.   See GGO, R.G. 7 G 12, Vol. 65, Despatch No. 81, Elgin to Grey, 13 August 1847, and GGO, R.G. 7 G 1, Vol. 117, Despatch No. 126, Grey to Elgin, 4 October 1847.

33.   *Ibid.*, Despatch No. 135, Grey to Elgin, 3 November 1847.

34.   In 1847 Glyns reported that new debentures were "unsalable" in London and throughout 1848 reported quotations well below par for Canadian 5 per cent debentures. See Finance, R.G. 19, Vol. 1155, Glyns to Bruneau, 24 March and 7 April 1848, *Glyn Mills Papers*, M.G. 24 D 36, Glyns to Ridout, 15 September 1848, Glyns to Hincks, 29 September 1848, and Glyns to Ridout, 27 October 1848.

35.   GGO, R.G. 7 G 12, Vol. 65, Despatch No. 101, Elgin to Grey, 20 November 1847, and Despatch No. 112, Elgin to Grey, 8 December 1847, and GGO, R.G. 7 G 1, Vol. 118, Despatch No. 151, Grey to Elgin, 6 January 1848, and "Copy," Trevelyan to Herman Merivale, Undersecretary of State for the Colonies, 20 December 1847, included in Despatch No. 151, Grey to Elgin, 6 January 1848. Also see Finance, R.G. 19, Vol. 2755, [Hincks] to Marshall, 28 March 1848.

36.   See GGO, R.G. 7 G 12, Vol. 65, Despatch No. 33, Elgin to Grey, 17 March 1848.

37.   See GGO, R.G. 7 G 1, Vol. 118, Despatch No. 197, Grey to Elgin, 14 April 1848, and GGO, R.G. 7 G 12, Vol. 65, "Copy," Minute of Council, 3 May 1848, included in Despatch No. 50, Elgin to Grey, 3 May 1848.

38.   See GGO, R.G. 7 G 12, Vol. 65, "Copy," Hincks, "Memorandum," 17 May 1848, included in Despatch No. 58, Elgin to Grey, 18 May 1848, and GGO, R.G. 7 G 1, Vol. 119, "Copy," Trevelyan to Merivale, 24 June 1848, included in Despatch No. 241, Grey to Elgin, 30 June 1848. Also see GGO, R.G. 7 G 1, Vol. 118, Despatch No. 197, Grey to Elgin, 14 April 1848, Vol. 119, "Copy," B. Hawes, Colonial Office, to Glyns, 14 April

1848, "Copy," Glyns to [?], 15 April 1848, "Copy," Glyns to Bruneau, 24 March 1848, "Copy," Merivale to Trevelyan, 26 April 1848, "Copy," Trevelyan to Merivale, 4 May 1848, included in Despatch No. 211, Grey to Elgin, 9 May 1848. Glyns had advanced a total of £40,000 stg on security of £80,000 stg debentures deposited at their house. Although that advance had been repaid, Hincks reached a similar arrangement with Barings to cover the July 1848 interest payments. See *Baring Papers*, M.G. 24 D 21, Vol. 1, Hincks to Barings, 7 September 1848, 148–150. By late 1848 he was back asking for another advance to meet interest payments. See Finance, R.G. 19, Vol. 2756, Hincks to Barings, 7 September 1848, Hincks to Glyns, 25 October and 1 November 1848.

39.   In 1846 the Canadian Legislature had complained bitterly about the repeal of the timber duties, asserting that protection was the "fundamental" and "universal" principle of empire. William Gladstone, then Colonial Secretary, observed that "Her Majesty's Government conceive that the protective principle cannot, with justice be described as the universal basis either of the general connection between the United Kingdom and its colonies, or even of their commercial connection." Gladstone argued that Australia had enjoyed considerable economic growth without any of the protective measures demanded by the Canadians. Revisions in timber duties in 1828, 1842, and 1843 had provoked similar prophecies of ruin, yet each time the Canadian timber industry had survived. The Canadians, Gladstone believed, had cried wolf once too often. GGO, R.G. 7 G 1, Vol. 113, Despatch No. 83, Gladstone to Cathcart, 3 June 1846. For examples of earlier protests, see GGO, R.G. 7 G 12, Vol. 56, "Copy," J. T. Brongeest, Chairman, Montreal Board of Trade, Petition, 7 April 1841, Merchants of Ottawa, Petition, 10 April 1841, and "Copy," William Walker, Chairman, Quebec Board of Trade, Memorial, 19 April 1841, included in Despatch No. 52, Sydenham to Russell, 24 April 1841, Vol. 58, Despatch No. 110, Sydenham to Russell, 26 August 1841, Vol. 63, Despatch No. 119, Bagot to Stanley, 12 May 1842, and Despatch No. 19, Bagot to Stanley, 27 January 1843. Nor, would it seem, did all Canadians believe that the repeal of protectionism would spell economic disaster. The *Globe* suggested that the "ruin" and "rapid decay" feared by so many Montreal merchants was a "ridiculous caricature" of the Canadian economy. The *Globe* asked, "Do they speak of Canada? Have the men who signed this [Annexation Manifesto] ever been out of Montreal?" The *Globe*, 20 October 1849, cited in *Free Trade, Annexation, and Reciprocity, 1846–1854*, ed. by Michael S. Cross (Toronto/ Montreal, 1971), 56–57.

40.   Careless, *The Union of the Canadas*, 120.

41.   See T. C. Keefer, *Philosophy of Railroads*, ed., with an introduction, by H. V. Nelles (Toronto, 1972). Information on Keefer is based primarily on Nelles' introduction.

42.   William Ormsby, "Francis Hincks," *Dictionary of Canadian Biography*, Vol. XI, 1881–1890, 406–416.

43.   GGO, R.G. 7 G 12, Vol. 63, Despatch No. 135, Bagot to Stanley, 13 June 1842.

44.   ECO, R.G. 1 E 1, State Book I, Vol. 71, Minute, 20 December 1848, 399.

45.   Inspector General [Hincks], "Memorandum on Immigration and on Public Works as connected therewith," ECO, R.G. 1 E 1, State Book I, Vol. 71, Minute, 20 December 1848, 400. This document is hereafter cited as "Memorandum on Immigration," 20 December 1848.

46.   "Memorandum on Immigration," 20 December 1848, 402.

47.   GGO, R.G. 7 G 1, Vol. 116, Despatch No. 47, Grey to Elgin, 1 April 1847.

48.   See GGO, R.G. 7 G 12, Vol. 65, Despatch No. 27, Elgin to Grey, 16 April 1847, and Despatch No. 22, Elgin to Grey, 26 March 1847.

49.   See GGO, R.G. 7 G 1, Vol. 116, Despatch No. 57, Grey to Elgin, 19 April 1847, and Despatch No. 65, Grey to Elgin, 3 May 1847.

50.   "Memorandum on Immigration," 20 December 1848, 404.

51.   *Ibid.*, 405.

52.   See Finance, R.G. 19, Vol. 2756, Hincks to Glyns, 7 September 1848, and Hincks to Barings, 7 September and 20 December 1848, *Baring Papers*, M.G. 24 D 21, Vol. 1, Dunn to Barings, 22 April 1848, and Hincks to Barings, 7 September 1848, and ECO, R.G. 1 E 1, State Book K, Vol. 70, Minute, 3 June 1848, 534–535.

53.   In 1845 Dunn, together with his 23-year-old French-Canadian wife and most of his children, had returned to England. See Cruikshank, "John Henry Dunn," 256.

54.   £20,000 stg in new 6 per cent debentures had been sold by Barings in January and February. Finance, R.G. 19, Vol. 2756, Hincks to Barings, 3 March 1848, and Hincks to Glyns, 3 March 1848.

55.   See ECO, R.G. 1 E 1, State Book J, Vol. 72, Minute, 30 July 1849, 275–276. In October 1848 Hincks had informed Barings and Glyns that "new arrangements will be made regarding our debentures" during the coming session. They were, as a consequence, to make no sales of the debentures in their hands, although those bonds would not be withdrawn as they were held as security for advances made to the province. Hincks also urged Barings and Glyns to make no sales under par; he much preferred to increase the interest paid to whatever was "required to command money." Finance, R.G. 19, Vol. 2256, Hincks to Glyns, 25 October 1848, and Hincks to Barings, 20 December 1848.

56.   See ECO, R.G. 1 E 1, State Book B, Vol. 62, Minute, 9 May 1843, 422–423.

57.   For example, in May 1850 the Bank of Montreal requested payment for £28,400 cy worth of matured Rebellion Losses and other debentures. Etienne-Paschal Taché, the Receiver General, sent a Bill of Exchange for only £8,400 cy, and the promise that "the balance £20,000 shall not be lost sight of." Taché paid this balance at the end of the month *after* the completion of debenture sales in Britain. Finance, R.G. 19, Vol. 1160, Taché to Alexander Simpson, Cashier, Bank of Montreal, 10 May 1850, Taché to James Leslie, Provincial Secretary, 10 May and 28 May 1850.

58.   "An Act for the Better Management of the Public Debt, Accounts, Revenue, and Property," 12 Vic. cap. 5, *Provincial Statutes of Canada*, 1849, 106–111. Also see Gilbert Norman Tucker, *The Canadian Commercial Revolution, 1845–1851* (New Haven, 1936), 79–80, and McArthur, "History of Public Finance," 172–173.

59.   ECO, R.G. 1 E 1, State Book I, Vol. 71, Minute, 27 December 1848, 433–434.

60.   Finance, R.G. 19, Vol. 1160, Viger to Leslie, 27 December 1848, Viger to D. Davidson, Manager, Bank of British North America, 28 December 1848, Viger to Simpson, 29 December 1848, Viger to Leslie, 3 January 1849, Viger to Simpson, 30 March 1849, Viger to Leslie, 13 April and 22 September 1849.

61.   See Province of Canada, *Report of Select Committee on the Subject of Public Deposits*, "Minutes of Evidence," Appendix EE, Questions Nos. 61, 62, 64, *Appendix to the Journals of the Legislative Assembly*, 1854–1855. The move to Toronto in 1850 provided an opportunity to reopen the question of the bank of deposit, and Hincks addressed letters of inquiry to the Commercial Bank and the Banks of Montreal, British North America, and Upper Canada. Hincks made it clear that "the Gov't [sic] will expect a certain amt. [sic] of accommodation from the Bank or Banks which shall have its account." Finance, R.G. 19, Vol. 2756, Hincks to Simpson, 8 December 1849, Hincks to Davidson, 8 December 1849, Hincks to F. A. Harper, Commercial Bank, 8 December

1848, and Hincks to Ridout, 8 December 1848. In the end the Bank of Upper Canada offered the "most advantageous" terms to the government, which in turn decided that "in future the Public Account be kept with that Institution." ECO, R.G. 1 E 1, State Book J, Vol. 72, Minute, 8 January 1850, 579–580.

62.   ECO, R.G. 1 E 1, State Book K, Vol. 70, Minute, 3 June 1848, 534–535.

63.   *The Elgin–Grey Papers*, ed. by Sir Arthur G. Doughty, Vol. 1 (Ottawa, 1937), 256.

64.   ECO, R.G. 1 E 1, State Book K, Vol. 70, Minute, 3 June 1848, 536–538, and State Book I, Vol. 71, Minutes, 16 August, 13 September, 4 October, 25 October, and 22 November 1848, 70, 131, 208, 270, and 322. Also see Finance, R.G. 19, Vol. 1160, RGO, [Viger] to Leslie, 24 October and 18 November 1848.

65.   Both pound currency and the equivalent dollar values were printed on the face of these debentures. Although it is clear that the government originally intended to issue debentures of less than $10 face value, only $10 and $20 debentures had been printed by June 1848. See Finance, R.G. 19, Vol. 2756, Hincks to Messrs. Rawdon, Wright, and Hatch, New York, 5 June 1848. All of the Orders-in-Council subsequent to that of 3 June 1848, including those ordering the redemption of these debentures, refer to $10 and $20 bonds. When the Receiver General ordered additional debentures printed in anticipation of a large issue in mid-1849, he ordered only $1, $2, and $5 face values. It is not clear if any of these smaller denominations were actually placed in circulation. Charlton's *Standard Catalogue*, the principal guide for numismatists, lists only $10 and $20 issues. See *1976 Standard Catalogue of Canadian Coins, Tokens, Paper Money*, ed. by J. E. Charlton, 24th Edition (Toronto, 1975), 128.

66.   Finance, R.G. 19, Vol. 1160, Viger to Hincks, 2 June 1849. Some of the correspondence between Viger and Hincks during the summer of 1849 was published in Province of Canada, G.-E. Cartier, Provincial Secretary, "Return to an Address from the Legislative Assembly, of 19th Ultimo; for Copies of Official Correspondence with Banks of Montreal and British North America, on the subject of Public Deposits, since the Publication of the Committee on Public Accounts, previous to the late adjournment," 11 April 1855, Appendix EE, *Appendix to the Journals of the Legislative Assembly*, 1854–1855.

67.   See Finance, R.G. 19, Vol. 1160, Viger to Hincks, 9 June and 16 June 1849.

68.   *Ibid.*, Viger to Hincks, 29 June 1849. The £19,500 was owed the Banks of Montreal and British North America.

69.   See Finance, R.G. 19, Vol. 1160, Viger to Ridout, 7 July 1849. Emphasis in the original.

70.   See ECO, R.G. 1 E 1, State Book I, Vol. 71, Minutes, 7 February and 12 March 1849, 487, 547, State Book J, Vol. 72, Minutes, 5 May, 9 June, 27 July, 29 August, 26 September and 14 December 1849, 76, 171, 269, 359, 416, 544, and State Book K, Vol. 73, Minute, 22 February 1850, 51.

71.   A decade later the province would begin selling public works to various municipalities. In 1863, for example, the province sold the Port Whitby Harbour and the Windsor and Scugog road to the County of Ontario for $48,000. See Finance, R.G. 19, Vol. 3375, Luther Holton, Minister of Finance, to John Ratcliffe, Warden, County of Ontario, 22 August 1863.

72.   "An Act to provide, by one general law, for the erection of Municipal Corporations, and the establishment of Regulations of Police, in and for the several Counties, Cities, Towns, Townships and Villages in Upper Canada," 12 Vic. cap. 81, *Provincial Statutes of Canada*, 1849. In addition to the general problem of distinguishing between local and

provincial works, Hincks had to deal as well with particular projects. The most difficult and convoluted problems revolved around the devolution of control of the York roads — Yonge Street, Dundas Street, and the Kingston Road. Originally trustees had been named to oversee the construction and operation of these roads but under the Union control was transferred to the newly created Board of Works. Later in 1849 Toronto offered to purchase the roads. Unhappy with the price offered, Hincks sold these roads to a private company headed by his friend, James Beaty. Although clear evidence was never produced, there was much in these arrangements which suggested that corrupt practices had thwarted Toronto's bid to own these roads. See Michael S. Cross, "The Stormy History of the York Roads, 1833–1865," *Ontario History*, LIV (1962), 1–24.

73.   "Memorandum on Immigration," 20 December 1848, 409–410.

74.   See GGO, R.G. 7 G 12, Vol. 54, Despatch No. 160, Thomson to Russell, 16 September 1840.

75.   This was not lost on Bagot, who soon appointed Hincks as Inspector General. See GGO, R.G. 7 G 12, Vol. 58, Despatch No. 113, Sydenham to Russell, 28 August 1841, and GGO, R.G. 7 G 12, Vol. 63, Despatch No. 135, Bagot to Stanley, 13 June 1842. Also see Ormsby, "Sir Francis Hincks," 154. Hincks also supported Sydenham's unsuccessful bid to create a provincial bank of issue. Sydenham intended to use profits from the issue of provincial notes to support public works construction, and this may have been the inspiration for Hincks' plan in 1848 to use special small denomination debentures to finance canal construction.

76.   Many of Sydenham's more conservative followers believed the legislation went too far. John Macaulay, for one, believed that the District Council proposal was "pregnant with much mischief" and commented in his inimitable fashion that "We all know that the air of this Continent is by no means too genial to Monarchy, & one would suppose that the Government would be the last to administer periodical draughts of exhilarating democratic gas to our people situated on the confines of the Great Republic — Yet we are to have about 40 unbridled little democratic assemblies meeting four times a year in Canada. I am perfectly confounded at the measure[.]" *The Arthur Papers*, Vol. 3, Macaulay to Arthur, 9 August 1841, 441–444.

77.   *Baring Papers*, M.G. 24 D 21, Vol. 1, Hincks to Barings, 23 April 1852, 504–510. Emphasis in the original.

78.   "Memorandum on Immigration," 20 December 1848, 412–414.

79.   *Ibid.*, 411.

80.   See GGO, R.G. 7 G 12, Vol. 65, Despatch No. 151, Elgin to Grey, 20 December 1848.

81.   See GGO, R.G. 1 G 1, Vol. 121, Despatch No. 315, Grey to Elgin, 24 January 1849.

82.   "Memorandum on Immigration," 20 December 1848, 415.

83.   Both George-Étienne Cartier, when introducing a petition from the St. Lawrence and Atlantic, and Hincks, when introducing the Guarantee Act, pointed out that state aid to railways was common practice south of the border, particularly in Massachusetts and New York. See *Debates of the Legislative Assembly*, Vol. 8, Part 1, 15 Feb. 1849, 696, and Vol. 8, Part 3, 11 Apr. 1849, 1825.

84.   See O. D. Skelton, *Life and Times of Sir Alexander Tilloch Galt*, ed., with an introduction, by Guy Maclean (Toronto, 1966), 20–25, and A. W. Currie, *The Grand Trunk Railway of Canada* (Toronto, 1957), 5–6.

85. See Gerald J. J. Tulchinsky, *The River Barons: Montreal Businessmen and the Growth of Industry and Transportation, 1837–1853* (Toronto and Buffalo, 1977), 149–150, Russell D. Smith, "The Early Years of the Great Western Railway, 1833–1857," *Ontario History*, LX (1968), 205–227, and Douglas McCalla, "Peter Buchanan, London Agent for the Great Western Railway of Canada," in *Canadian Business History: Selected Studies, 1497–1971*, ed. by David S. MacMillan (Toronto, 1972), 199–201.

86. See *Debates of the Legislative Assembly*, Vol. VIII, Part III, 1849, 1857–1861.

87. "An Act for Affording the Guarantee of the Province to the Bonds of Rail-way Companies on Certain Conditions, and for Rendering Assistance in the Construction of the Halifax and Quebec Railway," 12 Vic. cap. 29, *Provincial Statutes of Canada*, 1849, 213–215.

88. *Baring Papers*, M.G. 24 D 21, Vol. 1, "Extract from a Report of a Committee of the Honorable the Executive Council on Matters of State, dated 30th July 1849 approved by His Excellency the Governor General in Council on the same Day," 214–219. Also see ECO, R.G. 1 E 1, State Book J., Vol. 72, Minute, 30 July 1849, 275–276.

89. See Finance, R.G. 19, Vol. 1154, Barings to Taché, 3 May 1850.

90. See GGO, R.G. 7 G 12, Vol. 56, Despatch No. 214, Sydenham to Russell, 14 January 1841, Vol. 62, Despatch No. 34, Bagot to Stanley, 17 February 1842, and Despatch No. 77, Bagot to Stanley, 11 April 1842.

91. See "Memorandum on Immigration," 20 December 1848, 408.

92. GGO, R.G. 7 G 1, Vol. 96, "Memorial," 26 March 1841, included in Despatch No. 344, Russell to Sydenham, 26 March 1841. Also see GGO, R.G. 7 G 12, Vol. 56, Despatch No. 57, Sydenham to Russell, 6 May 1841.

93. GGO, R.G. 7 G 12, Vol. 62, Despatch No. 77, Bagot to Stanley, 11 April 1842.

94. "Memorandum on Immigration," 20 December 1848, 416.

95. Most of the province's good land had already been given away. As Bagot observed, "Formerly claims to land were created in the most lavish and improvident manner . . . almost everyone who applied obtained an order for land until it seemed as if the gov't [sic] had no other object but to divest itself as quickly as possible of all control over the unsettled portions of the Province." Bagot went on to argue that the problems resulted "not from Emigrants or Settlers or persons of the lower classes whose influence must at any time be unimportant, but from the wealthier and more powerful class who had made land speculation a trade and whose influence in the Legislative Council and Assembly, of which many of them were members, enabled them to resist any attempt to limit the creation of land rights." GGO, R.G. 7 G 12, Vol. 62, Despatch No. 77, Bagot to Stanley, 11 April 1842. The best general survey of land policies remains L. F. Gates, *Land Policies of Upper Canada* (Toronto, 1968). Also see David Gagan, "Property and 'Interest': Some Preliminary Evidence of Land Speculation by the 'Family Compact' in Upper Canada, 1820–1840," *Ontario History*, LXX (1978), 63–70, Leo A. Johnson, "The Settlement of the Western District, 1749–1850," in *Aspects of Nineteenth-Century Ontario: Essays Presented to James J. Talman*, ed. by F. H. Armstrong, H. A. Stevenson, and J. D. Wilson (Toronto, 1974), 19–35, and "Land Policy, Population Growth and Social Structure in the Home District, 1793–1851," *Ontario History*, LXIII (1971), 41–60.

96. "Memorandum on Immigration," 20 December 1848, 418–419.

97. Finance, R.G. 19, Vol. 2757, Hincks to Barings, [8] February 1851, and Hincks to Glyns, [8] February 1851.

98. *Ibid.*

Chapter 4
The Railway Mania

Money was poured out like water upon the
building of the Grand Trunk and Great
Western Lines, and, between 1852 and
1857, there was a period of speculative
mania which sent governments,
municipalities and corporations into
a wild rivalry of expenditure
and extravagance.[1]
— J. Castell Hopkins

In early 1849 the Reform government initiated a series of policies designed to end the short-term financial crisis and promote long-term growth. The Act for the Better Management of the Public Debt, the Guarantee Act, and the Municipal Corporations Act were not isolated initiatives; they were individual components of a coherent strategy which assumed that rapid economic expansion could best be encouraged by improving transport systems in the province. Improvements in internal transportation demanded state intervention either directly in the form of public works programmes or indirectly in the form of aid to railway companies. Not until the financial crisis eased, however, could one expect initiatives like the Guarantee Act or the Municipal Corporations Act to begin to have an effect.

  The provincial government decided in late 1848 to borrow £500,000 stg in Britain to help complete its canal system, to repay short-term debentures issued to pay accounts, and to redeem large issues of outstanding debentures due to mature in the near future.[2] In June 1849 Hincks journeyed to London to supervise personally the negotiation of this new loan, but the London capital market was in no mood to absorb new Canadian debentures. In May 1849 Canadian 5 per cent bonds had been quoted at only 88 to 90. Such large discounts convinced the government to up the ante: the new £500,000 stg issue would pay 6 per cent for 25 years.

  The process of creating a capital market proved difficult. Unlike debentures issued between 1843 and 1846, these bonds were not supported by imperial credit. Four per cent Canadian debentures carrying an imperial guarantee covering interest payments — but not principal — had sold quickly and easily. The imperial guarantee meant, according to George Carr Glyn, that investors responded as if these were "in fact an English security." Investors purchased such bonds "without any hesitation like an Exchequer Bill or any other Government Security."[3] The new issue was different; these securities stood on their own in a capital market reluctant during a period of tight money to invest in colonies. Without a British guarantee Barings and Glyns could arrange only one small sale of the new debentures in 1849.

With no success in Britain Hincks and Receiver General Louis-Michel Viger struggled to meet the government's obligations. In the absence of cash, money might still be raised by borrowing from those who had no choice but to lend. Employees and contractors who could not be paid with cash would be paid with interest-bearing debentures. This policy had been adopted in 1848, and the Act for the Better Management of the Public Debt had authorized all such issues. As the financial crisis reached its peak in mid-1849, the government again extended its use of small-denomination debentures issued "in lieu of money."[4] By February 1850 the new Receiver General, Étienne-Paschal Taché, again raised the limit on the total amount of these debentures to be issued as he had "reason to believe that further issues to a much larger amount will be required for the Public Service."[5] Fortunately, the financial crisis was about to end.

Hincks and the Reform Government, meanwhile, were under increasing pressure to cut spending with a retrenchment programme. Just as the crisis was ending Hincks gave in to this pressure; on 31 May 1850 he initiated a parliamentary enquiry into

> what further regulations and checks it may be proper ... to adopt for establishing an effective control upon all charges incurred in the receipt, custody and application of the public money, and what further measures can be adopted for reducing any part of the public expenditure without detriment to the public service.

Hincks's remarks in the Legislature suggest, however, that the Inspector General believed little should be expected from such an enquiry and commented that "if there was any branch of the public service, more than another upon which retrenchment could be effected, it was the contingent expenses of the Legislature."[6] At the same time Hincks assured the opposition that he "had never expressed himself as being opposed to retrenchment; but on the contrary, any saving that could be effected, consistent with the efficiency of the public service, should have his strenuous support."[7]

Mr. Boulton remained unhappy with the government's proposal to create a select committee, since its recommendations, as Hincks assured him would be the case, were not binding on the government. Fears that Hincks would sabotage the retrenchment process were, in the eyes of the opposition, quickly confirmed; when the First Report of the Committee was submitted at the beginning of July 8 of its 18 members[8] dissented. They argued that any reference to the Minutes of the Committee would show

> that the greater part of its proceedings has been rendered nugatory, and the vote previously taken reversed, by the amendments moved and carried by the Honorable Inspector General.[9]

It was not Hincks, however, who restricted the utility of the Select Committee.

At the first meeting of the Select Committee Hincks moved to begin immediately an examination of revenue and the administrative costs of collection to be followed by an examination of expenditures. Boulton then moved that the administrative heads of each government department be required to submit a complete return on all employees and their salaries, and that they then be called before the Committee to explain those returns. From this point on the Select Committee ignored the problems of revenue, the administrative costs of collection, and general expenditures and focused its attention instead on the civil service, salaries paid various officials including the Governor General, and the contingency expenses of each department. In preparation for its First Report the Committee confined its "labours by a careful review of the several duties assigned to the Chief Functionaries of the State, their position and emoluments."[10] Little came of the Select Committee enquiry in the short term, although seven years later the Civil Service Act imposed on public employees a far more uniform system of ranks and grades complete with salary maximums and minimums, created a Board to oversee the administration of a Civil Service Examination, and made that examination a necessary prerequisite for government employment.[11] No doubt the easing of financial restrictions during the summer of 1850 removed any pressure on the Committee to attempt more in the way of retrenchment.

Not until early March 1850 did Glyns place any of the £500,000 stg debenture issue — £2,000 in late March and another £2,000 in mid-April. Barings sold only £1,000 in mid-April. Then, finally, in May 1850 the news for which Taché and Hincks had been waiting arrived: £437,500 stg in debentures had been sold. Glyns commented that "it has taken some little time to bring the public mind to bear upon the satisfactory position of the financial State of the Province, but the favourable result of the operation is the best proof of its success." Barings were less sanguine and warned that the deal had been completed only after their efforts convinced investors that "no more would be offered in the market."[12] Some problems remained, but by October subscribers had made the final instalments on the debentures. By the end of the year Canadian 6 per cent and 5 per cent debentures were quoted at 105–106 and 96–97 respectively, rising to 107.5 and 97.5 by June 1851.

The government quickly transferred the proceeds from this loan to Canadian banks and immediately called in and redeemed all of the special small-denomination short-term debentures it had issued in 1848–1849, as well as other maturing securities. This left a large surplus of cash which remained on deposit in various domestic banks, most of it at 3 per cent interest.[13]

The government had weathered the financial storm of 1848–1849 with its credit intact. Indeed, it had created a new capital market for its securities. The price, however, was a sharp increase in the public debt from £3.8 million cy in 1847 to £4.5 million cy in 1850. In May 1850 the province had negotiated a £500,000 stg loan on the clear understanding that the total public debt would not be allowed to increase further. Uninhibited by its recent travail and apparently unconcerned about its recent promises to its British banking agents, the provincial government would soon authorize a new debenture issue of £400,000 stg as part of its programme of guaranteeing railway debts.[14]

Hincks, aware of the limits on Canadian credit, had introduced the Guarantee Act to encourage private investors to build the "public works" he believed necessary to stimulate economic growth. When Hincks raised the matter of a guarantee with the Executive Council in December 1848, he suggested that the province should guarantee half of the capital needed to construct railways. The financial crisis, however, forced a retreat. The government, in the eventual enactment, promised to guarantee only the interest — and not the principal — on railway loans. Hincks assumed that a provincial guarantee on the bonds of a private railway would ensure their marketability in London and other capital markets in much the same way as a similar imperial guarantee had led to easy sales of relatively low-interest provincial debentures during the 1840s.

The policy did not produce the desired results: bonds for the St. Lawrence and Atlantic Railway, the first of the railways to apply for the guarantee, could not be sold in London within acceptable margins.[15] Barings and Glyns commented in January 1851 that "there are many elements of distrust afloat which would militate against any attempt to realize a considerable amount of any Canadian securities."[16] Clearly one element of "distrust" involved doubts as to the profitability of Canadian railways. As James Price told Joshua Bates, a Barings agent in Boston, "that they would benefit the Colony there can be no question, but whether they would be profitable for some time to come is more doubtful."[17] Barings and Glyns were equally cold to appeals from the Great Western, but the latter had more luck raising money in late 1851 as a new plan to substitute railway debentures for shares produced somewhat better results.[18]

With the railways clearly needing more assistance than that provided by the Guarantee Act, the government reconsidered its position. The return of prosperity and the successful completion of the £500,000 stg loan provided the opportunity to extend greater assistance to the railways. No longer strapped for funds, Hincks returned to his earlier proposal to issue provincial bonds on behalf of the railway. He raised the matter with Barings and Glyns;[19] neither liked the idea. These bankers reminded Hincks that a large number — £600,000 stg in all — of Canadian 5 per cent debentures were due to mature in 1854 and 1855, and many British investors wondered if Canada had made proper arrangements for maturation. Indeed, many expected the government

will itself before many years become again a borrower and that therefore notwithstanding the improved conditions of the revenue of the Province it cannot be said that implicit confidence is entertained in the stability of Canadian credit.

Barings and Glyns did suggest that the government extend its guarantee to cover principal as well as interest on railway bonds, but only if the total amount to be guaranteed were limited. Moreover, they insisted that all railway bonds thus guaranteed be marketed only through their two houses. If the government agreed to extend the guarantee to principal and limit the total liability, Barings and Glyns would try to promote sales and reassure "friends" by purchasing the first £100,000 stg of St. Lawrence and Atlantic bonds at 85.[20] Both the government and the railway rejected this offer; an offer of 85 made little sense when the quotations for Canadian 6 per cent debentures stood at 103 and for Canadian 5 per cents at 94 to 95.

Hincks refused to abandon the idea of substituting provincial debentures for railway bonds. If the government was to extend its guarantee to cover principal as well as interest, there seemed no reason not to substitute provincial securities for private railway bonds since Canadian debentures commanded a higher price in the market. In April and again in May 1851 Hincks asked Barings and Glyns for their

advice, only to receive the same reply. Although admitting the substitution of government for railway bonds would increase the income from
sales, they reminded Hincks that previous

> assurances had left on our minds the impression which was shared by
> the subscribers to the last loan [the £500,000 stg loan in 1850] that the
> policy of the Government was to abstain from any increase of the Colonial
> Debt.

They did, however, increase their offer to buy the first £100,000 stg of
railway bonds from 85 to 98 if the government extended its guarantee
to cover principal as well as interest and limited the total liability to
£1 million stg.[21]

    The reservations of Barings and Glyns did not deter Hincks.
In August 1851 the Legislature passed the Main Trunk Line of Railway
Act. Although designed primarily to provide the legislative framework
for the much discussed intercolonial and its extension from Quebec to
Hamilton, this Act significantly modified the government's policy
towards all railway loan guarantees. Henceforth the government would
extend the guarantee to cover "the payment of the principal . . . as
well as to the payment of the interest thereon." More importantly,
Section XXII gave the government discretionary power to issue "Provincial Debentures for the amount to be guaranteed, or any part thereof."
These provincial debentures could be exchanged for the bonds of a
railway. The government also attempted to limit its total potential
liability by restricting not the amount to be guaranteed but the railways
that might qualify. The guarantee now applied only to the Grand
Trunk, the St. Lawrence and Atlantic, the Great Western, and the
Ontario, Simcoe, and Huron railways.[22]

    Receiver General Taché wasted little time in putting the
new policy into effect; he immediately sent Barings and Glyns the first
£100,000 stg of a proposed £400,000 worth of 25-year, 6 per cent debentures intended for the St. Lawrence and Atlantic account. At the same
time the government issued two drafts for £50,000 stg each, one on
Barings and the other on Glyns, in favour of John Young, Vice-
President of the St. Lawrence and Atlantic Railway. Barings and Glyns
reacted with surprise when the debentures arrived, but Taché reiterated that these were indeed *provincial debentures*. They were exactly
the same as the recent £500,000 stg issue marketed in 1850, and no
distinction, according to the Receiver General, was to be drawn between
the two issues. These debentures and others that followed sold quickly
and at premiums.[23] There followed in quick succession a £200,000 stg
issue for the Great Western Railway in October 1852, and a
£300,000 stg issue for the same line in August 1854.[24] Another

£270,000 stg guarantee would be granted to the Great Western in 1854 and 1855.

Although not intended to be part of the main trunk line, the Ontario, Simcoe, and Huron Railway was given special status because, according to Taché, it "had been commenced on the faith of the previous Act."[25] All preliminaries were quickly sorted out, and in early November 1852 the government authorized a £275,000 stg bond issue in favour of that railway. By July 1854 an additional guarantee brought the total for the Ontario, Simcoe, and Huron to £475,000 stg.[26]

These railways — the St. Lawrence and Atlantic, the Great Western, and to a lesser extent the Ontario, Simcoe, and Huron — were intended to be parts of a provincial railway system. It was this vision of a provincial rail system that had inspired the government in general and Francis Hincks in particular. The critical link in the system would be the Grand Trunk. Although the last line to qualify for the guarantee, its appetite for provincial debentures would prove unmatched.[27]

The Grand Trunk always saw itself as more than the middle link in a rail system of which the St. Lawrence and Atlantic constituted an eastern section and the Great Western a western section; rather it intended to merge Canada's railways into a single corporation. The first stage was the takeover of the St. Lawrence and Atlantic, whose stock was selling at a 40 per cent discount in December 1852. The Grand Trunk absorbed the line and exchanged its own stock for that of the St. Lawrence and Atlantic. This proved a boon to the stockholders of the latter company. By May 1853 St. Lawrence and Atlantic stock hit par; by June 1854 that stock was selling at a 22 per cent premium.[28] As part of the deal the Grand Trunk fell heir to an additional £67,500 stg guarantee authorized for the St. Lawrence and Atlantic, as well as £250,000 stg intended for the Quebec and Richmond Railway.[29] The original capitalization of the Grand Trunk, meanwhile, had included a proposed government guarantee of nearly £2 million stg, but in January 1853 Taché reported that

> there is every probability that this guarantee will not be claimed by the Company and that a proposal to abandon it has been already informally, and will be formally made. In this case the liabilities under the Railway Guarantee Act will be reduced to the small amount already stated [the £67,500 stg originally intended for the St. Lawrence and Atlantic].[30]

Such optimism proved fanciful.

In October 1853 the Grand Trunk qualified for its first £100,000 stg guaranteed loan. At the same time C. E. Anderson, the Deputy Receiver General, informed Barings and Glyns that the total amount to which the Grand Trunk would eventually be entitled "is as now understood to be £1,811,500 stg. one half of which will be ready for transmission from here by 1st December [1853]."[31] Over the course of the next several months debentures would be sold, and the proceeds turned over to the Grand Trunk. When Thomas Baring began to worry about the Grand Trunk's voracious appetite for capital, Hincks reassured him that

> you may rely upon it that in future there will be better management. We were *perfectly aware* of the state of things in England and have been taking every means practicable to keep down Expenditure. . . . We shall, however, in future be more cautious and all calls will be made subject to the approval of the Directors in London.[32]

Whatever restraints Hincks intended had little effect. By the spring of 1854 the Grand Trunk was requesting a further guarantee of £300,000 stg.[33] Although slow in acting, the Legislature proved very generous: in May 1855 the government authorized a further guarantee for £900,000 stg, transmitted the debentures to Barings and Glyns, and passed the proceeds on to the railway by the end of the year.[34] In mid-1855, then, outstanding debentures issued as part of the government's guarantee for railway loans totalled £3,456,500 stg, excluding the £900,000 which would be added to the total by the end of the year.

The government foresaw few problems in increasing the public debt to aid railway construction. The £500,000 stg loan in 1850 had left the province with substantial cash surpluses which it placed in term deposits with a variety of banks. Trade had revived, and revenue continued to flow into the treasury. In spite of the warnings from Barings and Glyns that a flood of new debentures would seriously injure Canada's credit, those bonds sold easily and at high prices. By the end of 1850 Canadian 6 per cent debentures were quoted in London at between 105 and 106; two years later £200,000 stg worth of debentures would be sold at 114.[35]

Hincks had two objectives when he introduced the Guarantee Act and later the Main Trunk Line of Railway Act: to ensure the construction of "public works" without increasing the public debt. The first objective was met, although the quality of the finished product, particularly in the case of the Grand Trunk, left much to be desired. The second objective could never be met in the atmosphere of largesse which existed at mid-century. After the passage of the Main Trunk Line of Railway Act provincial debentures were sold and the proceeds turned over to private companies (see Table 2). Obfuscatory distinctions between "direct" and "indirect" debts could not disguise the province's new liabilities. There would be no getting around this unpleasant

Table 2: Provincial Debentures Issued as a Guarantee to Various Railways, July 1855 (£1,000 stg)

Great Western Railway		
1 October 1852	£200.0	
3 July 1854	300.0	
17 November 1854	100.0	
15 January 1855	100.0	
1 June 1855	70.0	
	£770.0	£770.0
Ontario, Simcoe, and Huron Railway		
8 November 1852	£100.0	
9 April 1853	175.0	
28 November 1854	200.0	
	£475.0	475.0
Grant Trunk Railway System		
(a) St. Lawrence and Atlantic Railway		
28 October 1851	£300.0	
14 July 1852	100.0	
14 December 1852	60.0	
24 January 1853	7.5	
	£467.5	
(b) Quebec and Richmond Railway		
5 October 1853	£100.0	
17 August 1854	150.0	
	£250.0	
(c) Grand Trunk Railway		
2 March 1854	£100.0	
22 May 1854	100.0	
31 July 1854	110.0	
8 November 1854	50.0	
8 November 1854	174.0	
17 November 1854	26.0	
26 January 1855	498.8	
23 July 1855	122.5	
	£1,181.3	
		1,898.8
Amount Actually Released		£3,143.8
Amount Authorized but not yet		
Released to Grand Trunk		312.7
Total Guarantee		£3,456.5

Source: Finance, R.G. 19, Vol. 1162, [C. E. Anderson], "Memorandum of Provincial Guarantee to Various Railway Companies, Sterling," 25 July 1855.

fact when, in 1856, the various railways began defaulting on payments due to the government to cover the interest on these securities. The same would prove true of Hincks's attempts to shift to local authorities the financial obligations associated with the promotion of local works.

The modifications of the Guarantee Act led to a rapid increase in the total amount of provincial debentures placed in the market. New initiatives to enhance the credit of local governments created under the Municipal Corporations Act led to an equally sub-stantial increase in the province's debt. In 1848 Hincks noted that local projects should be built by local governments out of local revenue. To facilitate this process local municipal governments had to be created. It had been assumed that, with incorporation, the local tax base would suffice to ensure that loans for public works projects could be raised on the local credit. The Municipal Corporations Act proved insufficient as most municipalities could find no market for their debentures in the early 1850s.

This difficulty led Hincks to introduce the Consolidated Municipal Loan Fund Act for Upper Canada in 1852.[36] This Act allowed municipalities to raise money through the intermediation of the prov-incial government. It created a special "fund"[37] administered by the province; "provincial" debentures would be issued on this fund. The municipalities, after appropriate by-laws had been passed, could apply to the government for specific amounts, and the province would then issue debentures to municipal treasurers. Although the debentures paid 6 per cent interest, municipalities paid 8 per cent. In this way the province would be able to build a sinking fund, which in turn would secure the debt. Moneys raised, meanwhile, could only be used for transportation improvements; most went to railway construction, although some went to build bridges and roads. Hincks hoped that the "provincial" as opposed to the "municipal" character of these deben-tures would increase their market value; that in fact turned out to be the case. He also hoped, however, that the debentures would not increase the public debt; that proved to be impossible.

Debentures issued on the Consolidated Municipal Loan Fund were not secured by the Consolidated Revenue Fund and thus did not technically represent an increase in the provincial debt. Receiver General Taché stressed this point when, in early 1853, he alerted Barings and Glyns of their issue. Taché advised that

> no doubt they will in course of time be offered in your Market and you will exercise your own judgment regarding them . . . as there is no liability on the Provincial Revenue for such issues.[38]

Yet the government handled interest payments on the debentures in exactly the same manner as any other provincial issue. The Receiver

General paid coupons presented at his office with no reference to whether or not a particular municipality was in arrears. As C. E. Anderson, the Deputy Receiver General, explained, "they are in fact treated as if they were the coupons of bonds of the Consolidated Revenue Fund."[39]

By early 1855 12 municipalities which had borrowed a total of £498,000 cy were in arrears for nearly £18,000 cy.[40] In November Taché informed the Executive Council that the £1.5 million cy authorized had already been appropriated and that arrears in interest payments from municipalities now amounted to over £36,000 cy. He observed that £24,000 intended for the Sinking Fund had instead been used to pay interest. Taché also reported — a harbinger of things to come — that almost £500 cy had already been drawn on the Consolidated Revenue Fund to meet interest payments on Consolidated Municipal Loan Fund debentures. Taché demanded action be taken to correct this situation, but little could be done.[41]

Sectional differences, meanwhile, had not impeded Hincks' programme. The accepted division of the province into two units, each with its own civil law, school systems, and municipal institutions, restricted the application of the Municipal Corporations Act to Canada West. The larger cities in the eastern section, however, already held special charters which allowed them to tax and borrow on their own credit. Despite the problems already being experienced in Upper Canada, the Assembly extended its loan programme to Lower Canada. The Consolidated Municipal Loan Fund Act for Lower Canada was similar in all particulars to its counterpart in Upper Canada. The municipalities quickly took up the £1.5 million cy made available to them and fell into arrears on interest payments with similar speed. The Act for Lower Canada did little but multiply the province's financial problems.

Nor did these bonds do the provincial credit in London much good.[42] They began to move into the London market in haphazard fashion in 1856. The method of issuing the debentures ensured this result. The province did not market the bonds through its usual financial agents. Rather, the municipalities received the debentures and, in the majority of cases, used them to pay contractors; they in turn gave them to their bankers, who then put them on the market.[43] The net result was a depreciated price which helped dampen the market for all other Canadian securities.

The situation worsened in 1858 when the full impact of the depression began to be felt. Later, T. C. Baring summed up the situation when he observed:

> The interest on these Municipal Loan Fund Bonds is as you know guaranteed by the Province, though the guarantee is worded in so ambiguous

a manner as to leave it in doubt whether the Province could be legally compelled to pay. Of course more than half the Municipalities find themselves unwilling or unable (for many of those in Upper Canada are very hard up) to provide their own interest, and consequently one of the heavy items in Galt's financial statement this year [1859] was the amount required to meet this difficulty.[44]

Alexander T. Galt, the Minister of Finance, had already decided to remove the ambiguity once and for all. In 1859 he initiated a conversion of the debt.[45] Thus, 10 years after the passage of the Municipal Corporations Act and seven years after the Municipal Loan Fund Act for Upper Canada, both of which had been designed to avoid an increase in the public debt, the growing municipal debt became part of the provincial debt.

Throughout the 1850s the government continued to refer to its growing debt associated with various provincial and local transportation policies as an "indirect" debt. In its financial calculations the province preferred to consider only its "direct" debt, yet even here the government failed to take full advantage of the opportunities presented by prosperity to reduce liabilities. Had it done so perhaps the "indirect" debt would not have proven so burdensome in the longer term.

Certainly the opportunity to reduce liabilities existed. The first six years of the decade witnessed the rapid expansion of the Canadian economy. With the substantial increase in new arrivals in 1847–1848, the Province of Canada grew to 1.8 million by 1851. The rate of growth slowed somewhat during the 1850s, but population still increased by another 36 per cent, reaching 2.5 million in 1861.[46] Although below the peak years of the late 1840s, immigration continued to account for a portion of this growth. Between 1852 and 1857 an average of almost 30,000 immigrants arrived each year, but in 1858 and 1859 the number of new arrivals fell to 12,300 and 6,300 respectively.[47]

The increase in population and settlement helped expand the agriculture frontier in Canada West and promoted a rapid increase in Canadian exports. The railway construction boom combined with population growth to promote an equally rapid increase in imports. The government, meanwhile, relied upon the tariff for 80 per cent of its revenue; expanding trade thus ensured a healthy treasury. Although population growth led to new demands for expanded government and social services, revenues more than kept pace. The Consolidated Revenue Fund, as a result, ran substantial annual surpluses averaging £185,600 cy between 1850 and 1856 (see Appendix I). With such large surpluses one would expect the government to have reduced its liabilities significantly. Those liabilities were not, however, reduced; they increased.

The debt position of the Canadian government deteriorated steadily during these years (see Table 3).

Table 3: Public Debt of Canada, 1849–1856 (£1 million cy)

Year	Direct Debt	Indirect Debt	Total	Debentures Redeemed
1849	£4.09		£ 4.09	£.22
1850	4.51	£[.19]	4.70	.94
1851	4.45	.67	5.12	.74
1852	4.67	.92	5.59	.19
1853	4.62	2.86	7.48	.327
1854	4.35	5.36	9.71	.308
1855	4.31	7.15	11.46	.681
1856	4.70	7.49	12.19	.117

Source: Finance, R.G. 19, Vol. 3368, "Memo of Public Debt of Canada," January 1859, "Statement of the Public Debt from the year 1851 to 1860," *Report of the Minister of Finance, Public Accounts*, in *Sessional Papers*, Vol. XIX, No. 2, 1861, Sessional Paper No. 3: "Statement of Debentures Redeemed under Authority of Act 12 Vic., cap. 5, to 31 January 1853," Appendix (D), No. 41, *Appendix to the Journals of the Legislative Assembly*, 1854, Appendix (D), No. 27, *Appendix*, 1855, Appendix (30), No. 44, *Appendix*, 1856, Appendix (4), No. 30, *Appendix*, 1857.

Dollars in original documents have been converted to pounds cy. All calculations are my own.

The "indirect" debt of the government grew from £190,000 cy in 1850 to £7.5 million cy in 1856. Surprisingly the direct debt grew as well, from £4.5 million cy in 1850 to £4.7 million in 1856. In that year the total debt of the province stood at £12.2 million cy, a 215 per cent increase since 1849.

The government had the cash to reduce its direct debt during these years but did not do so. Part of the problem was financial miscalculations. In 1854 and 1855 a large portion of old Upper Canadian bond issues would mature. The £500,000 stg loan in 1850 had anticipated this maturation, and much of the cash from that loan remained on deposit in a number of banking institutions. Despite this, the government found itself short of cash and unable to redeem its debentures.

On 1 April 1854, £200,000 stg in 5 per cent debentures would mature. No sooner had the £500,000 stg loan been completed in May 1850 than Hincks ordered Barings and Glyns to start purchasing outstanding Canadian 5 per cent debentures.[48] In June 1852 Hincks informed Barings and Glyns that "it is absolutely necessary" to invest £100,000 for the Sinking Fund in provincial 5 per cents which were "so near maturity." Again in July 1852 Taché ordered Barings and Glyns to buy up to £50,000 stg of these debentures as long as the price did not exceed par. Glyns reported they were unable to find bonds at that price "nor can we see much prospect in the present state of our money market of our being able to do so."[49] As the maturation date drew nearer Taché again ordered Barings and Glyns to purchase at not more than par all 5 per cent bonds possible. Not until January and February did Barings and Glyns purchase a total of £11,000 stg of these debentures.[50]

The redemption process should have been simple enough despite the failure to purchase bonds in advance. The money needed for redemption was already in the bank. The government, however, chose to complicate the situation by launching a speculative adventure four months prior to the date of its bond maturation. Although it is not clear from whom Taché and Hincks got their information, they ordered Barings and Glyns to purchase up to £260,000 stg British Consols, which paid 3 per cent, "on the best terms that can be procured." According to Taché, "the intention of said investment was in the first instance for the purpose of reselling in the month of April next and redeeming the proceeds some £200,000 of 5 pCt [sic] Provincial Bonds due in London."[51] The cash that was used to purchase these Consols could have remained on deposit in Canada at roughly the same interest; the government already had a series of special deposits earning 3 and sometimes 4 per cent interest.[52] Yet the decision had been made, and the money transferred to London. Barings and Glyns began buying Consols in roughly £25,000 stg lots at between 94 and 96. These purchases were completed in January 1854.[53]

One month later the government tried to unload these Consols but found the price had fallen. They could not be sold, according to Barings and Glyns, without a "considerable loss" to the province. Taché, unable to sell the Consols, found himself having to negotiate a "short term loan" from his London agents to cover debenture redemptions.[54] This turn of events did not worry Taché who thought that the loan could easily be paid "avec l'argent que nous pouvons commander le 15 de Juin prochain. Le revenue, a l'ouverture de la navigation, sera très considérable." To reassure Hincks further, Taché added that

Il est [illegible] de remarquer les Recettes durant les mois de Mars, Avril, Mai & Juin 1853 ont été par les Douanes de £367,350, par Travaux Publics £28,634, Total £395,984. Et nous pouvons, je pense, sans aucune crainte compter sur le même montant à la même période de l'année présente.[55]

In the short term he was correct. With the temporary loan finalized, redemption of the province's debentures proceeded smoothly.

The provincial "chest" was in a healthy state in late 1854 and early 1855 (see Table 4). With almost £1 million cy on deposit,

Table 4: Cash at Credit of Province of Canada, 1 October 1854
          (£1,000 cy)

Institution	Amount at Interest	Rate (%)	Amount without Interest	Total
Bank of Upper Canada	£100.0	3	£202.0	£302.0
Bank of Montreal			8.6	8.6
Bank of British North America	75.0	4	1.6	76.6
Banque du Peuple	50.0	3	9.5	59.5
Commercial Bank, M.D.	100.0	3	11.8	111.8
Quebec Bank			1.3	1.3
City and District Savings Bank	11.0	4		11.0
Gore Bank			11.1	11.1
City Bank			40.6	40.6
Total Domestic	£336.0		£286.4	£622.4
Bank of England			£ .2	
Glyn, Mills			12.6	
Baring Brothers			1.9	
In 3 per cent Consols			335.7	
Total in Britain			£350.5	350.5
Total				£972.9

Source: Finance, R.G. 19, Vol. 1161, É.-P. Taché, Receiver General, "Statement of Cash,
at the Credit of the Government of Canada, subject to the Draft of the Receiver General
in the various Banking Institutions, or otherwise, in this Province on 1st October 1854,"
and Taché, "Statement of Cash at Credit of this Province in Europe subject to the Draft
or order of the Receiver General as on 1st October 1854," 20 October 1854.

including the overly optimistic face value quoted for the Consols, the
situation did not appear threatening. In addition, revenue for 1854 was
high. But hanging over this happy scene were £400,000 stg 5 per cent
debentures due to mature on 1 July 1855. There were also series of
other bonds due to mature during the year.

　　　　Taché's optimism about Consols was inappropriate. Only the
change in government in 1854 prevented him from buying more. Incred-
ibly, Taché informed Glyns that

> I should rather be disposed to purchase a further amount of Consols
> which with those already in hand would enable the province to meet the
> heavy payment for the redemption of Bonds maturing 1st July [1855].
> The funds having a tendency to improve, I am sorry that the contemplated
> purchase is not already made, as it is likely that the termination of the

present campaign would offer a good opportunity to dispose of the whole.[56]

The information upon which Taché based his opinions proved erroneous. The government would slip almost imperceptibly into deeper financial trouble at the end of the year, yet it held onto its Consols. This proved a mistake since 1855 brought a sharp reduction in customs revenue from £1.2 million to £813,800 cy as a consequence of the new Reciprocity Treaty (see Appendix I).

Most of the money earmarked for debenture redemptions remained tied up in Consols about which Taché continued to be inappropriately optimistic.[57] In February 1855 the government, as a result, decided to renew rather than redeem as much of its maturing debt as possible. It had long been the policy of the government to redeem all maturing debentures which it held on account of various funds in its control with new issues. In 1852, meanwhile, the Executive Council had authorized the Receiver General to redeem all debentures with less than 10 years to run to maturity with new 20-year bonds. Most of the debentures originally scheduled to mature in 1854 and 1855 held in the Sinking Fund, the Clergy Reserve Fund, the Indian Fund, and other accounts had already been replaced by new 20- and 25-year issues.[58] Now the government ordered new plates prepared in anticipation of "the large issue of Debentures that is likely to take place for new loans." Later, on 26 May 1855, the government ordered £200,000 stg 6 per cent, 25-year debentures sent to England in case they were needed for redemption purposes. These new 6 per cents would be used together with the Consols to redeem or renew the bonds maturing 1 July.[59] Not until later were Barings and Glyns able to unload £206,000 stg worth of the Consols at 91 and 91 1/8, considerably below the purchase price back in 1853. Unable to sell the remaining Consols at even that price, the government shifted them to the Bank of England to cover the payment for the imperial guaranteed loan's Sinking Fund.[60]

In addition to the loss absorbed in the resale of the Consols, the government had been required, as in 1854, to float another short-term loan on security of those bonds. These advances helped redeem debentures and were then repaid from the proceeds of the subsequent sale of Consols. This cost the government 2.5 per cent interest on the £180,000 stg borrowed.[61] Barings and Glyns, meanwhile, collected their usual brokerage and commission fees on all of these transactions. Thus ended Taché's speculative adventure in Consols.

Despite its difficulties, Canadian credit remained strong. The £200,000 stg 6 per cent debentures sent to cover the July 1855 redemptions sold at 110, a price under the market quotation but necessitated by the requirement that they be sold quickly and in one lump sum. Within the month £70,000 stg 6 per cents, part of the guarantee to the Great Western Railway, sold for 114.5. Although quotations for Canadian securities remained high for the rest of the year,[62] cash reserves available to the government had shrunk. The £622,000 held in domestic banks in October 1854 had been reduced to under £400,000 by June 1855.[63]

A change in government in 1854, meanwhile, had had no appreciable impact on government financial policy. This is partially explained by the continuity of tenure of both Taché as Receiver General and C. E. Anderson as Deputy Receiver General. During his career Taché demonstrated he could work with any party. Before 1841 he had devoted himself almost exclusively to his medical practice, although he had been a *patriote* in 1837. A follower of LaFontaine, he first entered the Legislative Assembly in 1841 as a strong advocate of an alliance with Hincks's and Baldwin's Upper Canadian Reformers. Taché made his political mark in 1846 when, during the debate on the militia, he commented that French Canadians were "in our habits, by our laws, and by our religion . . . monarchists and conservatives." He proclaimed that "the last cannon which is shot on this continent in defense of Great Britain will be fired by the hand of a French Canadian."[64] The Draper/Papineau government then named him Adjutant-General of Militia, Canada East. Taché resigned his seat in the Legislative Assembly, became a member of the Executive Council as Commissioner of Public Works, and was then appointed to the Legislative Council. Having been appointed by the Draper/Papineau administration, Taché remained a member of the Executive Council when Reform came to power in 1848 and after Hincks fell from power in 1854, serving as Receiver General from 1849 until 1856.[65] Having left the Receiver General's Office, Taché continued to serve in a variety of positions, including that of government leader on two occasions, throughout the Union period. He was replaced as Receiver General by a party chameleon like himself.

Joseph C. Morrison had emigrated to Canada from Ireland in 1830, studied law and was admitted to the bar in 1839, and soon built a healthy practice catering to commercial clients. In 1843 he had been named Clerk of the Executive Council and served the Council in its capacity as a Court of Appeal. First elected in 1848, Morrison represented Niagara after 1852 when he ran in a by-election in a seat vacated when Hincks resigned one of his two constituencies. Morrison first joined the Executive Council under Hincks in 1853 when he was named Solicitor General. According to his biographer, Morrison's career was "modeled on that of Francis Hincks, closely combining political office with the promotion of railways."[66] He had been one of the original directors of the Ontario, Simcoe, and Huron Railway and served as its President from 1852 until 1862. In 1853 he had acted as parliamentary agent for the Great Western and had chaired the merger meetings between the Toronto and Guelph and Grand Trunk railways. He was also closely connected both as a lawyer and as a politician with Isaac Buchanan and Samuel Zimmerman. During the mid-1850s Morrison became increasingly conservative in his politics. The Hincksite protégé joined the Liberal-Conservative government as Receiver General in 1856. Not surprisingly Morrison conducted business in much the same manner as Hincks and Taché before him.

The only significant difference in the conduct of financial affairs resulted not from changes in government or changes in ministers but from the more restricted manœuvrability that resulted from Taché's cash needs in late 1855. With the shortfall in revenue Taché began to tap the remaining funds held in special accounts. "The exigencies of the Public Service" led the Department to notify its bankers that term deposits would be withdrawn between 1 November 1855 and 1 January 1856.[67] The government did not liquidate all of these deposits, although as late as April 1856 unspecified "emergencies" made it seem likely the money would soon be needed.[68]

The government avoided liquidating all of its cash reserves by marketing a small debenture issue of £60,000 stg in September 1855.[69] Taché impatiently issued drafts drawn against these debentures before they could be sold.[70] Within six months the government returned to the market for a larger sum: £200,000 stg "to meet certain unforeseen exigencies of the Public Service." Morrison explained what those "unforeseen exigencies" were in his Memorandum to the Executive Council:

> The undersigned therefore looking to the large amount of Interest on the Public Debt of the Province due in England on 1st July and to be provided for by the Bank of Upper Canada say £141,828.12/2 stg respectfully suggests that he be authorized to draw on Messrs. Barings and Glyns each for *£50,000* stg to aid the Bank of Upper Canada in meeting the Interest above stated.

Four days later the government issued bills at 60 days for £100,000 stg.[71] The sale of new debentures would cover these drafts.

Although sales were slower than Morrison would have liked, the market for provincial issues, as has been mentioned, remained firm. The price quoted in late June was 112, but the first £100,000 stg of this issue sold in July at 113. Barings and Glyns placed the next £50,000 at 114.5 and the final £50,000 stg at 115. It should be noted, however, that these bonds enjoyed the advantage of being sold with one coupon having already matured: since the bonds were dated 1 January, the July interest payment had already "accrued." The government, meanwhile, immediately began drawing on the balance of the proceeds of these sales — £125,000 stg by mid-August 1856.[72]

Canada's credit rating, then, remained high throughout these years. Perhaps higher than it should have been given the signs of potential trouble. The province had survived the depression of 1848 by floating a £500,000 stg loan. Those funds had been used to redeem short-term domestic issues. The government liquidated what remained of the surplus through additional bond redemptions in 1854 and 1855 and through losses incurred in ill-advised speculation. Now in 1856 another bond issue had been sold to meet interest payments on the public debt. What made this development particularly ominous was that the government had borrowed to meet interest payments in a year when revenue was unusually high. During 1856 the tariff produced £1.0 million cy as compared to the pre-reciprocity peak of £1.2 million cy. Total revenue rose in 1856 to just over £1.2 million cy as compared to just under £1.4 million in 1854. The direct public debt had, remarkably, risen during a period — 1846–1856 — in which revenue had increased about two and a half times from £513,000 cy to £1.2 million cy (see Appendix I).

The direct debt had, at the same time, become only a third of the total debt. In order to promote railways the government had issued by mid-1855, as we have seen, an additional £3.5 million in provincial debentures. To this could be added another £3 million raised through the sale of "provincial" bonds issued on the two Municipal Loan Funds. In 1840 a debt crisis had been one factor promoting the Union of the Canadas. During its first year the Union had a total debt of £1.44 million. Fifteen years later the province had managed to increase its liabilities nearly twelve times. Its total debt now stood at £12.2 million cy. It had incurred this during a decade and a half of rapid growth and, with the exception of the short downturn in 1847 and 1848, sustained prosperity.

The economic depression of 1847–1849 had been relatively minor, yet it had provoked a major crisis for the government which had allowed its liabilities to increase rapidly. Responsible government had brought not restraint but greater largesse. The storm clouds looming on the financial horizon rolled over the province sooner rather than later. Indeed the next financial crisis was in the making even before the next economic depression became manifest.

On 1 January 1856 the Ontario, Simcoe, and Huron Railway defaulted on interest payments due on its guaranteed loan.[73] Between

April and June 1856 the government advanced a total of £383,000 cy to the Grand Trunk Railway. Then in July 1856 the government advanced another £100,000 cy to meet interest due on Grand Trunk bonds in London and £25,000 stg to meet interest due on bonds sold in Boston and New York. Two other advances for £14,900 cy and £12,500 cy soon followed in September to meet similar interest payments in Britain and the United States respectively.[74] The Great Western Railway, having already defaulted on its payment to the Sinking Fund in September 1855, now defaulted on its interest payments due 1 January 1857.[75] Exacerbated by railway defaults in 1856, the depression the following year provoked a crisis as severe as that in 1847–1849.

Notes

1.   J. Castell Hopkins, *Progress of Canada in the Century* (Toronto and Philadelphia, 1900), 332, cited in D. C. Masters, *The Reciprocity Treaty of 1854* (Toronto, 1963), 103.

2.   See Finance, R.G. 19, Vol. 2756, Hincks to Barings, 24 December 1849, and Hincks to Glyns, 24 December 1849. Hincks needed only £250,000 stg to meet "present requirements."

3.   *Glyn Mills Papers*, M.G. 24 D 36, George Carr Glyn to Hincks, 6 August 1849 and 5 April 1850.

4.   See above, Chapter 3, 72-73.

5.   Finance, R.G. 19, Vol. 1160, Taché to Leslie, 15 February 1850, Taché to Rawdon & Co., Engravers (N.Y.), 25 January 1850, and C. E. Anderson, Confidential Clerk, to Rawdon, 18 March 1850. Rawdon & Co. were the printers who handled all Canadian debentures. In 1853 Anderson's title of Confidential Clerk changed to Deputy Receiver General.

6.   *Debates of the Legislative Assembly*, Vol. 9, 31 May 1850, 339–340.

7.   *Ibid.*, p. 342.

8.   There was a suggestion that only the absence of a ninth member prevented his name from being added to the list of dissenters.

9.   *Debates of the Legislative Assembly*, Vol. 9, 9 July 1850, 1069.

10.   "First Report. The Select Committee appointed to inquire into the State of the Public Income and Expenditure of the Province, and to consider and report what further Regulations and Checks it may be proper in their opinion to make for establishing an effective control upon all charges incurred in the receipt, custody and application of the Public Money, and what measures can be adopted for reducing any part of the Public Expenditure, without detriment to the Public Service," Appendix BB, *Appendix to the Journals of the Legislative Assembly*, 1850.

11.   "An Act for improving the organization and increasing the efficiency of the Civil Service," 20 Vic., cap. 24, *Provincial Statutes of Canada*, 1857.

12.   Finance, R.G. 19, Vol. 1155, Glyns to Taché, 8 March, 22 March, and 5 April 1850, Glyns to Hincks, 3 May 1850, Vol. 1154, Barings to Taché, 19 April and 3 May 1850.

13.   See ECO, R.G. 1 E 1, State Book K, Vol. 73, Minute, 22 May 1850, 294, Finance, R.G. 19, Vol. 1154, Barings to Taché, 14 June, 12 July, and 1 November 1850, Vol. 1155, Glyns to Taché, 20 December 1850 and 13 June 1851, Vol. 1160, Taché to Barings, 25 May 1850, Taché to Leslie, 21 May 1850, [Taché] to Barings, 25 May 1850, Taché to Leslie, 23 May and 27 May 1850, Taché to B. M. Lemoine, Cashier, Banque du Peuple, 30 May 1850, Taché to [Jno.] Cameron, Cashier, [Com.] Bank of Toronto, 30 May 1850, Taché to Simpson, 31 May 1850, Taché to Glyns, [illegible] May 1850, Taché to Barings, 31 May 1850, Taché to Leslie, 31 May 1850, and Anderson to Ridout, 19 August 1850.

14.   Hincks first broached the question of the St. Lawrence and Atlantic with Glyns in November 1850. Finance, R.G. 19, Vol. 2757, Hincks to Glyns, 28 November 1850.

15.   See Albert Faucher, "Some Aspects of the Financial Difficulties of the Province of Canada," *Canadian Journal of Economics and Political Science*, XXVI (1960), 618.

16.   *Glyn Mills Papers*, M.G. 24 D 36 (A-540), Barings and Glyns to Hincks, 10 January 1851.

17.   See *Baring Papers*, M.G. 24, I D 21, Vol. 1, James Price to Joshua Bates, 8 July 1851.

18.   See McCalla, "Peter Buchanan, London Agent for the Great Western Railway of Canada," 201–203.

19.   Hincks originally outlined three ways of "improving the character of the Bonds": (a) to limit t grantee to only trunk lines, (b) to guarantee principal as well as interest, and (c) to make bonds convertible into stock of the company at par within perhaps five years following completion. See Finance, R.G. 19, Vol. 2757, Hincks to Barings, [8] February 1851 and Hincks to Glyns, [8] February 1851.

20.   *Glyn Mills Papers*, M.G. 24 D 36, Barings and Glyns to Hincks, 10 January 1851.

21.   Finance, R.G. 19, Vol. 2757, Hincks to Barings, 17 April 1851, *Glyn Mlls Papers*, M.G. 24 D 36, Glyns and Barings to Hincks, 23 May 1851, and Barings and Glyns to John Young, 23 May 1851. Hincks suggested that the amount guaranteed might be limited to £400,000 stg per annum, which would remove the problem of too many debentures being "thrown upon the market" at one time. Finance, R.G. 19, Vol. 2757, Hincks to Barings, 17 April 1851. Later, in his *Reminiscences*, Hincks notes Barings' and Glyns' insistence on limiting the total potential liability and then concludes that "[t]heir advice was followed, and the Provincial aid was limited to the main trunk line." Francis Hincks, *Reminiscences of his Public Life* (Montreal, 1884), 202. Similarly Currie suggests that Hincks agreed to the restrictions suggested by Barings and Glyns. See Currie, *The Grand Trunk Railway*, 9. The "restrictions" contained in the Main Trunk Line of Railway Act, however, were far broader than those which Barings and Glyns had in mind.

22.   "An Act to Make Provision for the Construction of a Main Trunk Line of Rail-way Throughout the Whole Length of This Province," 14–15 Vic. cap. 73, *Provincial Statutes of Canada*, 1851, 1951–1952. Before the final passage of the Act Hincks informed Barings that the first £100,000 stg to be issued on behalf of the St. Lawrence and Atlantic would be provincial debentures "of precisely the same character as the last issue." These should be sold quickly, according to Hincks, so that the "existing demands" of the railway could be met. Barings and Glyns could then study the legislation. See Finance, R.G. 19, Vol. 2757, Hincks to Barings, 23 June 1851.

23.   See Finance, R.G. 19, Vol. 1161, Taché to Rawdon and Co., 26 August 1851, Anderson to John Young, Vice-President, St. Lawrence and Atlantic Railway, 14 October 1851, Taché to Barings, 28 November 1851 and 9 January 1852, Taché to Glyns, 9 January and 10 January 1852, Taché to Barings, 10 January 1852, Taché to Glyns, 15 January 1852, and Taché to Barings, 15 January 1852. Also see RGO, "Memo relating to Exchange and Money transactions a/c [sic] St. Lawrence and Atlantic Railway Co.," 11 March 1852, "Memo of Exchange drawn on Messrs. Glyn, Mill, and Co., London, on a/22c of St. Lawrence and Atlantic Railway Company," [16 April 1852], and "Memo of Exchange drawn on Messrs. Baring Bros. and Co., London, on a/c of St. Lawrence and Atlantic Railway Company," [16 April 1852], *Baring Papers*, M.G. 24 D 21, Vol. 1, Young to Barings, 22 September and 18 October 1851, and Taché to Barings, 28 November 1851.

24.   See Finance, R.G. 19, Vol. 1161, Taché to Sir Allan MacNab, Chairman, Great Western Railway, 1 October 1852, Taché to Barings, 2 October 1852, Taché to Glyns, 2 October and 9 October 1852, Taché to Barings, 16 October and 27 November 1852, Taché to Glyns, 27 November 1852, Taché to Ridout, 27 November 1852, Taché to C. W. Harris, President, Great Western Railway, 2 December 1852, Anderson to Harris, 24 December 1852, Taché to A.-N. Morin, Provincial Secretary, 26 January 1853, Taché to Harris, 28 January 1853, Taché to Barings, 4 February 1853, Taché to Glyns, 4 February 1853 and 4 August 1854, Taché to Barings, 4 August and 9 December 1854, Taché to Glyns, 9 December 1854, Vol. 1155, Glyns to Taché, 5 November and 12 November 1852, Vol. 1154, Barings to Taché, 5 November and 12 November 1852, *Glyn Mills Papers*, M.G. 24 D 36, Glyns to Taché, 22 October, 12 November and 10 December 1852, Barings and Glyns to C. J. Brydges, Agent for the Great Western Railway of Canada, now in London, 24 August 1854, Glyns to Barings, 2 October 1854, Finance, R.G. 19, Vol. 1162, Taché to [W.] C. Stephens, Secretary, Great Western Railway, 16 February 1855, Taché to Glyns, 17 February 1855, Taché to Barings, 17 February 1855, Taché to Glyns, 24 March 1855, Taché to Barings, 24 March 1855, Anderson to Harris, 7 April 1855, Taché to Glyns, 4 June and 18 June 1855, and Taché to Barings, 18 June 1855. Barings and Glyns purchased on their own account the entire £300,000 stg issued in August 1854, the first £200,000 at 103 immediately, and the remaining £100,000 at 104 at 60 days. See *Glyn Mills Papers*, M.G. 24 D 36, Barings and Glyns to C. J. Brydges, 24 August 1854, Glyns to Barings, 2 October 1854, and Glyns to T. B. Smith, 5 January 1855.

25.   Finance, R.G. 19, Vol. 1161, Taché to Barings and Glyns, 14 January 1853.

26.   *Ibid.*, Taché to Morin, 12 November 1852, Taché to Barings and Glyns, 14 January 1853, Taché to Glyns, 24 March 1853, Taché to Barings, 24 March and 15 April 1853, Taché to Ridout, 15 April 1853, Taché to P.J.O. Chauveau, Provincial Secretary, 20 September and 19 December 1853, Taché to Glyns, 21 December 1854, Taché to Barings, 21 December 1854, Vol. 1154, Barings to Taché, 14 December and 17 December 1852, Vol. 1155, Glyns to Taché, 17 December 1852, *Glyn Mills Papers*, M.G. 24 D 36, Glyns to Hincks, 16 December 1852, and Glyns to Taché, 17 December 1852.

27.   The Grand Trunk had an equally voracious appetite for private capital. After John Ross, without prior consent, included the names of Thomas Baring and George Carr Glyn on the railway's prospectus, both allowed themselves, as D.C.M. Platt and Jeremy Adelman observe, "under protest and against their instincts" to become ever more intimately involved in the affairs of the line. D.C.M. Platt and Jeremy Adelman, "London Merchant Bankers in the First Phase of Heavy Borrowing: The Grand Trunk Railway," *Journal of Imperial and Commonwealth History*, 18 (1990), 217. As other investors proved reluctant to purchase stock in British North American trunk railways, Baring and Glyn became ever more committed financially as well.

28.   This episode, along with a similar windfall involving the consolidation of Toronto debentures given to the Ontario, Simcoe, and Huron Railway, brought Hincks before a special investigating committee charged with corrupt practices. Hincks was cleared of those charges. For Hincks's version see Hincks, *Reminiscences*, 344–353. Also see Currie, *The Grand Trunk Railway*, 14–15. Corruption would be one of the major issues in the 1854 general elections when the Hincks–Morin government fell from power. See Ormsby, "Sir Francis Hincks," 177–179, 191, George A. Davison, "The Hincks–Brown Rivalry and the Politics of Scandal," *Ontario History*, LXXXI (1989), 129–151, Careless, *The Union of the Canadas*, 185–186, and Donald Creighton, *John A. Macdonald: Young Politician* (Toronto, 1952), 196–197.

29.   See Finance, R.G. 19, Vol. 1161, Taché to B. Holmes, Vice-President, Grand Trunk Railway, 6 September 1853, Taché to Barings and Glyns, 14 January 1853, Anderson to Barings, 15 October 1853, and Anderson to Glyns, 15 October 1853. Only £100,000 stg in bonds for the Quebec and Richmond Railway remained to be sent to Barings and Glyns in late 1853.

30.   Finance, R.G. 19, Vol. 1161, Taché to Barings, 14 January 1853. Also see Currie, *The Grand Trunk Railway*, 18.

31.   Finance, R.G. 19, Vol. 1161, Anderson to Glyns, 15 October 1853, Taché to C. P. Roney, Managing Director, Grand Trunk Railway, 4 October 1853, Taché to T. A. Begly, Secretary, Board of Railway Commissioners, 4 October 1853, and Thomas [illegible] for the Receiver General, to Roney, 12 October 1853.

32.   *Baring Papers*, M.G. 24 D 21, Vol. 2, Hincks to Thomas Baring, 12 November 1853.

33.   Finance, R.G. 19, Vol. 1161, Taché to Brydges, 10 May 1854.

34.   *Ibid.*, Vol. 1162, Taché to Glyns, 12 May 1855, and Taché to Barings, 12 May 1855. In June 1855 the Inspector General went to London to make arrangements for the new loan, and the first packet of the new bonds followed between August and October 1855. See ECO, R.G. 1 E 1, State Book P, Vol. 78, Minute, 6 June 1855, 222, and Finance, R.G. 19, Vol. 1162, Anderson to Glyns, 6 August 1855, Anderson to Barings, 6 August 1855, Anderson to Glyns, 1 October 1855, and Anderson to Barings, 1 October 1855. The money was made available to the Grand Trunk beginning in December 1855. Finance, R.G. 19, Vol. 1162, Taché to Glyns, 24 December 1855, and Taché to Barings, 24 December 1855.

35.   See Finance, R.G. 19, Vol. 1155, Glyns to Taché, 12 November 1852, and Vol. 1154, Barings to Taché, 12 November 1852.

36.   "An Act to Establish a Consolidated Municipal Loan Fund for Upper Canada," 16 Vic. cap. 22, *Statutes of the Province of Canada*, 1852–1853, 48–59. The best discussion of the Consolidated Municipal Loan Fund is Albert Faucher, "Le fonds d'emprunt municipal dans le Haut-Canada, 1852–1867," in *Histoire économique et unité canadienne* (Montreal, 1970), 83–106.

37.   Although government bookkeepers kept the Municipal Loan Fund and the Consolidated Revenue Fund separate and distinct, there was no "fund" in the sense of moneys being paid into and out of distinct bank accounts as was the case with the Sinking Fund or the Clergy Reserve Fund. All debentures, receipts, and payments were handled by the Receiver General in the usual way. See above, pp. 100–101.

38.   See Finance, R.G. 19, Vol. 1161, Taché to Barings and Glyns, 14 January 1853.

39.   *Ibid.*, Vol. 1162, Anderson to George Crawford, M.P.P., 10 July 1856.

40. *Ibid.*, "Con: Mun: Loan Fund of U.C. Interest 8 % due 1st Jany 1855 and still remaining unpaid, by the undermentioned Municips: [sic]," [April 1855]. Anderson turned the question over to Attorney General John A. Macdonald for legal action but nothing came of this. Some money, however, did begin to trickle in; the Counties of Huron and Bruce, for example, paid £100 cy, the Township of Middleton paid £50, and the Town of St. Catharines paid £120. See Finance, R.G. 19, Vol. 1162, Taché to Macdonald, 23 April and 21 May 1855, Anderson to Macdonald, 4 June and 1 August 1855.

41. Finance, R.G. 19, Vol. 1162, Taché, "Memorandum," 22 November 1855. Also see Vol. 1162, Taché to Macdonald, 16 November 1855. These payments from the Consolidated Revenue Fund were not legal, and Taché demanded retroactive authority be provided to cover them.

42. When they reported the successful marketing of £200,000 stg debentures in late 1856 and early 1857, Glyns commented that the "forced sales" of Municipal Loan Fund debentures had made a very unfavourable impression on London money markets. See Finance, R.G. 19, Vol. 1162, Joseph C. Morrison, Receiver General, to Glyns, 9 February 1856.

43. See *ibid.*, 9 February 1857, Morrison, "Memorandum," 26 October 1857, Vol. 1157, Barings to Morrison, 5 February 1858, Barings to John Ross, Receiver General, 5 March and 30 April 1858, and Vol. 1158, Glyns to Ross, 28 April 1858.

44. *Baring Papers*, M.G. 24 D 21, Vol. 3, T. C. Baring to Thomas Baring, 16 April 1859.

45. *Glyn Mills Papers*, M.G. 24 D 36, "Private," George Carr Glyn to A. T. Galt, 15 April and 20 May 1859. See below, Chapter 6, 134ff.

46. *Historical Statistics of Canada*, ed. by F. H. Leacy, M. C. Urquhart, and K.A.H. Buckley, 2nd Edition (Ottawa, 1983), Series A2-14. All calculations are my own.

47. *Ibid.*, Series A350. All calculations are my own.

48. In 1850 Hincks believed the province should either buy as many of the outstanding 5 per cent debentures as possible under par, or intervene just enough to raise the price to par "and then renew them." Hincks preferred this second option "especially as out of the late loan, we shall have necessity to pay off a good deal in this Province." Finance, R.G. 19, Vol. 2756, Hincks to Glyns, 30 May 1850, and Hincks to Barings, 30 May 1850. Copies of these letters can also be found in *Baring Papers*, M.G. 24 D 21, Vol. 1, Hincks to Glyns, 30 May 1850 and Hincks to Barings, 30 May 1850. Also see ECO, R.G. 1 E 1, State Book K, Vol. 73, Minutes, 15 June, 26 September, 17 October, 21 October and 31 October 1850, 334, 466, 512, 520, 530, and State Book L, Vol. 74, Minute, 6 December 1850, 13.

49. Finance, R.G. 19, Vol. 2758, Hincks to Glyns, 19 June 1852, Hincks to Barings, 19 June 1852, and Vol. 1155, Glyns to Taché, 23 July 1852.

50. *Ibid.*, Vol. 1161, Taché to Barings, 3 December 1853, Taché to Glyns, 4 February and 11 February 1854.

51. *Ibid.*, Taché to Barings, 8 October 1853, and Taché, "Memo," 16 March 1854, *Baring Papers*, M.G. 24 D 21, Vol. 2, Anderson to Barings, 15 October 1853, and Taché to Barings, 19 October 1853. The original Order-in-Council authorizing the purchase passed after the Inspector General assured Cabinet that "there can be no danger of loss, as in the event of a still further decline in Consols, there can be no difficulty, looking at the present prosperous state of the Finances, in transferring the entire £260,000 to the credit of the Sinking Fund and paying the Provincial Debentures from other Funds." ECO, R.G. 1

E 1, State Book N, Vol. 76, Minute, 7 October 1853, 492. In December 1853 the government authorized Barings and Glyns *"at their discretion to pay off to the holders* any portion of the £200,000 of Debentures falling due on the 1st of April next." ECO, R.G. 1 E 1, State Book N, Vol. 76, Minute, 2 December 1853, 622–623. On this occasion Hincks explained that the decision to invest in Consols had been based upon "the impression that our fives could not be obtained at par." *Baring Papers*, M.G. 24 D 21, Vol. 2, Hincks to Thomas Baring, 2 December 1853.

52. Consols paid 3 per cent on their face value. A discounted purchase price of 94 produced an effective interest rate of 3.2 per cent.

53. Finance, R.G. 19, Vol. 1154, Barings to Taché, 11 November, 22 November, 13 December and 23 December 1853, and Vol. 1161, Taché to Glyns, 11 February 1854.

54. *Ibid.*, Vol. 1161, Taché, "Memo," 16 March 1854, and ECO, R.G. 1 E 1, State Book O, Vol. 77, Minute, 17 March 1854, 112–113.

55. *Ibid.*, Taché to Hincks, 18 March 1854. The first two £75,000 repayment instalments on 1 June and 1 July were paid out of current revenue. ECO, R.G. 1 E 1, State Book O, Vol. 77, Minute, 20 July 1854, 316–317.

56. *Ibid.*, Taché to Glyns, 30 September 1854.

57. *Ibid.*, 21 December 1854.

58. See ECO, R.G. 1 E 1, State Book M, Vol. 75, Minute, 18 March 1852, 69, State Book N, Vol. 76, Minute, 16 March 1853, 120–121, and State Book O, Vol. 77, Minute, 30 January 1854, 29.

59. See Finance, R.G. 19, Vol. 1162, Taché, "Memo," 27 February 1855, Taché, "Memorandum," 2 April 1855, Taché to Rawdon, 10 May 1855, Taché to Glyns, 12 May 1855, Taché to Barings, 12 May 1855, Taché, "Memorandum," 26 May 1855, and ECO, R.G. 1 E 1, State Book P, Vol. 78, Minute, 26 May 1855, 191–192. Taché had originally intended to use 5 per cent debentures. Also see Finance, R.G. 19, Vol. 1162, Taché to Glyns, 26 May 1855, Taché to Barings, 26 May 1855, Taché to Glyns, 4 June and 11 June 1855. If these debentures were not needed for redemptions, they were to be used as part of the guaranteed loans for the Grand Trunk.

60. Finance, R.G. 19, Vol. 1162, Taché to Glyns, 28 April and 11 June 1855, Anderson to Glyns, 30 July 1855, Anderson to Barings, 30 July 1855, Taché, "Memorandum," 27 December 1855, Taché to Glyns, 31 December 1855, Taché to Barings, 31 December 1855, Taché to C. E. Trevelyan, Secretary, H. M. Treasury, 31 December 1855, Taché to M. Marshall, Chief Cashier, Bank of England, 31 December 1855, Taché to Glyns, 28 January 1856, Taché to Barings, 18 February 1856, Taché to Glyns, 18 February 1856, and ECO, R.G. 1 E 1, State Book Q, Vol. 79, Minute, 29 December 1855, 70–71.

61. Finance, R.G. 19, Vol. 1161, Taché to Barings, 23 January 1855.

62. *Ibid.*, Vol. 1155, Glyns to Taché, 31 March 1854, Vol. 1162, Taché to Glyns, 9 July 1855, Taché to Barings, 9 July 1855, Anderson to Glyns, 25 August 1855, and Taché to Glyns, 17 December 1855.

63. *Ibid.*, Vol. 1162, Anderson, "Statement of Public Monies at Interest in Several Banks of the Province, by 1 June 1855," 5 June 1855.

64. Andrée Désilets, "Sir Étienne-Paschal Taché," *Dictionary of Canadian Biography*, Vol. IX, 1861–1870 (Toronto, 1976), 776–777.

65. *Ibid.*, 776.

66. "Joseph Curran Morrison," *Dictionary of Canadian Biography*, Vol. XI, 1881–1890 (Toronto, 1982), 618.

67. See Finance, R.G. 19, Vol. 1162, Taché to [R. Cassels], Manager, Bank of British North America, 5 July 1855, Taché to C. S. Ross, Cashier, Commercial Bank, M.D., Kingston, 5 July 1855, Taché to Lemoine, 5 July 1855, Taché to F. MacCulloch, Cashier, City Bank, 5 July 1855, Taché to Ross, 24 July 1855, Anderson to J. F. Bradshaw, Manager, Bank of Upper Canada, 24 July 1855, Anderson to Lemoine, 31 August 1855, Anderson to MacCulloch, 31 August 1855, Anderson to Cassels, 31 August 1855, Anderson to William Sache, Cashier, Molson's Bank, 31 August 1855, and Anderson to E. J. Barbeau, Actuary, City and District Savings Bank, Montreal, 31 August 1855.

68. See *ibid.*, Unsigned to Ross, 12 April 1855, Taché to Lemoine, 26 November 1855, and Taché to MacCulloch, 26 November 1855.

69. ECO, R.G. 1 E 1, State Book P, Vol. 78, Minute, 10 September 1855, 449. These debentures were for public works.

70. Finance, R.G. 19, Vol. 1162, Anderson to Glyns, 10 September 1855, Anderson to Barings, 10 September 1855, Anderson to Glyns, 24 September 1855, Anderson to Barings, 24 September 1855, Taché to Glyns, 12 November 1855, and Taché to Barings, 12 November 1855.

71. *Ibid.*, Morrison, "Memorandum," 28 May 1856, Morrison to Glyns, 2 June 1856, Morrison to Barings, 2 June 1856, and ECO, R.G. 1 E 1, State Book Q, Vol. 79, Minute, 30 May 1856, 308. The Order-in-Council mentions that the debentures in question were the £200,000 authorized on 3 May 1856. That order had authorized £100,000 for public works under 16 Vic. cap. 157 and 18 Vic. cap. 4, and a second £100,000 stg for seigneurial claims under 18 Vic. cap. 3. ECO, R.G. 1 E 1, Vol. 79, State Book Q, Minute, 3 May 1856, 276. Later in September Morrison told Glyns to expect another £100,000 stg debentures to cover the redemption of currency debentures in Canada. Finance, R.G. 19, Vol. 1162, Morrison to Glyns, 22 September 1856. By November this amount rose to £150,000, all of which was sold by February 1857. Morrison to Glyns, 3 November 1856, Morrison to Barings, 3 November 1856, Morrison to Glyns, 12 November 1856, Morrison to Barings, 12 November 1856, Morrison to Glyns, 24 November 1856, Morrison to Barings, 24 November and 29 December 1856, Morrison to Glyns, 29 December 1856, Morrison to Barings, 30 December 1856, Morrison to Glyns, 30 December 1856, Morrison to Barings, 5 January 1857, Morrison to Glyns, 5 January and 2 February 1857, Morrison to T. Lee Terrill, Provincial Secretary, 28 February 1857. The government sent an additional £50,000 in December 1856. Morrison to Glyns, 8 December 1856, Morrison to Barings, 8 December 1856, Morrison to Glyns, 13 December 1856, Morrison to Barings, 13 December 1856 and 26 January 1857, Morrison to Glyns, 26 January and 9 February 1857. No sooner had these securities been sold than another £146,000 was issued to cover redemptions. See Morrison, "Memorandum," 27 February 1857, Morrison to Barings, 28 February 1857, Morrison to Glyns, 28 February 1857, Morrison to Barings, 23 March 1857, Morrison to Glyns, 23 March 1857, Anderson to Ridout, 15 April 1857, Morrison to Glyns, 27 April 1857, and Morrison to Barings, 27 April 1857.

72. Finance, R.G. 19, Vol. 1162, Morrison to Glyns, 14 July and 21 July 1856, Morrison to Barings, 21 July 1856, Morrison to Glyns, 28 July 1856, Morrison to Barings, 28 July and 4 August 1856, Morrison to Glyns, 4 August and 11 August 1856, Morrison to Barings, 11 August 1856, Morrison to Glyns, 18 August 1856, and Morrison to Barings, 18 August 1856.

73. See *ibid.*, Taché to George-Étienne Cartier, Provincial Secretary, 20 February 1856, Anderson, "Statement showing the Obligation or Debt to the Government of the Ontario,

Simcoe, and Huron Railroad Company in detail, also the payments they have made etc, etc, being the Return asked for by The Hon. The Provincial Secretary in his letter of 8th May for the Information of the Legislative Assembly," 12 May 1856, and Anderson to Terrill, 30 August 1856.

74.   See *ibid.*, Anderson to Terrill, 30 August 1856, CEA [Anderson], "Memorandum of Advances to Grand Trunk Railway Co. since 1st April 1856," 23 October 1856, Morrison to Glyns, 14 July 1856, Morrison to Barings, 14 July 1856, Morrison to Glyns, 22 September 1856, Anderson to Jno. M. Grant, Secretary, Grand Trunk Railway, 22 September 1856.

75.   *Ibid.*, Morrison to Terrill, 28 February 1857, Anderson to Brydges, 10 March and 22 May 1857.

Chapter 5
Managing the Budget

As a young Country, a considerable outlay
from Public Funds becomes indispensable,
if we would develop those growing
resources, from which we are entitled to
expect, hereafter, an ample return of
National Wealth.
— William Cayley,
Inspector General, 1857[1]

In 1857 a severe depression ended a decade and a half of spectacular growth in the Province of Canada. Before beginning a discussion of the impact of that depression on the financial policies of the provincial government, it would be wise to pause and review the fiscal history of the province. Canada's public debt resulted from two specific policies: canal construction during the 1840s and railway guarantees during the 1850s. British investors, particularly during the 1850s, meanwhile, paid high premiums for ever larger issues of government bonds. One factor influencing their decision to do so was the apparently strong fiscal position of the government. Provincial finances appeared secure despite the crisis of 1837–1839 and 1847–1849. This becomes clear when we review the public accounts, more particularly the Consolidated Revenue Fund.

The Consolidated Revenue Fund included all of the ordinary items of expenditure, such as the Civil List and debt service charges, as well as most revenue. It excluded a number of major items of expenditure, including capital projects such as the canals, accounts for which were kept quite separate. A review of the Consolidated Revenue Fund demonstrates that, during the first 15 years of the Union, existing revenue programmes generated more than enough money to support the rapid expansion of all government services except the canal and railway programmes, which in turn were supposed to be self-financing.

At the time of union, Canada inherited civil institutions that remained small and uncomplicated. During the 1840s the province

completed the St. Lawrence canal system and welcomed increasing
numbers of new immigrants; both immigration and transportation
boosted the rate of growth. The final years of the decade witnessed a
minor interruption in the pace of economic development, followed during the 1850s by a period of even more intense and dynamic growth
fueled by a railway construction boom.[2] Between 1851 and 1861 the
population increased from 1.8 to 2.5 million.[3] The value of Canadian
exports increased from $13 million to $34.7 million, while the value of
imports increased from $21.4 million to $43.1 million.[4] This rapid
expansion in population and economic activity placed new demands on
the Canadian state.

Growth cost money: between 1842 and 1856 government
expenditures on the Consolidated Revenue Fund increased by
195 per cent.[5] Part of this increase resulted from the expansion of
established institutions and services to accommodate a larger population; part resulted from the creation of virtually new institutions.
Expenditures on the judicial system, for example, increased by
92.5 per cent during these years, while expenditures for civil government and the Legislature increased by 195 per cent. Much of this
increase came during the mid-1850s; costs associated with the Legislature, for example, rose from £47,800 cy in 1852 to £118,500 in 1856,
a reflection of the added costs associated with moving the capital back
and forth between Toronto and Quebec.

Simple growth, however, accounts for only part of the spending increases. The Province of Canada was different, not just larger,
by 1856. In both sections of the province some districts, parishes, and
townships were only just beginning to fill up with agricultural settlers,
yet the limits of frontier agricultural expansion in the older river- and
lake-front districts had been reached. Although the province remained
a largely rural society exporting primary products abroad, a larger and
more established population and economy in these districts made more
diverse demands for government services, which in turn led to a number of areas in which increases in government expenditures proved
spectacular. In 1857 William Cayley, the Inspector General, outlined
the peculiar problems faced by new countries:

> Our Population, annually increased by Immigration, compels more
> extended arrangements for the Administration of Justice, and the wants
> of Civil Government. Our Infant Enterprises need to be fostered by the
> aid of Public Funds, and our great productive resources nurtured and
> expanded, by the Erection of Public Buildings, the Construction of Light
> Houses on our Coasts, and Improvements of Harbours and Navigable
> Waters.
>   And independently of these inevitable Expenditures which burthen
> the Public Treasury of every young Country, we have from the same

Fund to draw means for the construction of Roads, the promotion of Agriculture, the support of Hospitals and other Charities, and the encouragement of Literary and Scientific Institutes, all of which in more populous and wealthy countries, are efficiently provided by individual enterprise and private benevolence.[6]

Certainly Cayley's description of a "young" country accurately describes Canada West; yet even in Canada East the abolition of seigneurial tenure and changes in the relations between church and state ensured that, although the Church would maintain control over many social services, increasing demands would be placed upon the public treasury.

Cayley isolated some but not all of the areas in which increases in expenditure had been most rapid during the first 15 years of the Union period. Spending on lighthouses and coastal services, for example, increased by nearly 1300 per cent, spending on agriculture increased 700 per cent, and spending on hospitals and charities increased by 300 per cent. Even more spectacular, however, was the 2300 per cent increase in militia spending. This increase occurred at the end of the period; spending on the militia jumped from only £2,200 in 1854 to £43,700 cy two years later. Such striking increases as these, however, had only a small impact on the general financial picture as the sums involved remained relatively small. Among these categories of expenditure, hospitals and charities accounted for by far the greatest absolute amount over the entire period, rising to £41,300 cy in 1856, yet this represented only 3.7 per cent of total expenditures.

None of these relatively new areas of expenditure were, from the perspective of government finance, as significant as education. The Union period witnessed the birth of the modern Canadian school system.[7] Canada West created new public and separate school systems, while in Canada East the Catholic and Protestant systems came to rely upon public rather than church financing.

At the time of union education cost the provincial government only £23,000 cy or 6 per cent of total expenditures. The new school Acts, passed during the first legislative session, ensured a rapid increase in expenditures to nearly £80,000 cy by 1845. Decisions to finance most schools through direct taxes at the local level eased the pressure on the provincial treasury; thus expenditures leveled off for the next decade. After 1853, however, expenditures again began to increase rapidly. By 1856 the provincial government was spending nearly £100,000 cy on education, an increase of 380 per cent since 1842.

The rapid expansion of expenditures on government and social services, so marked during these years, was paralleled by an expansion of public works. Despite the keeping of separate accounts for major capital projects such as the St. Lawrence canals, public works charged against the Consolidated Revenue Fund — roads, bridges, and buildings — accounted for a major portion of expenditure. In 1845 and 1846, for example, public works accounted for 15 per cent of all expenditures from the Consolidated Revenue Fund. After 1846 spending on public works fell dramatically from £83,000 to only £3,500 and remained at only 1 per cent of total expenditures until 1853. Spending increased sharply, reaching £116,300 and £99,600 in 1855 and 1856 respectively. This represented about 10 per cent of all expenditures.

In truth, public works projects accounted for a far larger portion of provincial spending. Major projects had been financed through bonded debts; interest payments on those debts were by far the single largest charge on the Consolidated Revenue Fund. In 1842 interest payments cost the provincial treasury £79,700 cy. This represented 21.3 per cent of total expenditures. With the negotiation of the new guaranteed loan, interest charges rose rapidly to £150,000 cy in 1846 and 1847 and to £225,400 cy in 1851. Between 1848 and 1851 interest accounted for about 35 per cent of all expenditures.[8] Marginal increases in the direct debt during the mid-1850s ensured that interest payments leveled off in absolute terms and declined relative to other items of expenditure. Despite this relative decline, interest remained the single largest charge on the treasury: in 1856 the £225,200 cy interest payments accounted for 20 per cent of all expenditures.

The direct debt had been contracted in the main to build canals; those canals, everyone had hoped, would be self-financing. Although the overly optimistic expectations of the 1840s never materialized, the canals nonetheless did become a source of new revenue. The government's income from its public works fluctuated annually with trade. Revenue rose sharply between 1842 and 1846, but then fell dramatically in 1847 and 1848. Economic revival brought a sharp increase in revenue, which reached a high of £77,600 cy in 1853; but between 1854 and 1856 reciprocity and reductions in rates brought revenue down. In the latter year public works produced £51,800 cy or 4.2 per cent of all revenues. Although a disappointing amount of money in light of the transportation rhetoric of the 1840s, public works generated more income in 1856 than all excise and territorial taxes combined. However, even at its peak between 1851 and 1854, public works did not produce enough revenue to meet the minimum annual payment for the Sinking Fund on the guaranteed loan.[9]

Despite high interest charges and modest revenue from its public works, the various demands placed upon the provincial treasury were well within the fiscal resources of the government. Although interest charges were high and expenditures for political, judicial, and social services increased substantially, all ordinary expenditures could be met through existing sources of revenue. Increasing population and a rapidly growing economy meant that revenues appeared to keep pace with expenditures; there seemed little need to opt for new or unpopular forms of taxation.

Throughout this period the government relied heavily upon tariffs against imported commodities to finance its operations. Revenue from tariffs rose sharply from £265,400 cy in 1842 to £429,700 in 1844. This represented 83.3 per cent of all revenue. In general the tariff continued to account for about 80 per cent of revenue, although income fluctuated annually with trade. During depressed years, such as 1847, tariff revenue fell to only 75.2 per cent of all revenue. During boom years, such as 1854, the tariff could account for as much as 85.3 per cent of revenue. In that year customs revenue peaked at £1.2 million before falling to £1 million in 1856, a result of the reciprocity agreement with the United States.

Rapidly increasing population and trade, then, ensured that provincial revenue rose by 238 per cent between 1842 and 1856, compared to only a 195 per cent increase in expenditures during these years. The substantial increases in customs revenue guaranteed that new sources of revenue, such as direct taxation, need not be considered. Indeed, increasing trade meant that other traditional sources of revenue, such as excise, would decline in importance.

In 1842 excise and territorial[10] taxes brought £32,000 and £25,800 cy respectively to the treasury. This represented 8.7 and 7.1 per cent respectively of all provincial revenue. Although moneys from these sources increased in absolute terms, the relative importance of both excise and territorial revenue declined significantly. By 1856 these two sources represented only 4.4 per cent of total revenue. Casual income from various fees, fines, and forfeitures, meanwhile, fluctuated markedly during these years, ranging from a low of 1.8 per cent in 1848 and 1853 to a high of 4.3 per cent in 1842. In 1855 and again in 1856 such revenue increased sharply to £53,700 and £89,700 cy respectively. By 1856 casual revenue accounted for 7.2 per cent of all provincial income.

The fiscal position of the Province of Canada, then, appeared extremely strong in 1856. Expenditures had increased substantially, yet revenue had increased even more rapidly. Although budgetary deficits had been accumulated in 1842, 1846, 1848, and 1855, the province had enjoyed healthy surpluses during most of these years. The accumulated surplus on the Consolidated Revenue Fund stood at £1.3 million cy by 1856, and to this could be added £773,000 cy plus accumulated interest which the province had paid into its Sinking Fund.

Although the Sinking Fund represented an expenditure on the Consolidated Revenue Fund, it remained an asset available to the province. Even the relatively large public debt was becoming progressively less burdensome as general economic growth ensured that debt service charges declined relative to both income and all other charges upon the treasury. Despite appearances, however, the provincial treasury remained vulnerable to sudden and unanticipated declines in revenue, as well as sudden increases in expenditure; the accounting practices and administrative systems of the period disguised as much as they illuminated.

Modern financial reporting begins with two basic statements: an income/expenditure statement that reflects total cash flows, and an asset/liability statement. The public accounts during the 1840s and 1850s appear to provide such statements, but in fact restrict themselves to the Consolidated Revenue Fund. Detailed statements on various projects, such as the St. Lawrence canals, were submitted to the Legislature separately; expenditures for construction of those canals were not reported in the Consolidated Fund. Despite these separate accounts, some items associated with capital projects, both revenue and expenditure, were listed in the statements of the Consolidated Revenue Fund. Revenue from tolls, for example, appeared as income, while interest paid on the accumulating debt appeared as an expenditure. The Consolidated Revenue Fund thus provides a very incomplete depiction of revenue, expenditures, and annual surpluses or deficits, making it extremely difficult to develop a clear picture of the province's real financial position.

Without clear and complete general statements on income and expenditures, assets and liabilities, the government was vulnerable in other ways as well. The over-reliance on customs duties ensured that huge deficits could be accumulated if trade suddenly collapsed. The province collected the bulk of its revenue during the spring and early summer. In any given fiscal year it would be virtually impossible to adopt effective alternative taxes to compensate for unanticipated shortfalls in revenue should trade decline sharply. Without the ability to implement effective taxation alternatives quickly, it would be equally difficult to effect short-term retrenchment measures. In 1857, for example, income from customs and from public works, both sensitive to general levels of economic activity, fell from £1.1 million to only £930,000 cy. Spending, however, continued to increase. This meant that a £133,500 cy surplus in 1856 became a £194,000 cy deficit in 1857.

Trade depressions threatened the provincial budget in other ways as well. Economic dislocations affected traffic on provincial rail and canal systems as surely as they affected government revenue.[11] This could have ominous consequences for government finance as the "indirect" debt represented a large portion of the province's total liabilities. In the case of the "direct" debt, the government failed to take full advantage of the opportunities presented by prosperity to reduce liabilities. The government's financial plans, meanwhile, failed to take account of the "indirect" debt. Although the latter represented that portion of the public debt for which there were corresponding debts owed the provincial government by various municipalities and railways, the province remained directly liable for all interest payments, as well as the principal on all debentures issued in its name. The province paid the interest on its "indirect" debt; the railways or municipalities in turn were to reimburse the Receiver General. The accounts of the Consolidated Revenue Fund reported neither the initial payments nor the reimbursements. Thus defaults by either the railways or the municipalities immediately translated into heavy demands upon the Consolidated Revenue Fund. Here was the Achilles heel of provincial finance. With revenue declining, budgeted expenditures increasing, and the railways and municipalities defaulting on guaranteed loans, Canada faced its most severe financial crisis to date. Renewed financial crisis ensured that the reform process, begun with Lord Sydenham, would continue to run its course. The end product of this process would be a more modern administrative and accounting system for managing government finance.

Financial administration in Canada involved exercises in crisis management, as well as in damage control. During the crises of 1837–1839 and again in 1847–1849 the government had been unable to anticipate problems and had instead reacted to events. Each crisis, as we have seen, had led to the adoption of a series of fundamental reforms and initiatives. In Lord Sydenham's case, better systems of administrative controls ensured that the Executive Council possessed the authority to define economic and financial policy, as well as the means to implement those policies. A new financial crisis at the end of the decade led Francis Hincks to propose a series of new economic initiatives. Those initiatives gave the province a set of coherent policy objectives, as well as a specific set of programmes designed to achieve those objectives. Better administrative and political controls, combined with a more integrated approach to economic and financial policy, resulted in a marked improvement over the more haphazard administrative and policy programmes of the pre-Union period, yet much remained to be done.

Administrative controls over departmental spending remained relatively lax, as the case of Upper Canada's Chief Super-

intendent of Schools illustrates. The government often advanced appropriated funds to its officials who in turn kept the money "in any Bank
they chose, and drew for it as they chose." In Egerton Ryerson's case,
such advances involved large balances of "upwards of £20,000."
Ryerson made no distinction between these funds and his private
accounts. Between 1851 and 1855 the Bank of Upper Canada paid
interest on this money to Ryerson who "felt . . . no more obligated to
account for any allowance the Bank was pleased to make on such
deposits than to account for any other private money." Ryerson believed
the interest he collected was simply "compensation" for acting as "treasurer and paymaster" for large sums disbursed by his office; he regarded
interest paid on government funds "as my own."[12] Ryerson was not
alone.

     Reform involved a number of general and specific questions.
To begin, the government needed to revamp its administrative structures. In particular, accounting practices appropriate to the pre-Union
period had become utterly inadequate. Public accounts, which reported
both budgetary surpluses and rapidly increasing debts, were obviously
inadequate. Between 1856 and 1859 the government adopted a number
of measures, beginning with the appointment of an Auditor General
and culminating in the revamping of the Inspector General's Office
— moves that substantially improved administrative practices.

     The early accounting practices of the provincial government
were both archaic and confused. The Receiver General received public
moneys, dispensed all cheques, and issued and kept records for all
debentures. Prior to 1849, as the Select Committee on Public Accounts
later observed, the Receiver General "kept no books of account. He
merely made memorandums and statements." After 1849 both the
Receiver General and the Inspector General were required to keep
books using double entry. Although compliance in the Receiver General's Office was ensured, bookkeepers at the Inspector General's Office
later reported that double-entry account books were kept "so far as
was practicable." This meant that the accounting practices of the two
offices were "essentially different"; the two sets of accounts, in the
words of the Select Committee, did not "assimilate."[13] At the end of
the fiscal year, meanwhile, the Receiver General submitted his
accounts to the Inspector General, who reviewed them before submit-
ting the public accounts to the Legislature. This review did not con-
stitute an audit in the usual sense of the term, nor did the submission
of accounts to the Legislature provide budgetary estimates or allow
effective budgetary control over government spending. In 1845 Charles
Metcalfe ordered the Deputy Inspector General to carry out an audit
of the public accounts, but his review proved superficial. No single set

of financial statements, meanwhile, provided a general picture of the government's financial position. Beginning in 1855, however, the government created the Office of the Auditor General, modernized accounting practices, and finally created a Department of Finance complete with the usual mechanisms of control, including the formal submission of budgetary estimates to the Legislature.

In 1855 John Langton became Auditor General. Immigrating to Canada in 1833, Langton had become a backwoods farmer in Sturgeon Lake before becoming a partner in the Mosson Boyd timber empire in 1849. Between 1851 and 1854 he unsuccessfully ran the Blyth Mills, an experience that, according to his biographer, "confirmed his distaste for a business career."[14] He was, meanwhile, very much a "community leader ... into everything — and kept the books for everything." In 1851 and 1854 he ran for the Legislative Assembly for Peterborough. Always concerned with finance he quickly established a reputation as a critic of the public accounts. After Macdonald named him Chair of the Board of Audit in 1855, Langton resigned his seat in the Assembly to become a career civil servant.

Langton had once described the public accounts as being in a "more curiously complicated state" than in any country.[15] On taking office he explained to his brother, "I expected to find a mess but the reality exceeded my expectations, especially as I have only yet got into the threshold of the dirtiest stall in the Augean stable — the Board of Works."[16] By the time he settled into his duties the collapse of trade in 1857 had created a financial crisis.

As revenue plunged, Langton reported that it was impossible to make reasonable estimates of either income or expenditures given the chaotic state of the public accounts. As he later explained:

> In former years these statements embraced only such payments and such revenues as belonged to the Consolidated Fund, and there was nearly an equal amount scattered through the separate statements of Special Funds, or which did not appear in detail at all, and could only be imperfectly gathered in the aggregate, from a comparison of the several items in the statement of Affairs of the year under consideration with those of the previous year.[17]

To correct this situation the government instituted a series of accounting reforms in 1858. Langton produced comparative statements for 1857 and 1858 to illustrate just how dramatically the old system had understated revenue, expenditures, and annual balances (see Table 5). The budgetary deficit in 1857 proved to be more than 500 per cent larger than originally reported in the public accounts. Henceforth the Legislature would be provided with general statements on income and expenditures and on assets and liabilities that clearly indicated the

Table 5: Income and Expenditures, 1857–1858 ($1,000)

	1857	1858
Old Accounting Practice		
Revenue	$ 5,353	$ 5,061
Expenditures	5,693	6,143
Balance	(340)	(1,082)
New Accounting Practice		
Revenue	10,583	10,271
Expenditures	12,688	11,403
Balance	(2,105)	(1,132)

Source: "Comparative Statement of the Expenditure and Revenue applicable to the Consolidated Fund, for the years 1857 and 1858, upon the principle of Statement No. 3, of the Public Accounts of 1857," and "Comparative Statement of the entire Payments and Receipts of the Province in the years 1857 and 1858, upon the principle of Statement No. 3, in the Public Accounts of 1858," in "Public Accounts for the Province of Canada for the year 1858," Appendix (5), *Appendix to the Journals of the Legislative Assembly*, 1859. Calculations are my own.

real financial state of the province. These would complement a number of detailed accounts on particular aspects of government operations which continued to form parts of the Inspector General's report.

No sooner had the new accounting system been put into place than the government reorganized the Inspector General's Office, renaming it the Department of Finance. To the old responsibilities of keeping accounts, ensuring their accuracy, and advising the Executive Council on both financial and economic policy, the new Minister added the responsibility of supervising and controlling departmental spending. Each Department submitted budgetary estimates to the Minister for general review and possible amendment. The Minister then prepared a budget to be submitted to the Legislature for approval. Such procedures introduced an element of financial planning and eliminated the spending autonomy of many Departments. No longer could Departments such as the Board of Works spend on their own initiative, leaving the Inspector General or the Receiver General to deal with the consequences. This process culminated in the Audit Act of 1864 which institutionalized the comptroller function within the Ministry of Finance.

The provincial government had little choice but to adopt such reforms. The hot-house atmosphere of rapid economic growth which characterized the first 15 years of the Union period ended with the depression. As economic growth slowed the province could no longer afford the lavish spending programmes of the past. Modern accounting practices provided the essential financial information that made budgetary control and realistic planning possible. The more restrictive economic environment of the late 1850s made other reforms equally desirable.

The economy, for example, needed a real currency. The province used pound currency for accounts.[18] Although most banks and some private merchants issued penny and half-penny tokens as well as notes in pound currency denominations, coins of all kinds circulated.[19] Each variety had to be rated through legislation, yet the actual rates of exchange varied considerably.[20] There was, meanwhile, no legal tender. Banks were obligated to redeem their own notes and tokens in specie, but no one was under any legal obligation to accept these notes or tokens in payment of goods and services. The problems encountered by customs collectors such as Thomas Parke illustrate the difficulties inherent in such a system.

Importers paid taxes and tolls with all manner of notes, coins, and tokens, and collectors like Parke established reasonable equivalents of value. All moneys collected had to be deposited in the government account at the Bank of Upper Canada. As Parke discovered in August 1856, the Bank sometimes refused to accept these deposits. Parke was incredulous that this "harassing system" could be perpetrated by the Bank's refusal of "good money." It turned out, however, that this was not all "good money." Parke had, for example, collected £300 in notes from the Bank of Stanstead. The Bank of Upper Canada refused to accept these, as the previous spring it "could find no such Bank." Gold coins collected by Parke turned out to have been the private production of a San Francisco merchant who used inferior gold and minted the coins with less than the standard weight.[21] Such a chaotic system was perhaps inevitable in a colonial frontier economy, but by the late 1850s the more developed province required a more modern system.

The province introduced new legislation making the dollar the currency of account, and arranged for the minting of an appropriate coinage. By April 1859 $356,000 in bronze and silver coins went into circulation through the banks, each bank receiving amounts proportionate to its paid-up capital.[22] Eventually $45 million worth of coins minted in 1858 and 1859 would be placed in circulation. Although Galt later reported that the failure to call in copper pennies and half-pennies delayed the adoption of the cent, the shift to decimal coinage proved a success.[23]

The Province of Canada had come a long way since that February day back in 1841 when the boom of cannon announced the union of Upper and Lower Canada to its unenthusiastic citizens. Although by no means the only reason, the Union was an administrative response to Upper Canada's financial difficulties. Sydenham had introduced administrative structures essential to the establishment of modern Cabinet government. These new administrative structures ensured greater political control, yet much remained to be done. Renewed financial crises, particularly in 1857, led to more reform initiatives. Precisely because financial options were more limited, there had to be more accurate accounting, tighter comptroller controls, and a more sophisticated employment of a wider range of economic levers available to the government. Alexander Tilloch Galt and his Liberal–Conservative colleagues would complete the process of administrative reform, providing the government with far greater control over the day-to-day management of its affairs.

Notes

1.   "Public Accounts for the Province of Canada for the year 1857," Appendix No. 4, *Appendix to the Journals of the Legislative Assembly*, 1858.

2.   As Currie points out, railway construction provided a major stimulus to growth, although immigration and the Crimean War were also important factors. He suggests that the Grand Trunk alone was providing £15,000 per day in wage payments during late 1854. See Currie, *The Grand Trunk*, 36–37. Also see L. H. Officer and L. B. Smith, "The Canadian–American Reciprocity Treaty of 1855 to 1866," *Journal of Economic History*, XXVIII (1968), 608–609.

3.   *Historical Statistics of Canada*, Second Edition, Series A2–14.

4.   *Trade and Navigation Reports*, Canada, cited in Officer and Smith, "The Canadian–American Reciprocity Treaty of 1855 to 1866," 600.

5.   The following analysis is based upon summary tables of the public accounts covering the period 1842–1857, submitted to the Legislature in 1858. Although individual entries do not always correspond exactly to the public accounts submitted in any particular year, the summary tables have the advantage of consistency over the period. The limited range of entries in the public accounts, particularly during the first years of the Union, and the changes in entries over time make comparisons based upon the annual reports extremely difficult. See "Public Accounts for the Province of Canada for the year 1857," Appendix No. 4, *Appendix to the Journals of the Legislative Assembly*, 1858. All calculations are my own.

6.   "Public Accounts for the Province of Canada for the year 1857," Appendix No. 4, *Appendix to the Journals of the Legislative Assembly*, 1858. Hodgetts mistakenly attributes these comments to Alexander Galt. See Hodgetts, *Pioneer Public Service*, 269–270.

7.   See *Canadian Education: A History*, ed. by J. Donald Wilson, Robert M. Stamp, and Louis-Philippe Audet (Scarborough, Ontario, 1970). The emergence of the school

system has generated a substantial literature in recent years, particularly on the motives and role of the state. The most recent and, to some degree, most challenging interpretation can be found in Bruce Curtis, *Building the Educational State: Canada West, 1836–1871* (London, 1988).

8.   In 1862 Galt suggested that this high proportion resulted in the main from relatively low expenditures on some items, particularly "our not having been required to make provision for the maintenance of an army and navy." See NAC, *Galt Papers*, M.G. 27 I D 8, Vol. 6, A. T. Galt, "Budget Speech," 1862, 5–6. Although there is some truth to this argument, debt service charges remained extraordinarily high, equivalent to modern Third World debt crisis situations. There are, however, few parallels between the Canadian debt in the 1850s and its impact and the contemporary debt crisis of the 1980s. In 1850, for example, debt service charges represented only 6 per cent of export earnings. This compares very favourably to the situation in debt crisis countries like Argentina, Mexico, or Brazil, where debt service charges in 1986 represented 50 per cent, 37 per cent, and 33 per cent of exports respectively. See Table 14.2, "External Debt Indicators, 1985–1986" in World Resources Institute, et. al., *World Resources, 1988–1989: An Assessment of the Resource Base that Supports the Global Economy with Data Tables for 146 Countries* (New York, 1988), 238–239. It should be remembered, however, that during the Union period Canada ran a balance of trade deficit. See below, Chapter 7.

9.   The minimum payment, according to the Act for the Better Management of the Public Debt, was £73,000 cy per annum, although in 1852 the province made a special payment of £219,000.

10.   Excise taxes were placed on the consumption of products such as alcoholic beverages and tobacco. In the main, "territorial" revenue came from rentals of ferries.

11.   Glyns certainly believed that the financial difficulties faced by the Grand Trunk Railway "arise very much from the disappointment about the traffic returns which continue so small." *Glyn Mills Papers*, M.G. 24 D 36, Glyns to Ridout, 25 September 1857. Earnings on the Great Western, meanwhile, collapsed from $1.2 million during the first half of 1856 to only $700,000 during the first half of 1859. Dividends fell as a result from 8.5 per cent in 1856 to 3.5 per cent in 1858. No dividend was paid in 1859. R. D. Smith, "The Early Years of the Great Western Railway," 222–225.

12.   "Minutes and Proceedings of the Committee, 18 May 1858 and 28 May 1858," Select Standing Committee on Public Accounts, Appendix No. 4, *Appendix to the Journals of the Legislative Assembly*, 1858. The appointment of John Langton as Auditor General led to the discovery of this practice; eventually Ryerson refunded nearly £1,400 to the province.

13.   "Second Report of Standing Committee on Public Accounts," Appendix JJ, *Appendix to the Journals of the Legislative Assembly*, 1854–1855. Also see Hodgetts, *Pioneer Public Service*, 99–108.

14.   Wendy Cameron, "John Langton," *Dictionary of Canadian Biography*, Vol. XII, 1891–1900 (Toronto, 1990), 527.

15.   Cited in Cameron, "John Langton," 527.

16.   John Langton to William Langton, Toronto, 17 April 1856, W. A. Langton, ed., *Early Days in Upper Canada, Letters of John Langton* (Toronto, 1926), 242–257, cited in *The Bank of Upper Canada*, 196.

17.   John Langton, Auditor General, "Public Accounts," Appendix No. 5, *Appendix to the Journals of the Legislative Assembly*, 1859.

18. In 1841, after a long debate over the adoption of the dollar, Canada opted for Halifax currency rated at 5s 1d to the dollar. Later, in 1850, Hincks restored the 5s rate. This legislation, according to McIvor, represented the key victory of the dollar over sterling as the basis of Canadian currency. Hincks' 1850 legislation also provided for the issue of silver coins for circulation, which would correspond in value to American coins and would be legal tender up to $10. Such coins, however, were not issued. See R. Craig McIvor, *Canadian Monetary, Banking and Fiscal Development* (Toronto, 1961), 41; Adam Shortt, "History of Canadian Metallic Currency," in *Money and Banking in Canada*, ed. by E. P. Neufeld (Toronto, 1964), 127–128, and Francis Hincks, "Hincks On Canadian Currency," in *Money and Banking in Canada*, 106–115. Also see Careless, *The Union of the Canadas*, 146.

19. See Shortt, "History of Canadian Metallic Currency," 116–131. Also see Angela Redish, "Why was Specie Scarce in Colonial Economies? An Analysis of the Canadian Currency, 1796–1830," *Journal of Economic History*, XLIV (1984), 713–728.

20. McCullough, *Money and Exchange in Canada to 1900*, provides a general account of exchange rates in the nineteenth century.

21. See Finance, R.G. 19, Vol. 3366, Thomas Parke, Collector, (Welland Canal, Port Colborne) to William Cayley, Inspector General, 4 August 1856, and Ridout to Anderson, 8 August 1856. The Bank of Stanstead had recently opened, but Ridout reported that its notes were circulating without the signature of any officer at the Inspector General's Office. The Bank would accept the gold coins at a 2 per cent discount.

22. See Finance, R.G. 19, Vol. 1163, T. D. Harrington, Deputy Receiver General, to the Cashier, Banque du Peuple, 27 December 1858. Similar letters were sent to 11 other banks. Also see Harrington to Thomas Graham, Royal Mint, 4 April 1859.

23. See Finance, R.G. 19, Vol. 3370, "Report of Honourable Minister of Finance upon Decimal System and Coinage Question," 19 December 1860.

Chapter 6
Sorting Out the Financial Legacy

The truth is that my difficulties,
financially, which have been sufficiently
great arising out of the position of the
Province when I assumed office, are
augmented every day by the necessity of
supporting interests [the Grand Trunk and
the Bank of Upper Canada] which it
would be most disastrous to allow
to succumb.
— A. T. Galt, 1859[1]

Administrative reforms provided the government with the management tools necessary to conduct financial affairs; adequate managerial tools, however, did not in themselves provide a solution to the financial problems inherited from an expansive decade. Finance Ministers in the Liberal-Conservative governments, first William Cayley and then Alexander T. Galt, had to grapple with three basic issues. Something had to be done about the Municipal Loan Fund. The government had to deal with the railways in terms both of arrears owed and of new demands for assistance. The additional expenditures occasioned by municipal[2] and railway defaults also created a budget crisis which had to be confronted. A large portion of the 1857 and 1858 deficit, meanwhile, would be financed through unfunded advances from Barings and Glyns. Some means had to be found to reduce those deficits and settle accounts with the London agents. These problems were intimately interrelated; none could be solved in isolation.

The government had to face these various financial difficulties during a period of increasing political turmoil. W. L. Morton has commented that "[i]nstability was the essence of Canadian politics";[3] at no time did this seem to be more true than during 1857–1858. The Macdonald/Taché government had been slowly but steadily losing strength until 1857, when the resignations of Joseph Cauchon, T. L. Terrill, François Lemieux, and Taché led to a new Macdonald/Cartier administration, a dissolution of the Assembly at the end of November, and a mid-winter election. In that election Cartier's *Bleus* returned 49 members compared to only nine *Rouges* and nine Independent Liberals. Macdonald's Conservatives, however, failed to carry a majority in Canada West and returned only 28 members. George Brown's *Globe* had spearheaded the campaign, complaining that the government was "refusing justice to Upper Canada, . . . despoiling the public chest for the benefit of the East . . . and in sacrificing the higher interests of the country at the shrine of Roman priestcraft."[4] Fully 33 Grit/Reform members had been elected in Canada West, denying the government a majority from that section. Reform strength in Canada West then combined with resentments in both sections at the decision to locate the permanent capital of the province in Ottawa to bring down the government. In July 1858, E.-U. Piché's motion that Ottawa be rejected was carried 64–50.

A new Brown/Dorion administration was sworn in at noon on 2 August 1858, only to be defeated on a want of confidence motion shortly after midnight the following morning. Three days later a new Cartier/Macdonald administration took office, greatly strengthened by the inclusion of Alexander Galt, entrepreneur, land and railway developer. Galt had been a *Rouge* who ran as an Independent Liberal in 1858 and now found himself one of the key players in a new Conservative/*Bleu* administration. His price for joining the government had been a commitment to British North American union. Frustrated in the short term, he was destined to wrestle with the financial legacy of Canada's earlier expansionist programmes. Despite the political upheavals, the outstanding characteristic of Galt's economic policy was to be continuity. He would simply follow the initiatives already established by William Cayley.

The first question addressed was the Municipal Loan Fund. The government confronted its "indirect" municipal liabilities and decided to convert the Fund into a more orthodox public debt. At the same time the government intended to shift the bulk of this debt from Canada to Britain. In 1858 a programme to redeem all outstanding Municipal Loan Fund debentures, as well as all currency debentures issued in Canada, was proposed. The government enjoyed one advantage: it controlled a large block of these debentures, held "in trust" for the educational, Indian, and other funds.[5] Yet the scheme required the sale of new provincial "Consols" in Britain. This would be a major financial operation involving "upwards of Two Millions Sterling falling due within six years, which may probably be dealt with."[6]

The government could contemplate such an operation because Canadian credit remained surprisingly strong during the first stages of the depression. As late as November 1857, Morrison found the state of the market "most satisfactory ... taking all things into consideration it is gratifying to the Province that its Credit stands so high."[7] In November quotations for Canadian 6 per cents stood at 108.5 to 109.5. Glyns expected they would soon fall, and indeed they did. Yet in December 1857 the province sold £500,000 stg worth of 6 per cent debentures at 103.[8] In total the province issued £646,000 stg during the year,[9] and in 1858 sent even more debentures to cover interest payments. These bonds sold for the remarkably high price of over 113.[10] With securities commanding such high prices, it seemed an auspicious moment for Galt, already headed for London to discuss British North American union, to open discussions with Barings and Glyns on a proposed conversion of the largest portion of the province's indirect debt.

In late summer 1858 new legislation, which called for the issue of Canadian Consolidated Stock, moved through the Assembly.[11] The Act for the Better Management of the Public Debt gave the province the power to call in and redeem outstanding debentures with new issues, but stipulated that the total debt was not to be increased as a result of such an operation.[12] The new legislation provided for the sale of any amount of the new "Stock," with the proceeds going to the redemption of all outstanding debentures including those for which there had been no direct liability. It also provided that the new Stock could be exchanged for Municipal Loan Fund debentures, the price of which would be established through public tender. The Consolidated Stock would pay 4.5 per cent interest and was consciously modelled on British Consols. Like their famous British counterparts, Canadian "Consols" would be "permanent" issues. The principal "shall not be paid off" before 1 January 1890 and after that date repayment would be at the discretion of the government, subject to one year's notice. If this proved successful, debt service charges each year would be reduced by an estimated £100,000 stg. Before Galt left for Britain, the Executive Council authorized him to negotiate arrangements with Barings and Glyns for the issue of Canadian Consols.[13] Negotiations, however, did not proceed as smoothly as Galt would have liked.

The London bankers would have preferred a clear commitment to avoid any increase in the provincial debt, although both "recognize[d] the wisdom" of the proposed conversion.[14] More importantly, they believed that the Act "cannot be advantageously worked but requires important amendments." These amendments included raising the interest paid on the new debentures from 4.5 to 5 per cent, shortening the term from 30 to 20 years, and creating a Sinking Fund of 0.5 per cent per annum to be invested only in the new issue. Galt in turn suggested the possibility of accepting Municipal Loan Fund bonds as payment for the new debentures, something not possible under the 1858 Act authorizing the conversion.[15] The provincial government eventually accepted these changes and new legislation was passed in 1859.[16] The most significant change in the new Act provided that Municipal Loan Fund debentures could be exchanged for new issues by Order-in-Council on whatever terms were recommended by the Minister of Finance.

A second Act, meanwhile, consolidated the two Municipal Loan Funds.[17] No new debentures could be authorized on the Upper Canada Fund, although those already authorized but not yet issued could be sold. Another £100,000, meanwhile, remained to be issued on the Lower Canada Fund. In order to recover some of this money the Act provided that municipalities pay to the Receiver General either 5 per cent of the assessed property value in the municipality or 6 per cent of the money raised by debenture sales authorized for that municipality. This money was to be the "first charge upon all the funds of the Municipality, for whatever purpose or under whatever By-Law they may have been raised."

The province would have to move slowly and cautiously with its debt conversion programme. George Carr Glyn had advised in April 1859 that "we do not think that you could undertake any advantageous operation for the conversion of the Debt during this year" and doubted that the province could get a loan at 5 per cent. In July Glyn again reported "the market here will not bear any large [?] for sale of Canadian securities."[18] Galt, however, intended to exchange depreciated Municipal Loan Fund bonds with Consols since this "would not be an increase in the Provincial Debt but merely an alteration in form attended by a reduction in Interest and therefore with benefit rather than injury to our credit."[19] The problem was the large "floating Debt" provided by Barings and Glyns, both of which were likely to place their own claims for payment of advances made on behalf of the provincial government ahead of the redemption of other debentures.[20]

Before the new 5 per cent Stock could be marketed the province had to deal with its outstanding unfunded debt. That debt accumulated throughout 1857 and 1858 as Barings and Glyns paid interest on sterling debentures and then waited for remittances. In early 1859 the province forwarded £350,000 stg worth of 6 per cent debentures to London for sale to cover these advances.[21] Although in February 1859 Galt issued bills for £100,000 stg against the proceeds to meet "the balance of the serious deficiency of last year," he wanted Barings and Glyns to withhold the bonds from the market until he could go to Britain following the legislative session.[22] Galt worried that the outbreak of war in Europe might lead to instability in capital markets. He recognized that he would be unable to settle advances the province owed Barings and Glyns without bond sales and suggested an unfunded temporary loan instead. Meanwhile, he still expected a price in the 110 range for these debentures.[23] As discussion progressed, the debt owed Barings and Glyns suddenly grew considerably larger when in June 1859 the Bank of Upper Canada informed the government that it was unable to remit £207,000 stg needed to cover the 1 July interest payment.[24] This announcement came hard on the heels of another Order-in-Council which authorized an additional £250,000 stg of debentures to be forwarded to the London agents. At this point the provincial account in Britain was overdrawn by £440,000 stg.[25]

Galt blamed his difficulties on the "necessity of supporting interests" that could not be allowed to collapse. The Grand Trunk and the Bank of Upper Canada were both experiencing financial difficulties. Both were also embroiled in a conflict with Glyns, which threatened to refuse payment for a £100,000 stg bill drawn on the bank by the railway. These pressures forced Galt "to conduct our English accounts differently from what I intended." By July the original £350,000 stg worth of debentures had been sold. This reduced the provincial debt owed Barings and Glyns to only £65,000, but to this would be added almost immediately the July interest payments on the public debt and the Municipal Loan Fund debentures. The outstanding liability owed Barings and Glyns, then, was £550,000 stg. Galt would require sales of another £500,000 stg and, if this could not be arranged, he hoped Barings and Glyns could provide a loan on security of those debentures.[26]

In Canada the government was able to move more quickly with its debt conversion programme. In July the Bank of Upper Canada exchanged £150,000 stg Municipal Loan Fund debentures for an equal amount of new bonds.[27] In October and November the government bought £183,000 Lower Canadian Municipal Loan Fund debentures at 94 and £45,000 at par from Trois-Rivières. The province also appointed Donald Lorn McDougall as the government broker in the redemption process.[28] The market in Britain, however, remained slow. Although Barings and Glyns placed £350,000 stg of 6 per cent debentures, both cautioned that "the demand is very limited and we agree with you that it is wise to defer for a time any attempt to negotiate a large sale."[29]

By the end of 1859 the government was ready to push its programme forward with greater urgency. During the next year it would require, in addition to almost £3 million in Municipal Loan Fund debentures, at least £400,000 stg to redeem "Feudal Tenure" debentures and debentures issued for government buildings in Ottawa. The government still owed Barings and Glyns £400,000 stg, against which they held as security 6 per cent debentures. Fortunately none of these expenses required immediate payment, and this allowed the government to place its new debentures on the market slowly and "periodically."[30] When Barings and Glyns reported that "the present time and state of the market offer as good a prospect of success as can fairly be hoped for,"[31] the province decided to move. On 23 November 1859 the Executive Council finally ordered the release of the new 5 per cent debentures and sent Galt to London to oversee their sale.[32]

In anticipation of redemption Galt had instructed all municipal treasurers to provide his office with complete information on all bonds placed by them or any that they continued to hold.[33] To facilitate conversion the Executive Council ordered that provincial debentures held in special trust accounts — except the Indian Fund — be surrendered with a view to their cancellation. Other securities held by these funds would be credited to a special "Trust Fund Investment Account." The various funds, now stripped of their assets, would be given a "credit in the Books of the Province" and would be paid 6 per cent interest or another rate ordered from time to time by Council.[34] Then, in late December 1859, the government offered to purchase all outstanding 6 per cent debentures and began the process of redemption, starting with $19,000 worth of Lunatic Asylum and $146,590 of Law Society debentures.[35] During February and March 1860 the government purchased or redeemed large amounts of debentures held in Canada.[36] Owners of Municipal Loan Fund bonds could exchange them at par for new 5 per cent debentures.[37]

Redemption of sterling debentures in Britain moved more slowly as the terms for purchase were less favourable. Although the government's offer to purchase outstanding 6 per cent debentures would expire on 30 June, most bondholders preferred to wait in order to cash the 1 July coupon.[38] Although Galt ordered a temporary halt to the conversion in mid-summer, in October the government renewed its original offer for 30 days.[39] By December 1860 Barings and Glyns reported that £2.3 million stg worth of 6 per cent bonds had been cancelled.[40]

The final step in the debt conversion process came on 1 January 1861 when the government began paying only 5 per cent interest on outstanding Consolidated Municipal Loan Fund debentures. At the same time it continued either to purchase at par or to exchange these outstanding debentures for other provincial 5 per cent issues.[41] Although this offer to redeem at par with 5 per cent interest would expire on 31 December 1861, the government extended the programme into the following year.[42]

To finance these purchases the government issued an initial £2.8 million stg in new "Consolidated Loan" 5 per cent debentures.[43] Although dated 1 January 1860, these bonds were all shipped to Britain during May and June.[44] Galt forwarded an additional £2.9 million between July and September 1860,[45] followed by another batch of new bonds in 1861.[46]

As Galt had explained earlier in the year, "It is a big figure I want. . . . It will be a capital operation, much the best we have ever attempted."[47] Indeed, it was; never had the government marketed so many debentures over such a short period. That the province could, in effect, unilaterally announce a reduction of interest on its outstanding debt and then complete its conversion so smoothly provides evidence of the more assured and assertive financial policies being pursued by the province by the early 1860s. Another example of the greater self-assurance of the province can be found in its changing relationship with the Grand Trunk Railway.

When the Grand Trunk was originally organized, some optimists believed that sufficient capital could be raised without reliance upon the government guarantees provided in the Main Trunk Line of Railway Act (1851).[48] Such optimism proved misplaced; by October 1853 government printers were hard at work preparing the first half of a £1.8 million stg bond issue under the guarantee to be shipped to Britain for sale on 1 December.[49] Both Barings and Glyns, meanwhile, became concerned about the railway's spending habits and their potential impact on provincial credit. Hincks in turn tried to reassure his London bankers: "We are *perfectly aware* of the state of things in England and have been taking every means practicable to keep down Expenditure." Although Hincks promised "in future to be more cautious,"[50] within the year the government extended new loan guarantees to the Grand Trunk.[51] Then, in early 1855, yet another £900,000 stg was promised to the railway.[52]

No longer willing after 1856 to issue additional government debentures, the government tendered other forms of assistance. Between 12 April and 21 June 1856 the government released to the Grand Trunk in Britain £315,000 stg. Then in July 1856 the government advanced over £100,000 cy to meet interest on £2.7 million stg debentures due 1 July, and another £14,900 to meet interest on £400,000 stg debentures due 1 September. The troubled railway received yet another advance of £25,000 stg in two instalments on 10 July and 22 September. Between 12 April and 22 September 1856, then, the government advanced over £540,000 cy to the Grand Trunk.[53] As the depression began, the government reached the limit of public largesse to the private railway.

In addition to straining relations between the government and the railway, the financial problems of the Grand Trunk Railway also complicated relations between the province and its London agents. Barings and Glyns had been handling all Canadian government business in Britain since the failure of Thomas Wilson and Company back in 1837 and had been named exclusive joint agents in 1848. During the late 1840s and early 1850s, both Barings and Glyns had advised caution; both, for example, had been decidedly unenthusiastic about the Guarantee Act and the guarantee provisions of the Main Trunk Line of Railway Act. They both feared that open-ended guarantees or the substitution of government for railway bonds would have a potentially disastrous impact on the provincial credit. In the case of Barings, however, the government connection led to an increasingly large involvement in the affairs of the Grand Trunk.[54] Glyns, meanwhile, was the London agent for the Bank of Upper Canada, the holder of the provincial account after 1849. As the bank entered a period of decline at the end of the 1850s, Glyns, as payment for their own claims against the bank, eventually took over the bank's claims on the Grand Trunk.[55] As both Barings and Glyns became increasingly involved with the Grand Trunk, roles were reversed. By the late 1850s the government became increasingly reluctant to provide additional aid, while Barings and Glyns became powerful lobbyists pushing the case for more funds. The Grand Trunk's voracious appetite for capital created a tangled web of financial dealings between the government, its London agents, and domestic banks.[56]

As government agents, Barings and Glyns enjoyed privileged access to the Minister of Finance, upon whom they pressed the claims of the railway. The government responded with a series of measures which, although providing some aid, avoided any additional increase in provincial liabilities. At the same time the government began to distance itself from the Grand Trunk. Under the Relief Act of 1856 the Grand Trunk could issue new preferential bonds, holders of which would be given precedence over Canada's claims against the company. Without this sacrifice of the provincial interest, everyone agreed, there would be no market for the new bond issue. The government in turn insisted that the proceeds of sales of the new preferential bonds be specifically earmarked for particular sections of the line; moneys raised could not be used for general purposes.[57]

Under the Act £2 million stg of the new preferential stock would be sold in the British market. The government later rejected a Grand Trunk proposal to release £100,000 stg to repay bank loans as inconsistent with the requirements of the Act that tied the proceeds of these bonds to specific sections of track. The Cabinet, however, then reversed its decision and authorized some limited sales in April 1858.[58] Indeed, new legislation in 1857 amended the Relief Act to allow the company to draw on the proceeds of preferential bond sales for any purpose, as long as amounts specified for particular sections of track were spent on schedule.[59] A year later, yet another Relief Act allowed the railway, by a two-thirds vote of shareholders, to raise new capital by preferential bonds without restriction.[60]

The 1857 legislation, meanwhile, had pushed the provincial claim even further into the background while severing the formal relationship between the government and the railway. The legislation deferred the provincial claim on company revenue to some unspecified future date when the railway became profitable. Moreover, the government would no longer appoint its own representatives to the railway's Board of Directors.[61] Originally, the government had felt that its guarantee entitled it to appoint six Directors and have its two London bankers sit on the British Board. This created clear conflicts of interest, however, since Directors of the company were now, as members of the Cabinet, providing aid to their railway.[62] Although a new arm's-length relationship between government and railway had clearly been established, this did not entirely end conflicts of interest as individual members of the government remained closely connected to the Grand Trunk.[63]

The deferral of provincial claims did not solve the Grand Trunk's financial difficulties, which grew worse as the initial stage of construction drew to a close.[64] Poor construction standards and the earlier decision to build a wider gauge system ensured that new capital would be needed to rebuild the recently opened line.[65] A proposal to issue £100,000 in new preferential bonds in 1858 had produced little revenue; Glyns observed that "[i]t is vain attempting to raise money for the Company under existing circumstances."[66]

The provincial government was sympathetic, but with capital markets tight and revenue declining, no further aid, either subsidies or loan guarantees, would be provided. The railway continued to pressure the government for additional relief, particularly in 1859.[67] Galt, however, politely refused: "[I]t is quite unnecessary to say that if a crisis occur, no possible assistance can be looked for from this side."[68] During his first term as Minister of Finance, Galt held to this position despite intense lobbying from both Barings and Glyns. The government was even less patient with the Great Western Railway, the other major recipient of guaranteed loans.

The financial problems of the Great Western revolved around a series of decisions to construct branch lines, which ate into the profits of the company, and its decision to acquire the Detroit and

Milwaukee Railroad Company. When the Bank of Upper Canada refused to advance money to the Detroit and Milwaukee, the Great Western shifted its account to the Commercial Bank. When the Commercial Bank, after two loans totalling £250,000 from the Great Western to the Detroit and Milwaukee, "positively prohibited" C. J. Brydges, Managing Director of the Great Western, from making any more advances, the latter still issued unsecured overdrafts worth $2 million, equivalent to half the capital of the bank. After arranging for the deposit of bonds to cover these overdrafts, Brydges switched the account back to the Bank of Upper Canada. The Commercial Bank never really recovered and collapsed within the decade.[69]

In February 1857, meanwhile, Morrison had had to repay £28,600 cy to the Bank of Upper Canada to cover the interest paid on debentures issued on behalf of the Great Western. Morrison demanded repayment from the railway and took the opportunity to remind Brydges that the company was also in arrears to the Sinking Fund.[70] Brydges, however, failed even to acknowledge receipt of this notice. The Receiver General became increasingly concerned as the date for the 1 July interest payment approached.[71] Although assured that arrangements had been made, the Bank of Upper Canada found itself in July 1857 without funds from the Great Western. The bank again had to apply to the province for reimbursement.[72] When the government threatened to place "the matter in the hands of the Attorney General for collection,"[73] it received only £20,000 of Municipal Loan Fund debentures as a payment to the Sinking Fund.[74]

Before the matter went to the Attorney General, the Great Western suggested clearing all its debts with the province. In September the company proposed paying off the entire £770,000 stg received under the Guarantee Act in four semi-annual instalments beginning 1 July 1858. This amount would be paid at par, with all securities held in the Sinking Fund accepted at par. The company also expected interest charges to be reduced as the outstanding debt was lowered. Morrison recommended immediate acceptance of this "very advantageous" plan. The Executive Council agreed, but warned the railway that it would expect "strict punctuality" in making payments.[75] It did not take long, however, for the deal to fall through.

Barings and Glyns received notice of this new arrangement for settling the Great Western account in April 1858 and were told to expect a first payment on 1 July.[76] Within the month, however, the Receiver General became "apprehensive [that] there may be a failure on the part of the Company"; as a precaution the Executive Council decided to forward £250,000 stg of provincial debentures to London. These debentures would be used to cover the 1 July interest on the public debt in the event that the Great Western did not deliver the money owed.[77] The Receiver General also sought assurances from the Great Western that the agreed £192,500 stg payment would be delivered on time in London.[78] Caution proved warranted and new squabbles soon erupted between the railway and the government.

When John Ross, who was the Receiver General from April to July 1858, complained about the Great Western's failure to make its first payment on 1 July,[79] Brackstone Baker, the London Secretary, suggested lamely that the deal had been contingent on the passage of an Act of the provincial Legislature rather than an executive order. Ross denied categorically that this was the case and observed that, on 2 October 1857, the Great Western's Board of Directors had agreed to act on the authority of an Order-in-Council.[80] In the end the Great Western Railway did pay two drafts issued on the railway for £77,800 stg each, which together with the Sinking Fund made up the first instalment on its repayment schedule.[81] Arrears of interest, however, remained unpaid. By November 1858 the Great Western still owed the government $116,700 for arrears in 1857 and 1858. When the government again demanded payment, Brydges responded that the railway would be unable "to repay at present any further amount of the loan of £770,000 Sterling."[82]

Initially the government adopted a tough stance towards the railway. It rejected all arguments for a suspension of the repayment agreement and informed Brydges that drafts on the company at 60 days in favour of Barings and Glyns would immediately be issued. The new Receiver General, George Sherwood, commented sternly, "I trust there will be no further attempt made to evade the agreement, and that the Drafts will be duly honoured."[83] When he informed Barings and Glyns that the drafts had been issued, however, Sherwood warned that the railway would likely default. Galt, however, believed, as he told Barings and Glyns, that the London Board would be able to find the money since "a failure on their part must necessarily involve proceedings that I fear would be prejudicial."[84]

The Great Western did not pay and, after first ordering Barings and Glyns to present their drafts again, the provincial government withdrew both.[85] Although the government rejected Brydges's contention that its agreement had been conditional upon legislation being passed in the Assembly, Galt agreed to meet with the Managing Director to discuss postponing all future payments.[86] In the end the government agreed to cancel its repayment agreement; but the question of arrears of interest remained.[87] Although the Great Western paid $59,100 in November 1859, it still owed considerable sums for back interest.[88] Unable to pay, Brydges proposed in early 1860 a three-year moratorium. The government "deeply regret[ted]" the troubles of the line, but believed "the causes which have produced this state of things are . . . passing away." Sure that the economy, and thus the prospects for traffic and revenue, were on the mend, Harrington, the Deputy Receiver General, informed Brydges that "the Government are not disposed to press unduly upon the company."[89] There was, however, to be no *de jure* moratorium. But by the end of the year, arrears owed the government for interest in 1857 and 1860 amounted to £71,300 cy, and the government was again pressing the railway for payment.[90] A solution was finally found when, in January 1861, it was agreed that the Postmaster General would pay $144,000 owed the railway directly to the Receiver General. This money would then be credited to the Great Western account at the Receiver General's Office.[91]

There remained the Ontario, Simcoe, and Huron Railway, which had also defaulted on interest due on guaranteed bonds in early 1856.[92] The government had asked for an immediate explanation and considered the company's response in June 1856.[93] In addition to the abysmal condition of the line and the imminent threat of seizure by the sheriff, the Directors reported that its debentures — quoted at 50 per cent discounts — were "unsalable" in London. Those debentures were the only means available to the railway for raising money. The railway's survival depended on an advance from the provincial government, which would be secured by £193,000 in securities and the cancellation of the government lien on the railway. Whatever its other problems, the Ontario, Simcoe, and Huron Railway did not lack political influence: its President, Joseph C. Morrison, was the Receiver General. The government approved this proposal and continued to pay interest due on guaranteed bonds.[94] By 1859, however, the financial situation demanded a more comprehensive settlement.

New legislation was passed in the Assembly in 1859 to vest control of the railway (now renamed the Northern Railway) in the Crown.[95] Under this legislation the province could either force a sale of the assets or run the line itself. Galt, however, believed neither of these options to be appropriate. He proposed instead a new bail-out scheme, not dissimilar to that reached with the Grand Trunk but providing the province with far greater control. The Executive Council in turn approved Galt's plan in May 1859.[96]

Under this scheme the Northern would issue £250,000 stg of preferential bonds.[97] In addition, the company would consolidate its existing debt by issuing second preference bonds. These securities would be exchanged for existing debentures, which would then be cancelled. The government then established an order of priority for earnings: (1) operating expenses, (2) first preference bonds, (3) second preference bonds, (4) interest on the provincial lien of $475,000,

(5) arrears of interest owed the province, (6) interest on mortgage bonds and arrears on all bonds issued prior to second preference debentures, and finally (7) dividends on share capital.

The government, meanwhile, would exert tight supervision over the Northern Railway. A list of subscribers for the first £100,000 preferential debentures had to be submitted to and approved by the provincial government on or before 1 August, and no further issue could be made without the sanction of the government. The capital raised was to be spent on repairs, on rolling stock, and on station and harbour facilities, and all of this work was to be done under the orders of officers appointed by the government.[98] The Cabinet added that "thereafter the Said Railway shall be maintained and worked to the entire satisfaction of the Government." The government also took control of the Toronto Station. All tariffs and tolls were to be subject to Cabinet approval. Finally, the Governor-in-Council would be the "sole judge of the performance or non-performance" of the agreement.[99]

This Draconian legislation accomplished its primary objective. It had allowed the government to force a sale of the line, but in reality there were no buyers. This left only one option: to take over the line as a public work. This too was unacceptable since the government, already pressed for funds, could not afford the necessary repairs to run the line. Current fiscal resources were clearly inadequate and the government could not increase the public debt beyond the proposed consolidation then being negotiated. Galt's alternative agreement ensured that the Northern could borrow on its own credit at minimal cost to the province. The government avoided having to foot the bill for repairs, yet at the same time provided itself with the necessary leverage to ensure that the disastrous performance of the past would not be repeated. The only cost to the province involved deferring its own claims on the line. Had the railway been forced into bankruptcy, those claims could not have been realized anyway. By 1865 the provincial government felt that, "now that the Road is in a more flourishing condition," it could begin collecting arrears.[100]

The railways were not alone in demanding provincial favours. As the depression of 1857 began, the provincial government came under increased pressure from protectionists who lobbied for changes in the tariff to "place one branch of Trade on as good a footing as another, and afford such a Security in investments for Manufacturing purposes, as would materially encourage home Industry."[101] The government faced even greater pressure from an Auditor General concerned more with revenue than trade.

John Langton advised William Cayley in mid-1858 that the budgetary deficit for the year was likely to be £587,000. Langton, the voice of gloom and doom, added that "this has all the appearances of a permanent deficiency upon our present basis, which no one can hope to meet by borrowing or by temporary expedients." Policies of retrenchment, including a suggested 30 per cent cut in the salaries of all government officials, would, Langton argued, still leave an annual deficit of over £300,000. Well aware of the province's dependence on customs duties, Langton rejected higher tariffs as a means of dealing with the deficit. He believed such a policy would produce little or no revenue given the trade depression.

Langton, an appointed rather than an elected official, could envision few alternatives. Expenditures could not be cut significantly, so additional income had to be raised; he suggested that "before we reach the end of the £600,000 we must come to direct taxation."[102] No politician, particularly the Inspector General in a vulnerable government, would contemplate direct taxes. Against the advice of his Auditor, Cayley raised the tariff on a wide range of luxury goods and manufactured products from 15 to 20 per cent.[103]

When Galt became Inspector General later in the year, the worst of the depression was behind him. It was possible for him to be a little more optimistic than Langton about the fiscal consequences of Cayley's new tariff structure and the subsequent prospects of avoiding future deficits. Expecting that the status quo would result in a much reduced deficit, Galt preferred to look at cost reductions rather than increased revenues to achieve a balanced budget. As Galt explained to Thomas Baring, he intended to "make all possible reductions in the Provincial Expenditure" before "meeting the then ascertained deficiency by taxation *if necessary*."[104]

Galt could not rely solely on "a speedy revival of Trade" combined with Cayley's new tariffs to meet all his budgetary objectives. The Cayley tariff, Galt explained, could at best only "arrest the deficiency, for the remainder of 1858."[105] Galt needed more than a reduced deficit or even a balanced budget if he was to deal successfully with the outstanding advances owed to Barings and Glyns and at the same time convert much of the existing debt. Galt required more revenue than the Cayley tariff could hope to provide; so, in January 1859, he began canvassing opinions both within and without the government on raising the tariff still further.

Galt faced a fiscal crisis, not a trade problem. He had no choice but to introduce a revenue tariff. At the same time, however, Galt toyed with protectionist notions. In the records of the Department of Finance, for example, can be found an undated and unsigned note in Galt's hand entitled "Political Economy." This essay clearly articulates most protectionist arguments.[106] Galt, it seemed, was preparing to alter his free trade views.

The historical debate may view "protectionism" as an industrial policy, but Galt's contemporaries employed the term more generally. They were at least as concerned with "protecting" the commercial system in which the province had invested so heavily. Galt certainly understood that tariffs could protect more than home manufacturers; customs duties could also be designed to protect import merchants in Canada East as well as the Grand Trunk Railway. To achieve this objective Galt proposed new *ad valorem* rates based upon the value of commodities at point of purchase rather than the value in country of origin.[107] As Galt later observed, *ad valorem* rates encouraged "the direct trade between Canada and all foreign countries by sea," securing "the benefits of this commerce . . . for our own merchants and forwarders."[108] Other observers concurred:

> Several merchants admitted to me today that it would to a great extent facilitate business, and the only objection I heard, with a single exception, was "that it favoured Montreal more than Upper Canada" in other words that it would drive the New Yorker out of the Canada market. To this I think there can be no objections if the U.C. Merchant can buy as well at Montreal as at New York. It is time we had a Canada Policy — and if there are no other or stronger reactions than those adduced by persons in favor of buying at New York — the true promoters of Canadian interests will support your views.[109]

Certainly the Montreal Board of Trade recognized that *ad valorem* duties were "better calculated to promote trade through our own Channels."[110] E. J. Charleton was even more blunt. He wanted a "national policy for the national advantage," but for him "national" seemed limited to Lower Canada. Charleton appealed to Galt as "the first lower Canadian finance Minister we have had since the Union," and argued that "the Reciprocity Treaty and the general commercial policy of your predecessors have sacrificed Lower Canada and the General trade of the Province to Upper Canada Agricultural interests." He fully anticipated that the proposed "ad valorem duties will be a boon to the St Lawrence route and a step in the right direction."[111] The Toronto Board of Trade, not surprisingly, recognized the "protectionism" of Galt's proposals; they were not so keen on the scheme.

Toronto merchants preferred specific duties, particularly on groceries and liquor "in accordance with the well known opinions of the commercial body of Western Canada who desire to have the option of two markets." *Ad valorem* duties, the Toronto Board observed, "would necessarily confine [trade] to the Ports of the Saint Lawrence."[112] Other Upper Canadians seemed less concerned by such a development. Jasper Gilkison of Hamilton, for example, agreed that

the tariff favoured the St. Lawrence rather than New York but concluded that "[i]f Montreal is benefited, so much the better."[113]

The favouring of importers along the St. Lawrence route
would protect more than the commercial interests of Lower Canada's
wholesalers and forwarders. Any system that favoured the ports of the
St. Lawrence would generate traffic for trunk railways. George Carr
Glyn, for one, recognized the benefits for his primary Canadian
asset: "It strikes us that your new Tariff will help the traffic of the
St. Lawrence and the G. [sic] Trunk. I congratulate you on your success
in parliament."[114] Contemporary opinion was that Lower Canada's
import merchants received at least as much protection as the province's
industrialists.

There is some evidence to suggest that the tariff, from the
point of view of the St. Lawrence commercial system, brought mixed
blessings. Galt's tariff raised the cost of reciprocity goods imported
from countries other than the United States while favouring those same
countries for non-reciprocity goods. To the degree that most reciprocity
products from the United States entered the country up-river, the effect
of the Galt tariff seems to have been to encourage a larger share of
reciprocity products to come from the United States and a larger share
of non-reciprocity products to arrive via the St. Lawrence from countries other than the United States. This is indeed what happened
between 1859 and 1862.[115]

As trade recovered, the value of all imports increased by
67.1 per cent between 1858 and 1862.[116] The sharp rise in reciprocity
imports accounts for the bulk of this increase: reciprocity goods
imported from the United States increased by 160 per cent, while reciprocity goods imported from all other countries increased by
64.1 per cent. Non-reciprocity imports from the United States, products
most affected by Galt's tariff, increased only 6.7 per cent, while such
imports from other countries increased by 75.1 per cent. Imports of all
commodities entering Canada by sea via the St. Lawrence system,
meanwhile, increased by 67.6 per cent during these years, roughly the
equivalent of the total increase in all imports.

Designed to protect the traffic of the St. Lawrence, the Galt
tariff attempted to respond to demands for protection of domestic manufacturers as well. In January 1859 Galt sent out a circular letter
asking for comments on his proposed tariff revisions. Although Galt
assured respondents that any revision in the tariff must make "adequate provision for the financial requirements of the Country," he also
sought opinions on "the classification of the several articles in the
specific and *ad valorem* lists — to the propriety of maintaining these
subdivisions — and also to the rates of duty now levied on the several

articles, in relation to their effect upon consumption and contraband trade as well as in the development of the manufacturing industries of the Province."[117] There can be little doubt that industrial protection was high on the agenda of most respondents. Nearly all the business organizations and private individuals who replied to the circular recognized and approved the protectionist elements in the new tariff proposals.[118] Not everyone, however, believed Galt's tariff would provide real protection.

All protectionists agreed that the "lowest possible rate" should be charged on raw materials in order to "encourage the industry of the Province." Galt, however, proposed raising the duty on many imported raw materials and semi-processed products from 2.5 and 5 per cent respectively to 10 per cent. The increased cost of such imports could negate any protection that might have been gained by higher tariffs on manufactured items.[119] The Kingston Board of Trade, although recognizing the revenue needs of the government, proposed that all items on the 10 per cent list should be reduced until they were on the free list by 1862.[120]

Although Galt recognized and tried to respond to these protectionist pressures, his primary commitment remained revenue. The huge budgetary deficits accumulated in 1857 and 1858 severely strained the financial resources of the province; the fiscal crisis necessitated a £350,000 stg bond issue in 1859 to cover those deficits. The province, meanwhile, was overdrawn in London for another £400,000 stg. In addition, Galt had committed the province to a debt conversion project that would require another £3 million debenture issue in 1859 and 1860. In 1859 Galt had to avoid a budgetary deficit. As he explained to Barings and Glyns in March, he intended to avoid "any resort to the money market for new funds, unless it be in payment of the advances made by your respective firms." His "whole policy" was "framed with a view to avoid any further demand on the London market."[121] Other supporters of the government made similar arguments. John Ross, for example, reported his conversations with the Duke of Newcastle and commented that

> I told the Duke we had to raise a certain amount of revenue for the purpose of paying our honest debts and supporting our Gov't [sic] Expenses and our tariff was arranged solely to effect that objective in a way least burdensome to our people and that *protection per se* would not be listened to by any large class in Canada.[122]

Galt consistently argued that his tariff was for revenue and only incidentally provided protection. Indeed, Galt on occasion suggested that "the Government have no expectation that the moderate duties imposed by Canada can produce any considerable development of manufacturing industry."[123]

Despite political difficulties in Upper Canada[124] and protests in Britain,[125] Galt had reason to congratulate himself by the end of the year. Whatever protectionism might have been built into his tariff, it certainly was not reducing imports. Galt was quick to point "with satisfaction" to statistics that demonstrated his "new tariff has not produced any disturbance of trade, nor checked importations."[126] A rapid recovery in trade, both imports and exports, combined with the higher duties to bring substantial revenue to the provincial treasury. As Cayley observed in October 1859, "[t]he Revenue is running up I am glad to see. . . . Times are mending with us but getting in old arrears is always a slow process."[127] Galt's tariff was precisely what he said it was — a revenue tariff that produced badly needed income for the government.

The clearest indication of Galt's intentions can be gleaned from his behaviour in subsequent years. By 1862 the economic crisis had eased; the economy had improved and the conversion of outstanding 6 per cent debentures, including the Municipal Loan Fund, had in the main been carried through successfully. Budgetary deficits, however, remained. In that year Galt projected a deficit of over $5 million. At the same time, he asserted that "as you increase the duties you diminish the consumption" and tempt smugglers.[128] In the circumstances Galt promised "to remove those high duties which are calculated to defeat revenue."[129]

American increases in duties on tea, sugar, molasses, and coffee allowed Galt to raise specific duties on these commodities without fear of encouraging smuggling. This, he believed, would produce $1.5 million in additional revenue "which will probably suffice for all our wants."[130] Additional revenue from specific duties allowed Galt to lower the general rates. In his budget speech Galt argued that

> I think in fact that it is absolutely necessary this reduction should be made, because I find from the experience of past years that as the duty has been augmented the consumption has diminished. . . . [I]t is not so much to the effect upon the revenue that I would draw attention as to the fact that we have now an opportunity of reinvigorating our trade by reducing the duty on foreign goods. . . . [W]e must seek to get the utmost amount we can, coupled with unrestrained and unembarrassed trade.[131]

To George Carr Glyn Galt commented,

> I will not conceal from you that adopting this course I feel that I shall encounter the most serious opposition as being somewhat in advance of the intelligence of the country, but now that the American Tariff has

afforded me the means of doing so, I can no longer [consent] to be the apparent advocate of a system to which my own judgement is wholly opposed.[132]

To Thomas Baring he added: "The measures proposed by the Government will I trust give satisfaction in England, and remove the complaint made against our Tariff as Protective."[133]

The Ministry, however, fell before the Legislature implemented Galt's proposed tariff changes. His successors believed the revenue needs of the government would not allow tariff reductions. They intended to deal with deficits by bringing "the expenditures of the Country within the income at the earliest practicable period," hopefully within the year. New estimates approved in September 1862 cut over $400,000 from government expenditures and William Howland, the Minister of Finance, promised to cut another $1 million.[134]

Galt is best known for his 1859 tariff reforms, which provoked a contemporary and subsequent historical debate about their protectionist aspects. Ministers of Finance design policies to solve problems: Galt faced a fiscal crisis, not a trade crisis. He provided the best assessment of his tariff in his original budget speech, in which he said that his object was threefold: to generate revenue, to create a system favourable to the St. Lawrence route, and to provide incidental protection to manufacturers.[135] Therein lies its significance: what made Galt unique was his consideration of both the trade and revenue implications of his tariff proposals. He designed a revenue tariff that provided as much protection as possible to existing economic interests, including Lower Canadian import merchants and railways, consistent with the fiscal needs of the government.[136]

Responsible government had coincided with an acute financial crisis in 1847–1849 which led the Reform government to reassess all programmes and policies. Hincks's new proposals remained consistent with established policy objectives and orientations. Rather than suggesting new directions, Hincks provided a more integrated economic strategy accompanied by a range of specific tactical initiatives. These strategies, however, remained relatively crude and unsophisticated. They led, moreover, to the compounding of debts and a new financial crisis in the wake of the depression of 1857. This in turn forced another re-evaluation of policies and programmes. As in 1848–1849, there were few startling initiatives. Rather, there were modifications more consistent with existing financial and fiscal limits. Precisely because financial options were more limited, there had to be a more sophisticated employment of a wider range of economic levers available to the government. Alexander Tilloch Galt and his Liberal–Conservative colleagues also developed a far more sophisticated understanding of the interrelationship between fiscal, economic, and commercial policies. Fiscal problems continued to plague the province, but after 1862 the government faced these problems with a better appreciation of the complexities of financial management and with administrative structures that allowed its members to exert far greater control over their own destinies.

Notes

1. *Galt Papers*, M.G. 27 I D 8, Vol. 10, "Private," Galt to Thomas Baring, 14 July 1859.

2. By the end of 1857 arrears from municipalities for interest on the Municipal Loan Fund stood at £161,700. Finance, R.G. 19, Vol. 1163, RGO, "Statement showing the amt [sic] of Loans borrowed by the Municipalities of U.C. under 16 Vic., cap. 22, interest and contingencies due by same up to date," 2 December 1857.

3. W. L. Morton, *The Critical Years: The Union of British North America, 1857–1873* (Toronto, 1964), 11.

4. *Globe*, 23 November 1857, cited in Morton, *The Critical Years*, 15.

5. A. T. Galt, *Canada: 1849–1859* (Quebec, 1860), 29.

6. *Galt Papers*, M.G. 27 I D 8, Vol. 1, "Private," Galt to Thomas Baring, 16 August 1858.

7. Finance, R.G. 19, Vol. 1163, Morrison to Glyns, 2 November 1857.

8. *Ibid.*, Anderson to Glyns, 23 November 1857, Anderson to Barings, 28 December 1857, and Anderson to Glyns, 28 December 1857.

9. *Ibid.*, [RGO], "Memorandum of Sterling Debentures issued in 1857. £646,000 stg." [February 1858]. Morrison reported in January that £622,200 of the debentures sent to London had been sold. Finance, R.G. 19, Vol. 1163, Morrison to Glyns, 25 January 1858.

10. *Ibid.*, John Ross, Receiver General, to Barings, 17 May and 26 July 1858, Ross to Barings, 26 July 1858, and George Sherwood, Receiver General, to Barings, 6 September 1858.

11. "An Act to Make More Advantageous Provision for the Redemption of Provincial Debentures and the Consolidation of the Public Debt, and for Other Purposes," 22 Vic. cap. 84, *Provincial Statutes of Canada*, 1858. Also see McArthur, "History of Public Finance," 178–179.

12. See above, Chapter 3, 71.

13. ECO, R.G. 1 E 1, State Book T, Vol. 82, Minutes, 31 August and 9 September 1858, 101–102, 104–105.

14. See *Galt Papers*, M.G. 27 I D 8, Vol. 1, Barings and Glyns to Galt, 5 August 1859.

15. Finance, R.G. 19, Vol. 3376, Galt to Barings and Glyns, 16 November 1858.

16. "An Act to Amend the Act of 1858, to Make More Advantageous Provision for the Redemption of Provincial Debentures and the Consolidation of the Public Debt," 22 Vic. cap. 14, *Provincial Statutes of Canada*, 1859.

17. "An Act Further to Amend the Consolidated Municipal Loan Fund Acts," 22 Vic. cap. 15, *Provincial Statutes of Canada*, 1859. In addition this Act provided that funds under the "Seignorial Amendment Act of 1859," which were due the Townships, would be paid out of the Lower Canada Municipal Loan Fund. See Section 5.

18. *Glyn Papers*, M.G. 24 D 36, "Private," George Carr Glyn to Galt, 15 April 1859, and *Galt Papers*, M.G. 27, I D 8, Vol. 1, "Private," George Carr Glyn to Galt, 15 July 1859. In April Glyns assured Galt that additional advances would be made rather than forcing sales of debentures. Within the next several months large sales were completed, yet new advances were still necessary. In July 1859 Galt forwarded another £250,000 stg worth of debentures to Barings and Glyns as security for loans. Finance, R.G. 19, Vol. 3376, Galt to Barings and Glyns, 14 July 1859.

19. Finance, R.G. 19, Vol. 3376, Galt to Barings, 7 March 1859.

20. *Ibid.*, Galt to Barings and Glyns, 16 May 1859.

21. *Ibid.*, Galt to Glyns, 10 January 1859, Galt to Barings, 10 January 1859, Galt to Barings and Glyns, 7 February 1859, Galt to Glyns, 14 February 1859, Galt to Barings, 14 February 1859, Galt to Barings and Glyns, 16 May and 14 July 1859; Vol. 1163, Harrington to R. T. Pennefather, 12 February 1859, Sherwood to Glyns, 14 February 1859, Sherwood to Barings, 14 February 1859; Vol. 1164, Sherwood to Glyns, 9 May 1859, Sherwood to Barings, 9 May 1859, Harrington to Pennefather, 14 May 1859, Harrington to Glyns, 16 May 1859, Harrington to Barings, 16 May 1859, Harrington to Pennefather, 11 June 1859, Sherwood to Glyns, 13 June 1859, and Sherwood to Barings, 13 June 1859.

22. Finance, R.G. 19, Vol. 3376, Galt to Barings and Glyns, 7 February 1859, Galt to Glyns, 14 February 1859, and Galt to Barings, 14 February 1859.

23. Finance, R.G. 19, Vol. 3376, Galt to Barings and Glyns, 16 May 1859.

24. *Ibid.*, 16 May and 6 June 1859, Vol. 1164, Harrington to Ridout, 21 May and 4 June 1859, Harrington to Glyns, 6 June 1859, Sherwood to Ridout, 13 June 1859, Sherwood to Glyns, 13 June 1859, and Sherwood to Barings, 13 June 1859.

25. ECO, R.G. 1 E 1, State Book U, Vol. 83, Minute, 6 June 1859, 106, Finance, R.G. 19, Vol. 3376, Galt to Barings and Glyns, 6 June 1859; Vol. 1164, Sherwood to Barings, 11 July 1859, [Sherwood] to Glyns, 11 July and 18 July 1859, and Sherwood to Barings, 18 July 1859. Barings and Glyns requested smaller denominations and these were later substituted for the £250,000 originally sent. See Finance, R.G. 19, Vol. 1164, Harrington to Barings, 9 September 1859, Harrington to Pennefather, 28 October 1859, Harrington to Glyns, 28 October 1859, and Harrington to Barings, 28 October 1859.

26. *Galt Papers*, M.G. 27 I D 8, Vol. 10, "Private," Galt to Thomas Baring, 14 July 1859.

27. ECO, R.G. 1 E 1, State Book U, Vol. 83, Minutes, 11 July and 14 July 1859, 221, 230; Finance, R.G. 19, Vol. 3376, Galt to Barings and Glyns, 14 July 1859; Vol. 1164, Sherwood to Glyns, 11 November 1859, and Sherwood to Barings, 11 November 1859. The new debentures paid 6 per cent interest. Also see Baskerville, *The Bank of Upper Canada*, 196.

28. Finance, R.G. 19, Vol. 1164, Harrington to C. Alleyn, Provincial Secretary, 31 October 1859, Harrington to the Provincial Secretary, 8 November 1859, and ECO, R.G. 1 E 1, State Book U, Vol. 83, Minutes, 22 October, 11 November and 29 November 1859, 361, 414, 483.

29. *Galt Papers*, M.G. 27 I D 8, Vol. 1, Barings and Glyns to Galt, 5 August 1859; Finance, R.G. 19, Vol. 3376, Galt to Barings and Glyns, 26 June and 29 August 1859;

Vol. 1164, Sherwood to Barings, 4 July 1859, and Sherwood to Glyns, 4 July 1859. Galt was pleased that the price of Canadian debentures "continues high," and supported the policy of "only making such moderate sales as do not depress the market." Also see *Galt Papers*, M.G. 27 I D 8, Vol. 1, "Private," George Carr Glyn to Galt, 16 August 1859.

30.   Finance, R.G. 19, Vol. 3376, Galt to Barings and Glyns, 24 October 1859.

31.   *Galt Papers*, M.G. 27, I D 8, Vol. 1, "Private," George Carr Glyn to Galt, 4 November 1859, "Private," Thomas Baring to Galt, 4 November 1859, and Ross to Galt, 4 November 1859.

32.   ECO, R.G. 1 E 1, State Book U, Vol. 83, Minute, 23 November 1859, 463–464.

33.   See Finance, R.G. 19, Vol. 2764, Galt to the Treasurers of the Various Municipalities of Upper and Lower Canada, 7 November 1859.

34.   ECO, R.G. 1 E 1, State Book U, Vol. 83, Minute, 23 November 1859, 453–455.

35.   See Finance, R.G. 19, Vol. 1164, George Reiffenstein, Clerk, RGO, to Alleyn, 30 December 1859.

36.   See, for example, Finance, R.G. 19, Vol. 1164, George Sherwood to The honble [sic] The Executive Council, [7] February 1860, Srwood to Cassels, 9 February 1860, Harrington to Cassels, 7 March 1860; Vol. 2764, Galt to Barings and Glyns, 3 March 1860; ECO, R.G. 1 E 1, State Book U, Vol. 83, Minute, 7 February and 15 February 1860, 641, 656; State Book V, Vol. 84, Minutes, 17 July 1860, 308.

37.   See Finance, R.G. 19, Vol. 1164, Harrington to A. Cameron, Cashier, Bank of Toronto, 26 March 1860.

38.   See *Galt Papers*, M.G. 27 I D 8, Vol. 2, Thomas Baring to Galt, 3 April 1860.

39.   ECO, R.G. 1 E 1, State Book V, Vol. 84, "Copy," Galt to Barings and Glyns, 11 July 1860, and "Copy," Barings and Glyns to Galt, 14 July 1860, included in Minutes, 2 August and 11 October 1860, 341–343, 424–425, and Finance, R.G. 19, Vol. 3376, Galt to Barings and Glyns, 12 October 1860.

40.   Finance, R.G. 19, Vol. 1164, Reiffenstein to [Dickenson], 8 January 1861. In December 1860 the government also ordered Barings and Glyns to take the January interest payments out of the Consolidated Loan Fund Account. The "unsettled state of financial affairs in the United States" convinced Galt that he should avoid any transfer of funds from Canada that would "reduce seriously the balances held in this country." Finance, R.G. 19, Vol. 3375, Galt to Barings and Glyns, 4 December 1860.

41.   See Finance, R.G. 19, Vol. 3376, Galt to Barings an Glyns, 11 January 1861; Vol. 1164, Harrington to J. D. Nutter, Agent, Provincial Bank of Canada, Montreal, 25 January 1861, and Harrington to U.-I. Tessier, President, La Banque Nationale, 9 June 1861. As Galt observed, these bonds had "rarely if ever been quoted at par" and the offer to purchase at par would offset any possible objection to the lowering of interest to 5 per cent.

42.   See Finance, R.G. 19, Vol. 1165, Harrington to Glyns, 14 June 1861, Harrington to Barings, 14 June 1861, and Reiffenstein to B. [M.] LeMoine, Cashier, Banque du Peuple, 4 July 1861, Harrington, "Memo," 1 February 1862, Harrington to C. M. Arnold, Cashier, Niagara Bank, 3 February 1862, Harrington to E. T. Taylor, Manager, Bank of Upper Canada, 1 March 1862, and ECO, R.G. 1 E 1, State Book X, Vol. 86, Minute, 3 February 1862, 38.

43.   ECO, R.G. 1 E 1, State Book V, Vol. 84, Minute, 16 May 1860, 146–147.

44.   Finance, R.G. 19, Vol. 1164, Sherwood to Barings, 5 May 1860, Sherwood to Glyns, 5 May 1860, Sherwood to Barings, 22 June 1860, and Sherwood to Glyns, 22 June 1860.

45.   See *ibid.*, Harrington to Glyns, 14 September 1860.

46.   In October 1860 the government ordered another £2.2 million bonds printed. Finance, R.G. 19, Vol. 1164, Harrington to George Mathews, Engraver, Montreal, 15 October 1860. Also see Vol. 1165, Harrington to Glyns, 9 August 1861, Harrington to Barings, 9 August 1861, Harrington to Glyns, 1 November 1861, Harrington to Barings, 1 November 1861, Harrington to Glyns, 8 November 1861, Harrington to Barings, 8 November 1861, Harrington to Glyns, 22 November 1861, Harrington to Barings, 22 November 1861, Harrington to Glyns, 27 December 1861, and Harrington to Barings, 27 December 1861. In March Galt ordered Barings and Glyns to sell up to £150,000 stg of the 5 per cent debentures to settle outstanding balances due their firms. See Finance, R.G. 19, Vol. 3376, Galt to Glyns and Barings, 21 March 1861. Then in June 1861 the Cabinet authorized another £300,000 of the 5 per cent debentures to cover expenses under the Supply Bill. Half of these were ordered sold in October. The government also sold a number of the new debentures to domestic banks. See ECO, R.G. 1 E 1, State Book W, Vol. 85, Minutes, 13 June, 2 October, 8 November, and 15 November 1861, 242, 423, 480–481, 503–504.

47.   *Galt Papers*, M.G. 27 I D 8, Vol. 2, Galt to [S.] Smith, Friday Night [January 1860].

48.   Finance, R.G. 19, Vol. 1161, Taché to Barings and Glyns, 14 January 1853. According to Currie, Hincks originally offered to guarantee one half of the capital necessary to the railway, but then tried to limit the guarantee to £3,000 stg per mile. The company prospectus called for the issue of £1.8 million stg in debentures which were "convertible" into provincial securities. Total capitalization would be £9.5 million stg. See Currie, *The Grand Trunk Railway*, 8, 13, 18.

49.   Finance, R.G. 19, Vol. 1161, Anderson to Glyns, 15 October 1853.

50.   *Baring Papers*, M.G. 24 D 21, Vol. 2, Hincks to Thomas Baring, 12 November 1853. Emphasis in the original.

51.   See Finance, R.G. 19, Vol. 1161, Taché to Glyns, 31 July 1854, Taché to Barings, 31 July 1854, [Taché] to Glyns, 4 August 1854, Taché to Barings, 4 August 1854, Taché to Glyns, 19 August 1854, and Taché to Barings, 19 August 1854.

52.   *Ibid.*, Vol. 1162, Taché to Glyns, 12 May 1855 and Taché to Barings, 12 May 1855. These bonds were forwarded to London during August and September 1855. See Anderson to Glyns, 6 August 1855, Anderson to Barings, 6 August 1855, Anderson to Glyns, 1 October 1855, and Anderson to Barings, 1 October 1855. Also see ECO, R.G. 1 E 1, State Book P, Vol. 78, Minute, 6 June 1855, 222.

53.   Finance, R.G. 19, Vol. 1162, CEA, "Memorandum of Advances to the Grand Trunk Railway Co. since 1st. April 1856," 23 October 1856. The last advance of £25,000 helped the Grand Trunk "meet certain engagements on this side of the Atlantic." Morrison to Glyns, 14 July 1856, Morrison to Barings, 14 July 1856, Morrison to Glyns, 22 September 1856, Anderson to Jno. M. Grant, Secretary, Grand Trunk Railway, 22 September 1856.

54.   Both Thomas Baring and George Carr Glyn were original members of the Board of Directors of the Grand Trunk, representing their partners' financial interests. See Careless, *The Union of the Canadas*, 143.

55.   As a result of this the bank was able to reduce its debt to Glyns by $890,000. See Baskerville, *The Bank of Upper Canada*, cxliii.

56.   The best analysis of the convoluted dealings of the Bank of Upper Canada, the government, the railway, and Barings and Glyns can be found in Baskerville, *The Bank of Upper Canada*, particularly cxxxii–cxliii, and P. A. Baskerville, "The Pet Bank, the Local State and the Imperial Centre, 1850–1864," *Journal of Canadian Studies* 20 (1985), 22–46.

57.   "An Act to Grant Additional Aid to the Grand Trunk Railway Company of Canada," 19–20 Vic. cap. 111, *Provincial Statutes of Canada*, 1856.

58.   See ECO, R.G. 1 E 1, State Book S, Vol. 81, Minutes, 3 April and 12 April 1858, 466–467, 504–507. Also see Finance, R.G. 19, Vol. 1163, Anderson to Glyns, 19 April 1858.

59.   "An Act to Dispense with Government Directors in the Grand Trunk Railway Company of Canada, and to Facilitate the Completion of the Company's Works from Rivière du Loup to Sarnia," 20 Vic. cap. 11, *Provincial Statutes of Canada*, 1857. This Act extended the deadlines for construction of specified sections by one year.

60.   "An Act to Amend the Acts Relating to the Grand Trunk Railway Company of Canada," 22 Vic. cap. 52, *Provincial Statutes of Canada*, 1858.

61.   See "An Act to Dispense with Government Directors in the Grand Trunk Railway Company of Canada, and to Facilitate the Completion of the Company's Works from Rivière du Loup to Sarnia," 20 Vic. cap. 11, *Provincial Statutes of Canada*, 1857.

62.   Currie, *The Grand Trunk Railway*, 39.

63.   Peter Baskerville suggests that the unpopularity of the Grand Trunk forced the government to find less direct ways of aiding the ailing line. Politically it was easier to aid the bank of Upper Canada and through the Bank indirectly aid the Grand Trunk. "The government and the London agents," Baskerville argues, "came to the bank's aid for one primary reason: in prolonging the bank's existence they saw a last opportunity to save the Grand Trunk and protect their immense investments." Baskerville, *The Bank of Upper Canada*, cxxxviii.

64.   Glyns reported in September 1857 that quotations for 6 per cent debentures of the Grand Trunk stood at only 75 to 78, "a state of discount which precludes the Directors from operating." *Glyn Mills Papers*, M.G. 24 D 36, Glyns to Ridout, 25 September 1857.

65.   See Currie, *The Grand Trunk Railway*, 54–56. The Great Western also suffered from spiraling costs, faulty materials, and poor construction standards. See Smith, "The Early Years of the Great Western Railway," 216–221.

66.   *Glyn Mills Papers*, M.G. 24, D 36, George Carr Glyn to Galt, 23 November 1857. The release of the preferential bonds had originally been authorized in early October 1857. See Finance, R.G. 19, Vol. 1162, Morrison, to Sir C. P. Roney, Secretary, Grand Trunk Railway, 7 October 1857.

67.   *Galt Papers*, M.G. 27 I D 8, Vol. 1, "Private," Ross to [Galt], 19 August 1859, "Confidential," George Carr Glyn to Galt, 23 August 1859, Thomas Baring to Galt, 23 August 1859, "Private and Confidential," Ross to Galt, 23 August 1859, "Private," Ross to Galt, 25 August 1859, "Private," Galt to Ross, 9 September 1859, "Private," Ross to Galt, 13 September 1859, George Carr Glyn to Galt, 20 September 1859, "Private," Ross to Galt, 24 September 1859, "Private," Ross to Galt, 27 September 1859, Barings to Galt, 30 September 1859, "Private," Galt to Ross, 3 October 1859; Vol. 10, "Confidential," Galt to George Carr Glyn, 9 September 1859, "Confidential," Galt to Thomas Baring, 9 September 1859, "Confidential," Galt to George Carr Glyn, 3 October 1859, and "Confidential," Galt to Thomas Baring, 10 October 1859.

68. *Galt Papers*, M.G. 27 I D 8, Vol. 10, "Private," Galt to George Carr Glyn, 1 March 1860 and "Private," Galt to Thomas Baring, 1 March 1860.

69. See Max Magill, "The Failure of the Commercial Bank," in *To Preserve and Defend: Essays on Kingston in the Nineteenth Century*, ed. by Gerald Tulchinsky (Montreal, 1976), 169–173. C. J. Brydges came to Canada in 1852 as Managing Director of the Great Western Railway. In December 1861 he also became superintendent of the Grand Trunk Railway. He maintained his dual positions with the two companies until late 1862, when he resigned from the Great Western to become the General Manager of the Grand Trunk, a position he held until 1874. See Alan Wilson and R. A. Hotchkiss, "Charles John Brydges," *Dictionary of Canadian Biography*, Vol. XI, 1881–1890 (Toronto, 1982), 121–125.

70. Finance, R.G. 19, Vol. 1162, Morrison to Terrill, 28 February 1857, and Anderson to Brydges, 10 March 1857.

71. *Ibid.*, Anderson to Brydges, 22 May 1857.

72. *Ibid.*, Anderson to Brydges, 29 May 1857, and Anderson to Terrill, 29 July 1857.

73. *Ibid.*, Anderson to Brydges, 26 August 1857.

74. *Ibid.*, Anderson to W. R. Stephens, Secretary, Great Western Railway Co., 3 September 1857.

75. *Ibid.*, Anderson to Brydges, 2 September 1857, Morrison, "Memorandum," 10 September 1857, and ECO, R.G. 1 E 1, State Book S, Vol. 81, Minute, 14 September 1857, 21–23.

76. Finance, R.G. 19, Vol. 1163, Anderson to Barings, 12 April 1858, and Anderson to Glyns, 12 April 1858.

77. ECO, R.G. 1 E 1, State Book S, Vol. 81, Minute, 14 May 1858, 584.

78. Finance, R.G. 19, Vol. 1163, Anderson to Brydges, 17 May 1858.

79. *Ibid.*, Ross to the Chairman, Great Western Railway, London, 7 June 1858, Ross to Glyns, 7 June 1858, Ross to Barings, 7 June 1858, Ross to Glyns, 12 July 1858, and Ross to Barings, 12 July 1858.

80. *Ibid.*, Ross to Brackstone Baker, Secretary, Great Western Railway, London, 12 July 1858.

81. *Ibid.*, Ross to the Chairman, Great Western Railway, London, 24 July 1858, Ross to Glyns, 24 July 1858, and Ross to Barings, 24 July 1858.

82. *Ibid.*, Harrington to Bridges [sic], 26 November 1858. Also see Harrington to Bridges [sic], 13 November and 18 November 1858.

83. *Ibid.*, Sherwood to Bridges [sic], 6 January 1859.

84. *Ibid.*, Sherwood to the Chairman, Great Western Railway, London, 10 January 1859, Sherwood to Barings, 10 January 1859, Sherwood to Glyns, 10 January 1859; Vol. 3376, Galt to Glyns, 10 January 1859, and Galt to Barings, 10 January 1859.

85. *Ibid.*, Sherwood to Glyns, 21 February 1859, Sherwood to Barings, 21 February 1859, Sherwood to Glyns, 7 March 1859, Sherwood to Barings, 7 March and 23 April 1859, and Sherwood to Glyns, 23 April 1859.

86. *Ibid.*, Sherwood to Bridges [sic], 22 January 1859, and Harrington to Brydges, 23 February 1859.

87.   *Ibid.*, Vol. 1164, Harrington to Brydges, 17 May 1859, Harrington to W. Stephens, 12 October 1859.

88.   *Ibid.*, Reiffenstein to W. Stephens, 18 November and 2 December 1859.

89.   *Ibid.*, Harrington to Brydges, 3 March 1860.

90.   *Ibid.*, Harrington to Brydges, 7 November 1860, and Harrington to W. Stephens, 3 December 1860.

91.   *Ibid.*, Harrington to W. Stephens, 3 December 1860, Harrington, "Memo," 22 December 1860, Harrington to W. Stephens, 28 January 1861; Vol. 1165, Harrington to W. Knapp Henderson, Assistant Secretary, Great Western Railway, 3 February 1862, and Harrington to William [Whiter], Secretary, Post Office Department, 5 February 1862.

92.   *Ibid.*, Vol. 1162, Taché to Cartier, 20 February 1856, and Anderson, "Statement showing the obligation or debts to the Government of the Ontario Simcoe and Huron Railroad Company in detail, also the payments they have made etc., being the Return asked for by the Hon. The Provincial Secretary in his letter of 8th May for the Information of the Legislative Assembly," 12 May 1856.

93.   Finance, R.G. 19, Vol. 2760, William Dickenson, Deputy Inspector General, to J. C. Morrison, President, Ontario, Simcoe, and Huron Railway, 27 February 1856, and ECO, R.G. 1 E 1, State Book Q, Vol. 79, Minute, 14 June 1856, 325–327.

94.   Finance, R.G. 19, Vol. 1162, Morrison to Glyns, 21 February 1857, Anderson to Terrill, 23 July 1857; and Vol. 1163, Sherwood to Alleyn, [?] January 1859.

95.   "An Act Relating to the Northern Railway Company of Canada," 22 Vic. cap. 89, *Provincial Statutes of Canada*, 1859. Also see Baskerville, "Transportation, Social Change, and State Formation, Upper Canada, 1841–1864," in *Colonial Leviathan*, 244–247.

96.   ECO, R.G. 1 E 1, State Book U, Vol. 83, Minute, 12 May 1859, 33–46.

97.   The issue of preferential bonds had been provided for in the Northern Railway Act. See Section 2, "An Act Relating to the Northern Railway Company of Canada," 22 Vic. cap. 89, *Provincial Statutes of Canada*, 1859.

98.   During the early 1850s the Board of Railway Commissioners had been given the responsibility of overseeing construction and ensuring adherence to legislative standards. Its most interesting intervention came in 1852 in the case of the Northern: the railway was forced to requalify for aid after upgrading construction standards. See Baskerville, "Transportation, Social Change, and State Formation, Upper Canada, 1841–1864," in *Colonial Leviathan*, 237.

99.   ECO, R.G. 1 E 1, State Book U, Vol. 83, Minute, 12 May 1859, 33–46.

100. Finance, R.G. 19, Vol. 1166, Harrington to F. W. Cumberland, Managing Director, Northern Railway, 28 August 1865.

101. *Ibid.*, Vol. 3367, Petition from "The Manufacturers and Mechanics of Montreal" [1857]. The Cayley and Galt tariffs have been the subject of an extensive historical literature. Until recently most, but not all, historians emphasized the revenue aspects of the tariff, including Skelton, *The Life and Times of Alexander Tilloch Galt*, Easterbrook and Aitken, *Canadian Economic History*, and Gordon Blake, *Customs Administration in Canada: An Essay in Tariff Technology* (Toronto, 1957). More recently Tom Naylor, *The History of Canadian Business, 1867–1914*, Vol. 1, *The Banks and Finance Capital* (Toronto 1975) and William L. Marr and Donald G. Paterson, *Canada: An Economic*

History (Toronto, 1980) argue that the tariff was for revenue. Those advocating traditional arguments that the tariff was protectionist include Edward Porritt, *Sixty Years
of Protection in Canada, 1846–1907: Where Industry Leans on the Politician* (London,
1908) and Orville John McDiarmid, *Commercial Policy in the Canadian Economy* (Cambridge, Mass., 1946). Recent literature has renewed the debate and insists that the Galt
tariff provided effective protection for manufacturers. See, in particular, D. F. Barnett,
"The Galt Tariff: Incidental or Effective Protection?," *Canadian Journal of Economics*
IX (1976), 389–407, Gregory S. Kealey, *Toronto Workers Respond to Industrial Capitalism, 1867–1887*, (Toronto, 1980), and A. A. den Otter, "Alexander Galt, the 1859
Tariff, and Canadian Economic Nationalism," *Canadian Historical Review* LXIII (1982),
151–178. Ben Forster provides the best recent assessment of the tariff in *A Conjunction
of Interests* (Toronto, 1986). Forster is concerned in the main with the rise of protectionism in Canada but recognizes the divisions within the business community. He
argues that the Cayley and Galt tariffs were designed primarily as revenue tariffs to
solve the pressing financial difficulties facing the government. Galt, however, tried to
balance conflicting protectionist interests, giving as much protection as possible consistent with the revenue needs of the government. This analysis supports the Forster
interpretation.

102. Finance, R.G. 19, Vol. 3376, Auditor's Office to Cayley, 27 June 1858.

103. Forster, *A Conjunction of Interests*, 40.

104. *Galt Papers*, M.G. 27 I D 8, Vol. 1, "Private," Galt to Thomas Baring, 16 August
1858.

105. *Ibid.*

106. Finance, R.G. 19, Vol. 3368, "Political Economy" [January 1859]. Forster also attributes this note to Galt. See Forster, *A Conjunction of Interests*, 44, footnote 52.

107. See Masters, *The Reciprocity Treaty*, 66.

108. Galt, *Canada: 1849–1859*, 35–36.

109. Finance, R.G. 19, Vol. 3368, "Private," R. Spence to Inspector General, Saturday
[January 1859].

110. *Ibid.*, John G. Dinning, Secretary, Montreal Board of Trade, to Galt, 19 January
1859. Also see G. B. Forsyth, Chairman, Quebec Board of Trade, to Galt, 31 January
1859. Also see Forster, *A Conjunction of Interests*, particularly 43–44, 47–48.

111. See *Galt Papers*, M.G. 27 I D 8, Vol. 1, E. J. Charleton to Galt, 20 February 1859.

112. Finance, R.G. 19, Vol. 3368, Charles Robertson, Secretary, Toronto Board of Trade,
to Galt, 3 February 1859.

113. *Ibid.*, Jasper Gilkison to Galt, 21 March 1859.

114. *Glyn Mills Papers*, M.G. 24 D 36, "Private," George Carr Glyn to Galt, 15 April
1859.

115. See below, Chapter 7.

116. The following information is drawn from "Tables of the Trade and Navigation of
the Province of Canada for the year 1858," Appendix (No. 6), *Appendix to the Journals
of the Legislative Assembly*, 1859, "Tables of the Trade and Navigation of the Province
of Canada for the year 1860," Sessional Paper No. 2, *Sessional Papers*, 1861, "Tables of
the Trade and Navigation of the Province of Canada for the year 1862," Sessional Paper
No. 2, *Sessional Papers*, 1863. All calculations are my own. For a general discussion of
Canada's external trade, see below, Chapter 7.

117. Finance, R.G. 19, Vol. 3376, Galt, "Circular," 6 January 1859. The circular was sent to the presidents of the Hamilton, Toronto, Kingston, London, Ottawa, Montreal, and Quebec Boards of Trade.

118. See Finance, R.G. 19, Vol. 3368, Dinning to Galt, 19 January 1859, James Shannon, Secretary, Kingston Board of Trade, to Galt, 27 January 1859, and Forsyth to Galt, 31 January 1859.

119. See, for example, Finance, R.G. 19, Vol. 3368, "Memorial of the Undersigned Merchants and Manufacturers of the City of Montreal," Frothingham and Workman et al., to Galt, 11 March 1859 [41 signatures appeared on this Memorial], William Rodden to John Rose, 7 February 1859, George Peck to Galt, 7 March 1859, and W. S. Macdonald to Galt, 17 March 1859.

120. *Ibid.*, Edward Berry, President, Kingston Board of Trade, to Galt, 15 March 1859. As Forster points out, many protectionist manufacturers protested against Galt's tariff as finally implemented. Indeed, protectionist-merchant Isaac Buchanan led the opposition attacks. See Forster, *A Conjunction of Interests*, 46–48.

121. Finance, R.G. 19, Vol. 3376, Galt to Barings and Glyns, 7 March 1859.

122. *Galt Papers*, M.G. 27 I D 8, Vol. 1, "Private," Ross to Galt, 29 August 1859.

123. Galt, *Canada: 1849–1859*, 34.

124. T. C. Baring reported to Thomas Baring that Galt's tariff had been received so badly in Upper Canada that there was talk of a "political crisis and change of Ministry." See *Baring Papers*, M.G. 24 D 21, Vol. 3, T. C. Baring to Thomas Baring, 17 March 1859.

125. In anticipation of criticisms that he was raising duties, Galt suggested to George Carr Glyn that Canadian duties had in fact declined from a general rate of 13 per cent to only 10 per cent in 1857 despite some increases on particular commodities. "I make these few remarks now," he told Glyn, "in case the article in the *Economist* should have given you or Mr. Baring any uneasiness." *Galt Papers*, M.G. 27 I D 8, Vol. 1, "Private," Galt to George Carr Glyn, 17 January 1859.

126. Galt, *Canada: 1849–1859*, 36–37. Galt went on to suggest that "reductions in the scale of duties can only take place as the increasing population and wealth of Canada swell the importations." *Ibid.*, 41.

127. Finance, R.G. 19, Vol. 3369, Cayley to Galt, 20 October 1859.

128. *Galt Papers*, M.G. 27 I D 8, Vol. 6, Galt, "Budget Speech" [1862], 18, 21.

129. Finance, R.G. 19, Vol. 3376, Galt to Barings and Glyns, 6 January 1862.

130. *Galt Papers*, M.G. 27 I D 8, Vol. 10, "Private," Galt to George Carr Glyn, 7 February 1862. Galt went on to comment: "I do not intend to increase the rates on goods, in the first place, because I consider them high enough for revenue, and secondly because my doing so would cause unpleasant feeling in England when we desire to avoid any cause of offense."

131. *Ibid.*, Vol. 6, Galt, "Budget Speech" [1862], 31.

132. *Ibid.*, Vol. 10, "Private," Galt to George Carr Glyn, 19 May 1862.

133. *Baring Papers*, M.G. 24 D 21, Vol. 3, Galt to Thomas Baring, 19 May 1862. Galt had earlier commented that his new budget proposals would "show by the general spirit of our legislation, the desire we have always felt to harmonize in policy as well as in sentiment with our fellow subjects in Great Britain." Finance, R.G. 19, Vol. 3376, Galt to Barings and Glyns, 6 January 1862.

134. *Ibid.*, William Howland, Minister of Finance, to Barings and Glyns, 19 September 1862.

135. See Toronto *Globe*, 12 and 14 March 1859. Throughout the controversies that raged over his tariff proposals Galt never deviated from this explanation of his purposes. To manufacturers upset that the tariff provided too little protection Galt proved, in the words of the Hamilton *Spectator*, "obdurate." He repeated that "revenue must be had" and duties would be set accordingly. See *Spectator*, 12 March 1859. He repeated these same arguments to the British government when it forwarded complaints that the tariff provided too much protection.

136. Forster portrays Galt in more Machiavellian terms. Various business groups were divided both within the manufacturing community and between manufacturing and commercial interests. As a member of a relatively weak government, Galt attempted, according to Forster, to "divide and conquer" with his tariff. Forster, *A Conjunction of Interests*, 49.

Chapter 7
Trade, Finance, and the Limits
of Frontier Growth

We might anticipate very shortly in the
future the same sort of financial revulsion
which has been experienced in all
countries that have traded
beyond their means.
— A. T. Galt, Budget Speech, 1866[1]

Between 1857 and 1862 the government weathered a financial crisis, reformed its administrative structures, and initiated a number of new policies that demonstrated it was master of its own house. From this perspective the province looked strong, stable, and assured. The reality was different. The Canadian economy as then structured could not pay its way from its own earnings. The limits of frontier growth within the province, meanwhile, had been reached, and thus the conditions that had allowed the economy to ignore structural imbalances no longer obtained.

In 1866 Alexander Galt delivered an unusual budget speech. For the first time since he had become Minister of Finance in 1858 the government had run a budgetary surplus during the previous year. That surplus resulted from the sharp increase in imports which boosted customs revenue. The increase in imports had been accompanied by a sharp increase in exports without which, according to Galt, there would have been much cause for concern. Although Canadian finance ministers were not in the habit of discussing the balance of trade, Galt at least was aware of the potential dangers. Trade deficits, he warned, led inevitably to "financial revulsion." After sounding this alarm, Galt ended on an optimistic note:

> If the same prudence characterizes the people of Canada in the future
> as in the past — if we import no more than we have the ability to pay

for — we shall not be exposed to those revulsions of trade which are now the source of misery and anxiety in many countries.[2]

This remark leads one to wonder if the Minister of Finance had read his reports on trade and navigation. Canada had imported far more than it had exported in each of the eight years since Galt first became Minister of Finance. Between 1858 and 1865 the cumulative trade deficit ran to fully $67.5 million. While Canada may have had the "ability to pay" for its imports, the money had clearly not come from export earnings.

It has long been customary to view Canada as a staple producer with an export-driven economy. Although Harold Innis, the originator of the staple model, notes the dependence of frontier societies on imports from the metropolis, "the fundamental assumption of the staple theory," as Melville H. Watkins observes, "is that exports are the leading sector of the economy and set the pace for economic growth."[3] For the staple model, imports are significant only as a partial explanation of why colonial economies concentrate on staple production. As Innis argues, "Goods were produced as rapidly as possible to be sold at the most advantageous price in the home market in order to purchase goods essential to the maintenance and improvement of the current standard of living."[4]

As rich and profitable as the fur trade might have been, New France never exported enough fur to cover its imports. This situation continued during the period of British dominance. Indeed, many traditional studies of the economy during the early years of the British regime present a picture of an utterly unworkable economy without commenting on precisely how accounts were made to balance and economic collapse avoided. The general answer to the question of how this economy financed its trade deficit is readily apparent, although there are remarkably few detailed studies of the colony's balance of payments.

Canada's large trade deficit did not produce a balance of payments crisis, one reason being that it was likely much smaller than official figures would indicate, a result both of smuggling and of incomplete data collection in a pre-statistical age.[5] Capital, meanwhile, flowed into this economy in a variety of ways. Immigrants arrived. Not all were dirt-poor, and even those who were brought their capacity to labour with them. That labour rapidly created wealth by transforming wilderness into productive commercial enterprises. Private investors put additional capital into the economy. Although some capital flowed out as profit to metropolitan interests, some remained, part of the slow process of domestic accumulation. By far the largest source of capital, however, was the state. The imperial authorities paid soldiers and officials, constructed public buildings, and helped improve infrastructure and develop economic enterprises. They did this with Treasury funds to which the colonists made few contributions.

The imperial state made the colonial economy run as it did. W. J. Eccles, for example, long ago pointed out that the "military establishment ran the fur trade a close second as the economic mainstay" of New France.[6] Similarly R. Craig McIvor observed that British efforts to establish sterling in its colony required it to pump specie into the economy through its military payments.[7] The specie flowed out just as rapidly to pay for imports.

The Conquest had brought trade disruptions, but the period of adjustment had proved short. Nor had it taken long for the new imperial metropole to assume its traditional function of financing its colony's trade deficit.[8] Paul McCann has demonstrated that, although the trade deficit was less than traditionally assumed, it remained substantial; Quebec ran a cumulative deficit on its current account of £433,900 stg between 1768 and 1772.[9] British military and civil spending during these years totalled £376,619, leaving a deficit of only £70,700 which could be balanced by a variety of other means.[10]

Even after the American Revolution and later the War of 1812, imperial spending in British North America remained substantial. As late as 1828 spending on the military establishments at Kingston and Halifax was over £330,000 stg.[11] To this could be added sums spent on the empire's civil establishment, as well as major public works projects such as the Rideau Canal. By the time of the Union, however, the slow process of imperial disengagement in British North America was already well advanced. The suppression of the rebellions and the studied rejection of responsible government were rear-guard actions by a Colonial Office already committed to reducing its North American liabilities.

Although colonial officials would not countenance overt separation, they had already come to the conclusion that British North America was not something worth spending much money on. The colonies would have to pay their own way. Upper Canada's financial problems would not be solved by the British taxpayer; the best the Colonial Office offered was a guarantee to pay interest, but not principal, on a new Canadian loan should the province default. In the end Canada paid both interest and principal on time and in full; not a penny of Treasury funds ever crossed the Atlantic to help pay for Canada's St. Lawrence canal system. Although the British military stationed in Canada continued to be paid by the Commissary, all other government officials, including the Governor, depended on the colonial Legislature.

It is in this context that Canadians moved in the 1840s and 1850s to improve their export performance. Trade deficits can be attacked by increasing exports, limiting imports, or both. What is remarkable about the Union period is the degree to which restricting imports seems never to have been considered. At no time did the government see imports as a source of economic weakness.

The cynic would see a conflict of interest at work which produced a government blind spot on the question of import control. The single most important decision-maker on economic questions was the Inspector General/Minister of Finance; the men who filled this position invariably came from the ranks of the import-merchant/ banker/railway-promoter community. Four men in particular dominated economic policy during the Union period: Francis Hincks, William Cayley, Alexander Tilloch Galt, and Luther Holton. Between them they occupied the Office of Inspector General/Minister of Finance for 21 of the 26 years of the Union. Hincks, Cayley, and Holton made their way into the economic and political elite by way of the counting houses of the empire and local colonial importing and forwarding firms.[12] In the case of Holton and others, commercial connections stimulated an interest in transportation improvements, an interest that translated into directorships for railway companies. Here they joined forces with men like Alexander Galt.[13] These were men whose private interest lay in trade and traffic for their railways. All looked to an increase in the volume of trade as a source of personal profit. As ministers of the Crown their private interests dovetailed nicely with their public concerns.

Potential conflicts of interest, however, do not adequately explain why Inspectors General and Ministers of Finance failed to address directly Canada's trade deficit. Despite the intimate connection between public policy and the private sector in Victorian Canada, men like Galt could and did distinguish between public and private interests when the two clearly conflicted. Galt's studied refusal to provide additional aid to the Grand Trunk after 1859 provides at least one demonstration of the degree to which public concerns dominated natural inclination.

A far more potent factor, which lay at the root of trade and financial policies, was the antipathy towards direct taxation shared by all British North Americans. As W. L. Morton has suggested, "[T]he mid-Victorian passion for economy ... was matched only by the British North American horror of taxation."[14] Most provincial politicians believed that even the hint of direct taxes was the quick route to certain electoral defeat. As long as politicians feared to introduce direct taxation, the government remained almost totally dependent on customs duties to finance civil administration. As long as government finance remained dependent on customs duties, any policy designed to restrict imports was ludicrous. Indeed, so important were customs duties to the structure of government finance that ministers could on occasion appear blinded to the realities of trade.

William Howland, for example, presented the general view in explaining the government's budgetary deficit in 1862. The Civil War had, he asserted, "diminished demand for our staple products," which in turn "produced a corresponding check upon the purchasing power of our people, and a corresponding loss to the principal sources of our revenue."[15] Although total exports had declined from $34.7 to $31.7 million between 1861 and 1862, it is difficult to place the blame on the Civil War since exports to the United States increased during these years. Imports, meanwhile, far from declining because of reduced purchasing power, increased sharply from $43.1 to $48.6 million. In 1862 the Province of Canada ran up one of the largest balance of trade deficits in its history, yet the Minister of Finance commented only about the loss of revenue which he believed resulted from a decline in imports. Howland, it would appear, paid no more attention to his reports on trade and navigation than did Galt.

Canada depended upon tariffs, and few people saw any need to consider alternative sources of revenue. British North Americans shared a basic optimism about their economic prospects common in frontier settlement colonies. Only the most jaded observers believed that deficits — either trade, balance of payments, or budgetary — might prove permanent; most preferred to believe that the natural resource allocation of the country provided almost unlimited potential for short- and long-term development. The extraordinary reliance upon credit in private business circles is best exemplified in the career of Isaac Buchanan, who had an unquestioned faith in the growth ethic.[16] The transportation rhetoric is best exemplified in Thomas Keefer's *Philosophy of Railways*, which subscribed to this same philosophy of growth.[17] Government financial and economic policy is best articulated by Francis Hincks, who also had unquestioned faith in the unrivalled economic potential of Canada's frontier.

Canadians did not perceive a trade problem during the Union period because they believed that immigration and settlement ensured the rapid expansion of exports. The government pursued policies to encourage a more rapid increase in exports not as a possible solution to a looming trade crisis, but simply as part of its settlement and development strategy. It was in this context that Canadians pressured the British government during the 1840s to protect Canada's export sector.

Imperialism, more particularly the Corn Laws and Timber
Duties, provided Canadian products with preferential access to over-
seas markets. During the early 1840s Canadians won concessions, such
as the Canada Corn Act, which further enhanced Canadian export
potential.[18] Such strategies were linked to transportation projects,
aimed as they were at capturing a share of the through traffic between
the American Midwest and Britain.[19] Measures like the Canada Corn
Act ensured a degree of processing in the colony that would enhance
export performance by adding value to re-exported products.

The strategy of relying upon imperial solidarity to enhance
export performance, however, unravelled after 1846 as Sir Robert
Peel's Tories opted for free trade. That decision produced much consternation on this side of the Atlantic;[20] the Annexation Manifesto
demonstrated the degree to which the patriotism of many lay in their
pocketbooks. The Manifesto also signalled the generally accepted
notion that the best alternative to lost imperial advantage lay in
expanded continental trade.[21] As the first efforts at reciprocity proved
fruitless, and as subsequent export performance demonstrated that
Canadian trade with Britain did not depend upon imperial protection,
the enthusiasm for a negotiated "most favoured nation" access to the
American market waned, but it did not disappear.[22] When in 1854 a
more propitious opportunity presented itself, Canada opted for reciprocity.

The Reciprocity Treaty negotiated in 1854 and ratified in
February 1855 should have been highly beneficial to the Province of
Canada.[23] The treaty provided free trade in all natural products, American access to the Atlantic fisheries of British North America, and
equalization of tolls on Canadian and American ships using the
St. Lawrence system. The bulk of Canada's export products would now
have access to a continental market of over 30 million. At the same
time the bulk of Canada's imports would not be affected by the treaty.
Reciprocity, all believed, could only improve an already strong export
performance with minimum financial consequences for the government, which continued to collect customs duties on most of the province's American imports. Whether reciprocity would improve an
already poor trade performance was debatable.[24]

Exports of reciprocity goods to the United States nearly doubled between 1854 and 1855, rising from $8.5 million to $16.5 million.
Although declining temporarily during the depression of 1857, reciprocity exports to the United States remained high for a decade (see
Figure 1). Exports of these products then hit an artificial high in 1866
as Canadians rushed to beat the repeal date. Although exports declined
from this peak, they remained as high in 1867 as at any time during

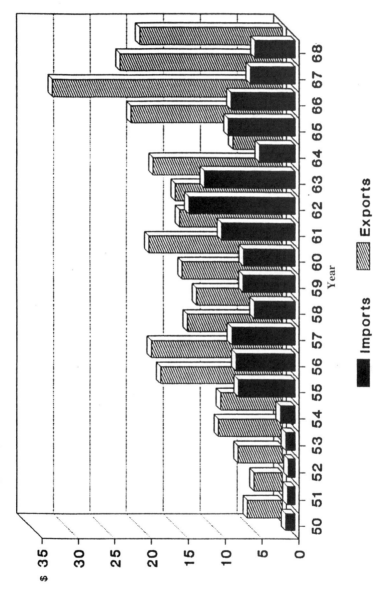

Figure 1: Trade in Reciprocity Goods with the United States, 1850–1868 ($ Million)

Imports   Exports

Year

Source: Officer and Smith, "The Canadian–American Reciprocity Treaty," Table 1, 600. Figures for 1850–1883 cover 12 months ending 31 December; for 1864 cover six months ending 30 June; for 1865–1868 cover 12 months ending 30 June.

the life of the treaty. Reciprocity imports from the United States, meanwhile, rose even faster than exports during the first year of the treaty, increasing 300 per cent in a single year from a mere $2 million in 1854 to $7.7 million in 1855.[25] Reciprocity imports continued to increase at a much reduced rate until the depression, recovered during the first years of the Civil War, then fell sharply after 1862.

Despite the more rapid rate of growth in reciprocity imports compared to that of exports during the first year of the treaty, the sharp increase in total volume ensured that Canada's surplus in reciprocity trade with the United States grew in 1855 (see Figure 2). The surplus did not, however, continue to grow at anywhere near the pre-reciprocity rate. The surplus in Canada's favour then fell sharply during the depression in 1857. It recovered slowly before falling even more sharply during the first years of the Civil War. Except for the artificial peak in 1866, the repeal of the treaty, as we have noted, had little impact on exports. However, reciprocity imports fell sharply. As a result, Canada's surplus in reciprocity trade with the United States was greater in 1867 and 1868 than at any time during the first decade of the Reciprocity Treaty.

Both reciprocity and its repeal, it would seem, benefitted Canada. The treaty led to a sharp jump in the volume and value of trade. This new and much higher level of trade was easily maintained during the life of the treaty, a fact which meant that the surplus in Canada's favour increased despite the more rapid increase in imports compared to exports. After the treaty's repeal, exports remained high, imports fell, and the surplus, as a result, rose even higher than during the life of the treaty. Such an optimistic assessment, however, requires some qualification.

Some of the increased flow of reciprocity goods between Canada and the United States represented a diversion from other markets and sources of supply rather than an absolute increase in trade. L. H. Officer and L. B. Smith suggest that almost all of the increased trade with the United States between 1854 and 1855 was trade creation rather than trade diversion.[26] Although there was a small decline in both reciprocity imports and exports from countries other than the United States in 1855, this proved temporary. By 1856 reciprocity exports and imports from other countries had returned to their previous level. Imports and especially exports of such goods to other countries, however, increased only marginally in subsequent years despite the rapid increase in Canadian economic activity in general and trade in particular. The reciprocity decade, as a result, witnessed a sharp shift to a continental trading system that was, not surprisingly, most noticeable in the case of reciprocity imports. Between 1850 and 1854

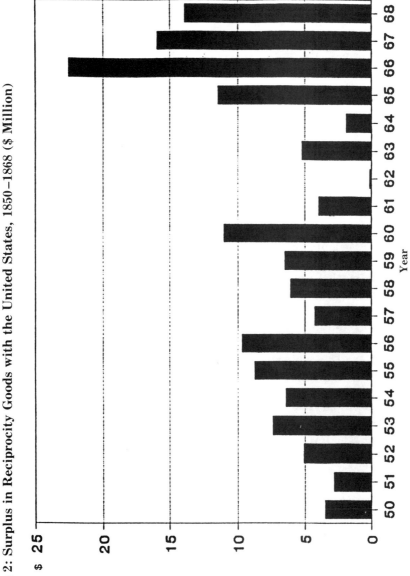

Figure 2: Surplus in Reciprocity Goods with the United States, 1850–1868 ($ Million)

Source: See Figure 1.

reciprocity imports from the United States represented about 45 per cent of all such imports. In 1855 the United States supplied 71 per cent of these products. During the period of the Reciprocity Treaty, the United States supplied substantially more than half of all reciprocity imports in all but two years. The same story emerges in the case of reciprocity exports, although here the original dependence on the American market was more pronounced and, as a result, the shift was less sharp. Perhaps reflecting the continued depressed state of the British market, 87 per cent of Canadian exports that were later covered by the treaty found their way to the American market in 1850. Between 1851 and 1854 this figure fell to about 70 per cent, before jumping to fully 92 per cent in 1855. Reciprocity exports to the United States remained above 83 per cent of all such exports until the final year of the treaty, yet even in 1866 the United States absorbed 80 per cent of all reciprocity exports.

The overwhelming importance of the continental market in reciprocity products, both imports and exports, strengthened Canada's continental attachment in all trade (see Figure 3). Between 1850 and 1854 roughly 40 per cent of all Canadian trade was with the United States. This figure jumped sharply to 58 per cent of all imports and 67 per cent of all exports with reciprocity. In the case of exports the American market remained critical, absorbing significantly more than half of all exports in all but two years. Imports, however, readjusted. Between 1856 and 1863 the percentage of all imports from the United States ranged from a low of 49 per cent in 1861 to a high of 54 per cent in 1858. The percentage fell to 44 per cent in 1864 and 1865, and to under 40 per cent between 1866 and 1868, roughly the same as the level during the pre-reciprocity period.[27]

These shifts also affected the distribution of Canadian exports between reciprocity and non-reciprocity goods. Canada, to be sure, remained an exporter of primary products. Between 1850 and 1854 non-reciprocity commodities accounted for about 12 per cent of all exports. Between 1855 and 1862 they fell to only about 6 per cent, ranging from a low of 4.4 per cent to a high of 7.5 per cent. With the treaty under threat and eventually repealed, Canadian exports again became slightly more diversified. Between 1863 and 1867 non-reciprocity products accounted for about 14 per cent of all exports, ranging from a low of 11.3 per cent to a high of 15.7 per cent.

These shifts in trade had some benefits for Canada's balance of trade deficit (see Figure 4). Canada's trade position deteriorated significantly during the early 1850s; the trade deficit increased from $5 million in 1850 to nearly $10 million in 1853 and to almost $20 million a year later. In 1856 and 1857 the deficit stood at almost

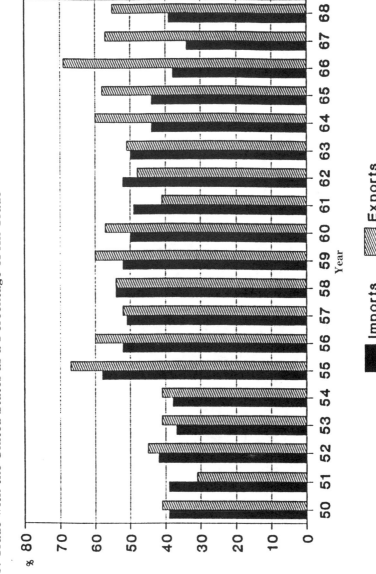

Figure 3: Trade with the United States as a Percentage of All Trade

Source: See Figure 1.

$14 million, before falling to $7 million in 1858 and only $2 million in 1860. The Civil War coincided with a substantial increase in the deficit, although there were wide annual variations ranging from a low of $3.5 million in 1866 to a high of $17 million in 1862. With the end of the reciprocity period, the deficit rose to $14 million in 1867.

Despite the annual fluctuations the basic problem remained. Canada ran a balance of trade deficit which grew substantially larger during the 1850s. To some extent development policies encouraged short-term growth in the deficit: the railway construction boom of the early 1850s no doubt contributed to the rapid increase in imports during those years. The trade deficits of the early 1850s represented investments as well as consumption, and those investments helped stimulate economic growth, which in turn helped increase exports. During the latter years of the decade and into the 1860s Canada's trade situation steadily improved as a result. Despite this improvement, however, substantial deficits on visible trade continued to accumulate.

Although precision in a pre-statistical era is impossible, it is clear that Canada's balance of payments was closer to equilibrium than its balance of trade. As in the past, the state played the critical role: government spending, more than any other single factor, kept this economy moving. During the Union period the provincial government assumed the traditional imperial role of raising funds abroad to be spent in the colony. The only other institutions to invest similarly large sums were the railways,[28] and, as we have seen, railway capital flowed into the economy via state encouragement and intervention and much of it eventually became a provincial liability.

There was one critical element that made the Union period fundamentally different from the colonial past. Imperial spending during the pre-Union period — or, more accurately, the pre-1830 period — came without long-term liabilities. Imperial expenditures represented a permanent addition to the capital of the colony, although in truth much of this capital flowed out of the colony to pay for imported commodities. Imperial spending helped ensure the maintenance of a relatively high standard of living even when domestic capital for investment accumulated painfully slowly. Provincial spending during the Union period played the same role. Capital raised in Britain was distributed within the colonial economy, with most of this capital flowing out relatively quickly to pay for imported commodities. But unlike imperial spending, provincial spending came with a liability attached — the mounting public debt. That debt had to be serviced in the short term and presumably repaid in the longer term. As the debt accumulated an ever-larger share of new capital never reached the colony at all; it flowed back almost immediately to the imperial centre in the

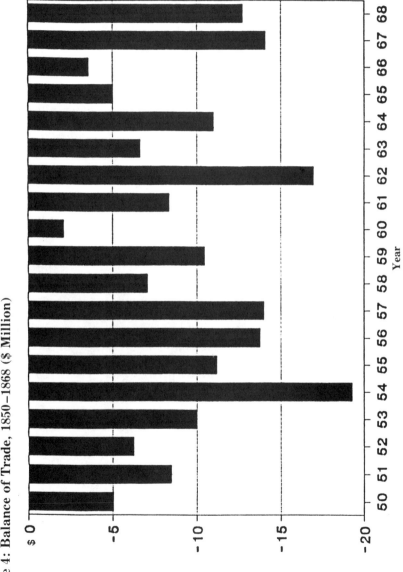

Figure 4: Balance of Trade, 1850–1868 ($ Million)

form of interest payments. By the mid-1850s the Canadian government was already acquiring new bonded debts for the sole purpose of paying interest on its existing liabilities. As debentures issued during the late 1830s and early 1840s began to mature, renewal of debts always resulted in an increase in total liabilities even when, as was the case with Galt's Consols, interest rates fell marginally. When credit abroad could no longer be obtained, the government began to borrow domestically.

By 1860 the Canadian economy had become dependent upon the steady flow of credit. This system relied upon the continued strength of the dominant growth ethic. As long as imperial money lenders, like their colonial partners, believed in the almost unlimited potential of frontier resources, new credit would be readily available. Despite severe financial crises in 1837–1839, 1847–1849, and 1857–1859, crises accompanied by short-term credit squeezes, the growth ethic prevailed. Colonial politicians like Hincks and Galt had been consistently more sanguine and optimistic than their London agents about the willingness of investors to gamble on Canada's economic prospects, and they had been proven correct. During the 1840s, the 1850s and into the 1860s British investors willingly paid high premiums for ever more substantial volumes of Canadian securities. As long as this continued Canadian accounts could be made to balance.

The depression of 1857 and the continued difficulties of the Grand Trunk shook the complacent optimism of Canadian "boosters" and their London allies. Although eventually successful, Galt's conversion of part of the public debt proved far more difficult to arrange than previous ventures into the London capital market. In this case, British investors accepted lower interest rates because it was to their advantage to exchange depreciated securities for Consols at par. Unlike previous debenture issues, however, the Consols produced almost no new capital for distribution in the domestic economy either for consumption or for new investment. Nor was much new development money likely to be made available, for the conditions that had promoted the credit system no longer obtained.

By 1860 much wild land remained in the colony,[29] yet settlement in relatively remote townships was already well advanced.[30] New colonization roads, as J.M.S. Careless points out, were already pushing north into the Canadian Shield "in ignorance of the vast extent of this stern barrier."[31] As the frontier began to close, the belief in unlimited growth waned. The financial history of the 1860s involved the attempt to come to terms with this new reality and the new-found reluctance of British investors to pour capital into the Province of Canada through the agency of the provincial government. Confederation would eventually re-create a frontier vision and help overcome investor hesitancy, but in the early 1860s Confederation was not yet an option.

The adjustment for a province grown accustomed to easy credit would be difficult. In this context the Galt tariff represented a first step in a new "austerity" programme for the Canadian consumer. With credit to pay for trade deficits harder to obtain and with revenue to service earlier commitments more difficult to find, the Cayley and Galt tariffs effectively lowered Canadian standards of living in order to meet foreign obligations. In his 1862 budget proposals, Galt intended to increase the duty on "leading articles of consumption of the whole people, in order to sustain our revenue and arrest the great falling off that has already taken place."[32] These tariffs were not adopted as a means of attacking imports in order to eliminate a trade deficit. Rather, they were to raise the cost of those commodities to the Canadian consumer, thus increasing the cost of living, in order to pay foreign creditors. The Galt tariff was to some degree the nineteenth-century version of modern austerity measures by which many debtor countries lower domestic standards of living and maintain economic policies to promote exports in order to meet external obligations.

Notes

1.   *Galt Papers*, M.G. 27 I D 8, Vol. 6, Galt, "Budget Speech, 1866," 5–6.

2.   *Ibid.*

3.   Melville H. Watkins, "A Staple Theory of Economic Growth," *The Canadian Journal of Economic and Political Science* XXIX (1963), 144.

4.   Harold A. Innis, *The Fur Trade in Canada: An Introduction to Canadian Economic History*, Revised Edition (Toronto, 1956), 384.

5.   Jean Lunn suggested, for example, that in some years illegal exports accounted for one-half to two-thirds of all beaver produced in New France. Jean Lunn, "The Illegal Fur Trade Out of New France, 1713–60," Canadian Historical Association, *Annual Report* (1939), 65. Also see Officer and Smith, "The Canadian–American Reciprocity Treaty of 1855 to 1866," 605–607.

6.   W. J. Eccles, "The Social, Economic and Political Significance of the Military Establishment in New France," *Canadian Historical Review*, LII (1971), 1.

7.   McIvor, *Canadian Monetary, Banking, and Fiscal Development*, 41, and Redish, "Why was Specie Scarce in Colonial Economies?," 713–728.

8.   As Fernand Ouellet observes, Quebec's huge trade deficit during the early 1760s was "partially compensated for by the metal currency which was shipped to the colony for the payment and upkeep of the troops." Fernand Ouellet, *Economic and Social*

History of Quebec, 1760–1850: Structures and Conjonctures, trans. by the Institute of Canadian Studies (Ottawa, 1980), 55.

9.   Paul McCann, "Quebec's Balance of Payments, 1768–1772: A Quantitative Model," M.A. Thesis, University of Ottawa, 1982, Table 3.8, 119.

10.   *Ibid.*, Table 4.1, 141.

11.   Eccles, "The Social, Economic and Political Significance of the Military Establishment in New France," 22.

12.   Hincks had been born in Cork, Ireland, had trained in the counting houses of Belfast, had opened an import-wholesale business when he immigrated to York, and later had become Cashier of the People's Bank. William Ormsby, "Francis Hincks," *Dictionary of Canadian Biography*, Vol. XI, 1881–1890, 406–416. Cayley had been born in St. Petersburg, Russia, and was well connected in the banking community. Paul G. Cornell, "William Cayley," *Dictionary of Canadian Biography*, Vol. XI, 1881–1890, 165–167. Holton, born in Leeds County, Upper Canada, had lived since the age of seven in Montreal with his uncle, a Vermont-born general merchant. In 1836 he had joined the import-forwarding firm of Henderson and Hooker, eventually emerging as senior partner in Hooker and Holton. Later he had liquidated his interests in the forwarding trade in favour of railway development, which had brought him into partnership with Galt, David Lewis Macpherson and Casimir Gzowski. H. C. Klassen, "Luther Hamilton Holton," *Dictionary of Canadian Biography*, Vol. X, 1871–1880, 354–358. Only Galt had no background in the import trade. He had come to Canada as the local agent for the British North American Land Company. Efforts to promote settlement had led to his promotion of the St. Lawrence and Atlantic, which provided entry into the banking and railway promotion community of Montreal. Skelton, *Life and Times of Galt*, and A. A. den Otter, *Civilizing the West: The Galts and the Development of Western Canada* (Edmonton, 1982), 10–19.

13.   Holton and Galt, together with David L. Macpherson, were partners in the St. Lawrence and Atlantic and the Quebec and Richmond, and held the original charter for the Toronto and Guelph. They were also partners with C. Gzowski's construction contractors. See Currie, *The Grand Trunk Railway*, 11–12, 14. For a more extended discussion of the intermingling of political and railway interests see George A. Davison, "Francis Hincks and the Politics of Interest, 1831–1855," unpublished Ph.D. thesis, University of Alberta, 1989, pp. 127–178.

14.   Morton, *The Critical Years*, 123. Morton made this comment in connection with his discussion of Gladstone's refusal to support new guarantees for the intercolonial railway.

15.   William P. Howland, "Report of the Minister of Finance of Canada," Sessional Paper No. 10, *Sessional Papers*, 1863.

16.   Douglas McCalla comments that Buchanan's "initiatives, based mainly on his persistent faith that Upper Canada would expand, were for twenty years vindicated by its swift development," but eventually this vision proved "inappropriate for changed circumstances." Douglas McCalla, *The Upper Canada Trade, 1834–1872: A Study of the Buchanans' Business* (Toronto, 1979), 150. McCalla's analysis demonstrates the centrality of credit in the business world of pre-Confederation Canada; "ample credit support was," he shows, "vital to the functioning of the distinctive frontier long-credit system." *Ibid.*, 152, passim.

17.   See above, Chapter 3, 67.

18.   In 1842 and 1843 the Montreal Board of Trade demanded that British duties on a wide range of Canadian agricultural exports be removed and argued that Canadian

produce "ought to be regarded with especial favor." This position was supported by Bagot who argued the Canadian case in his correspondence to the Colonial Office. See Montreal Board of Trade, "Petition," 1 February 1842, included in GGO, R.G. 7 G 12, Vol. 62, Despatch No. 39, Bagot to Stanley, 21 February 1842, and Vol. 63, Despatch No. 245, Bagot to Stanley, 13 December 1843.

19. See, for example, GGO, R.G. 7 G 12, Vol. 64, Despatch No. 7, Cathcart to Gladstone, 28 June 1846. The repeal of the Corn Laws would, the provincial government believed, eliminate any prospect of luring trade away from American routes and into the St. Lawrence. This would, according to the Executive Council, leave the provincial government with no means of repaying the guaranteed loan.

20. Cathcart reported in 1846 that the proposed adoption of free trade "created a very general impression throughout Canada that the Home Market would at the termination of three years be effectively closed against Canadian Products." See GGO, R.G. 7 G 12, Vol. 65, "Confidential," Despatch No. 1, Cathcart to Gladstone, 11 June 1846.

21. In 1849 Lord Elgin blamed the depression on a combination of the denial of preference for Canadian produce in Britain and the discrimination these products faced in the United States, "the nearer and hardly less important market." See GGO, R.G. 7 G 12, Vol. 65, Despatch No. 69, Elgin to Grey, 15 June 1849. There is an old and very traditional literature on this point running from Adam Shortt, "Economic History, 1840–1867," in *Canada and Its Provinces*, Vol. 5, 185–257, through Tucker, *The Canadian Commercial Revolution*, to standard textbook versions, such as Easterbrook and Aitken, *Canadian Economic History*, 362, passim. Considerable attention has been paid, however, to the British American League, which provided a dissenting voice foreshadowing the National Policy. The League believed the future lay in protectionism to stimulate infant industry and British North American union. The League, however, was generally ignored by most contemporaries and, as G. A. Hallowell comments, "disappeared with little perceptible trace." Gerald A. Hallowell, "The Reaction of Upper Canadian Tories to Annexation and the British American League," *Ontario History*, LXVII (1970), 53–54. Also see, for example, Tucker, *The Canadian Commercial Revolution*, 108–112 and Creighton, *John A. Macdonald: Young Politician*, 142–144.

22. As J.M.S. Careless has observed, many in Canada East saw reciprocity as of little benefit to themselves, while even the *Globe* saw the treaty as a "qualified benefit in the existing state of prosperity." Careless, *The Union of the Canadas*, 138. Also see Easterbrook and Aitken, *Canadian Economic History*, 365–369.

23. Most historians believe that reciprocity was a great boon to the Canadian economy. See Masters, *The Reciprocity Treaty*, and S. A. Saunders, "Reciprocity Treaty of 1854: A Regional Study," *Canadian Journal of Economics and Political Science* II (1936), 41–53. This traditional optimistic view has been challenged by Officer and Smith, "The Canadian–American Reciprocity Treaty," 598–623.

24. Robert E. Ankli argues that reciprocity represented a "British North American attempt to increase its exports while limiting increases in imports," but the success achieved during the decade was largely independent of the treaty. Robert E. Ankli, "The Reciprocity Treaty of 1854," *Canadian Journal of Economics* IV (1971), 2.

25. As Officer and Smith observe, the "import boom" during these years was stimulated in the main by rapid immigration and the railway construction boom. They suggest that, "[a]t best, Reciprocity can just have reinforced it." See Officer and Smith, "The Canadian–American Reciprocity Treaty," 608–609. D. C. Masters, meanwhile, notes that there is some suggestion that the Americans provided an inflated value for their goods. If this is the case, then the swing in favour of American exports would be even more pronounced. See Masters, *The Reciprocity Treaty*, 109.

26.   Officer and Smith, "The Canadian–American Reciprocity Treaty," 601.

27.   Masters argues that American opposition to the treaty resulted in the main from its failure to increase the export of non-reciprocity products and suggests that the Cayley and Galt tariffs had much to do with this result. See Masters, *The Reciprocity Treaty*, 117. It should be noted, however, that the decline was relative, not absolute. The Galt tariff was designed to favour the St. Lawrence route. See above, Chapter 6, 240–243.

28.   See Douglas McCalla, "Railways and the Development of Canada West, 1850–1870," in *Colonial Leviathan*, 199.

29.   David P. Gagan observes that, at a time when Upper Canadians looked to annexation of the West and the opening of new agricultural frontiers as an outlet for population increases, there was demographic decline in long-settled areas such as Peel County where land in two of its five townships remained vacant. David P. Gagan, *Hopeful Travellers: Families, Land, and Social Change in Mid-Victorian Peel County, Canada West* (Toronto, 1981), 40, passim. That vacant wild land, however, had long since been alienated from the Crown.

30.   William Shannon, for example, demonstrates that, in frontier townships such as Collingwood, where settlement had been considerably slower than in neighbouring Natawasaga and St. Vincent, a settlement boom occurred in the 1850s. See William Shannon, "Brokers, Land Bankers and 'Birds of Evil Omen': Colonial Land Policies in Upper Canada: Collingwood Township, 1834–1860," M.A. Thesis, University of Ottawa, 1989.

31.   J.M.S. Careless, "The Place, the Office, the Times, and the Men," 20.

32.   *Galt Papers*, M.G. 27 I D 8, Vol. 6, Galt, "Budget Speech," [1862], 24.

Chapter 8
Towards Confederation

The borrowing process has unfortunately
been employed too generally and too long,
encouraging unnecessary expenditure, and
relieving the community from the burdens
which it should be made to bear as the
consequence of its own acts. The time has
come when another method must of
necessity be pursued. Instead of taxing our
credit, and so transferring the burden
from ourselves to posterity, it is desirable
that we should now tax our available
resources to an extent indicated
by the deficiency.
— William Howland
Minister of Finance, 1863[1]

As difficult as the adjustment to slower growth might have been, the provincial government had not yet exhausted its fiscal and credit options. The financial policies of the previous quarter-century had successfully shifted the Canadian public debt from this side of the Atlantic to Britain. This process helped free domestic capital for other investments, which had in turn helped facilitate economic growth. It also meant that as the credit squeeze in London tightened, the government could, in the short term at least, turn again to domestic sources to finance its activities. Credit was needed because, although there would be no new major public works projects, nor new relief measures for private railways, the province found it impossible to balance its books (See Appendix II).

As the economic crisis of 1857–1858 took hold the government introduced austerity measures to control expenditures. In August 1858 the Executive Council informed each department that

> it is necessary that the greatest possible reduction be made in the outlay
> under the charge of the various Departments of the Government . . . each
> Head of Department of the Government do lay before Your Excellency

in Council, at the earliest possible day an Estimate of the proposed outlay till 31st December next, distinguishing between those items which do not admit of any possible reduction, and such as might admit of reconsideration.[2]

Cost cutting brought expenditures in 1859 down to $9.7 million, a reduction of over $2.5 million. Expenditures in 1860, however, jumped sharply to $21 million, a result of a special $6.5 million payment to the Sinking Fund. When this extraordinary expenditure is subtracted from the total, expenditures remain $3.3 million higher than in 1858. After 1860 the government successfully held its expenditures in check. During the last year of its existence the province spent $12.9 million. This was only slightly higher than expenditures in 1858.

It required considerable effort to hold total expenditures in line. Galt's debt conversion programme, combined with the government's now habitual need to issue debentures in order to service the public debt, ensured that interest charges absorbed an ever-larger portion of total expenditures. Between 1855 and 1862 outstanding liabilities increased from $52.1 million to $72.7 million. Assets held against this debt in various Sinking Funds also rose but at a much slower rate. Net liabilities as a result increased during these years by over $20 million. Although some of this increase went to permanent works, $14.4 million resulted from budgetary deficits.[3] Most of the new securities sold after 1859 paid lower interest than redeemed bonds, yet debt service charges could not be reduced. Twenty-seven per cent of provincial spending in 1858 went to pay interest. This increased to 34 per cent in 1862 and to 34.7 per cent in 1863. Keeping total expenditures in line meant, in other words, sharp cuts in many items of ordinary expenditure, particularly in the costs of the Legislature and in public works.

In addition to holding expenditures in check, Galt had also introduced his revenue tariff in 1859 in an effort to balance the budget. Revenue from customs duties increased from $3.4 million in 1858 to $4.5 million in 1859 and to $4.8 million in 1861. The government increased excise and territorial taxes as well and revenue from these sources rose from $139,000 and $415,000 respectively in 1858 to $346,000 and $679,000 respectively in 1861. Total revenue increased 23 per cent during these years, rising from $8 million in 1858 to $10 million in 1861 then falling to only $8.4 million in 1862. This was clearly insufficient to meet the government's needs. Although Galt's 1859 budget brought the deficit down from $3.1 million on ordinary expenditures and revenue to only $1.5 million, the deficit ballooned to $5.3 million in 1860. To this could be added the $6.5 million payment to the Sinking Fund. Between 1858 and 1859 the total deficit, including debenture sales and redemptions, rose from $1.1 million to $2 million. Over $30 million in debenture sales in 1860 provided the government with a total budgetary surplus of only $2.7 million, which disappeared in 1861 and 1862 when the government ran a cumulative deficit of $2.9 million. When Galt ended his first term as Minister of Finance, Canada was in as precarious a financial position as at any time in its history. The province had been kept afloat by the willingness of British investors to buy Canadian securities and the willingness of Barings and Glyns to continue to advance additional funds to the province.

Although acting on behalf of the province since the failure of Thomas Wilson and Company in 1837, Barings and Glyns had not been named joint "agents" until 1848 when the province sought and received advances from these London houses to cover interest due on the public debt. When in late 1848 Glyns agreed to advance only half of a requested £40,000 stg, Hincks had turned to Barings. On this occasion he explained

> that that house [Glyns] has always been looked upon in the same light as your own. Both pay the interest on a portion of our debt, charging the same commission for doing so, and I can see no ground for one being looked on, more than the other, as agents of the Province. I must confess therefore, that I was much disappointed at finding that your House was unwilling, at a time when, owing to unavoidable circumstances, the Province is in temporary embarrassment, to advance us £20,000.[4]

Hincks threatened to explore the possibility of finding another agency in London if Barings did not continue to provide the advance: "[O]ne thing is to my mind clear and I shall repeat it. The Canadian Government must obtain the services of an eminent House in London."[5] It was in this context that Hincks, Barings, and Glyns reached a formal agreement on the joint agency which was then confirmed in the Act for the Better Management of the Public Debt.

All government debentures marketed in Britain passed in equal amounts through the houses of Barings and Glyns, as agents. They also paid interest on all debentures. In addition to these various brokerage services, for which they received a commission, Barings and Glyns frequently invested on their own account. The government expected its agents to help facilitate government operations by purchasing securities, if necessary, to encourage other investors. The province also expected Barings and Glyns to advance moneys when needed. This most commonly involved the advance for short periods of any moneys necessary to meet interest payments until remittances could be sent from Canada. There was, however, no agreement that set precise terms governing the level and cost of this "accommodation."

Galt corrected this lacuna in 1858 and negotiated a new formal agreement, which provided a line of credit totalling £250,000 stg to be shared by the two agents. Any advance beyond £125,000 stg from either Barings or Glyns would be subject to special arrangements. Barings and Glyns agreed to pay 4 per cent interest on all balances in their hands at the credit of the province, while the province would be charged 5 per cent on amounts advanced. The province also agreed to provide debentures for sale as security for these advances.[6]

It would not take long for the province to tap this line of credit to the full; indeed, they would almost always be overdrawn. The government relied on such advances to pay interest on its debt in Britain, and only rarely did remittances follow to repay Barings and Glyns. Invariably debentures had to be sold to balance these accounts. On occasion this could complicate other financial programmes; in 1859, for example, the province's proposed issue of 5 per cent Consolidated Stock, as we have seen, had to wait for the sale of £350,000 stg in 6 per cent debentures to cover such advances. As the depression eased, the new Consolidated debentures began to be used not only to raise new funds but also to clear advances owed Barings and Glyns.[7]

So long as quotations for these securities remained relatively high, Barings and Glyns showed no concern about the province's overdrawn account. But in 1862 the market began to soften,[8] and both houses became increasingly nervous about the huge deficit in the provincial account. Galt also worried about financial developments, particularly the unstable situation in New York capital markets that resulted from the Civil War. As Galt explained to William Hamilton Merritt, "I fear we may very soon have a serious financial crisis arising out of the state of the New York money market, and prudence dictates that the Government like individuals should watch coming events."[9]

In May 1862 the government again played out what had become a spring and fall ritual. Galt informed Barings and Glyns that funds to meet the 1 July interest payments might not be forwarded on time. In early June the government forwarded instead £325,000 worth of debentures to cover anticipated advances.[10] As usual, Barings and Glyns covered the interest payments, but on this occasion they pointed out that "our present cash advance much exceeds the stipulated amount." With no demand for Canadian securities, both were "anxiously" awaiting news from the Minister of Finance.[11] Both wanted cash, not more debentures.

The government was able to respond with cash. The Receiver General, James Morris, immediately began buying sterling exchange from various banks to be remitted to London — on 8 September 1862, $100,000 from the Quebec Bank, and $600,000 from the Bank of Upper

Canada, both at 9.5 per cent. A week later the Receiver General purchased another $200,000 in sterling exchange.[12] Morris then remitted
£55,800 stg to Glyns and £45,300 to Barings in mid-September with
the promise to remit more within the month.[13] By November 1862 a
total of £245,000 stg had been transferred to London.[14] The decision
to send cash corresponded with a change in government.

Although issues of sectional rivalry, constitutional reform,
and schools underlie the party divisions and political instability of the
last decade of the Union period, it remained true that complaints of
financial extravagence and corruption were central features of opposition politics from the mid-1850s. This was the issue that brought the
government down in 1862. When Cartier brought in his Militia Bill,
L.-V. Sicotte, a *Bleu* politician who had broken with the government
over the location of the new capital in Ottawa, led the attack by arguing
that Canada with its huge deficits should not bankrupt itself by assum-
ing larger costs for defence.[15] The new John Sandfield Macdonald/
Sicotte government, which assumed office in May 1862, pledged itself
to "double majority, cheap, efficient government, and pragmatic
reform."[16] Although led by moderates, the government counted among
its supporters *Rouge* leader A. A. Dorion as well as the Grit William
P. Howland who took over the Finance portfolio. Howland, in turn,
promised not just economy but retrenchment, in order to balance the
budget.[17] Despite such promises, however, little changed in the basic
thrust of government policy.

John Sandfield Macdonald was as much a graduate of the
Grand Trunk fraternity as Galt, John A. Macdonald, or George Cartier.
Back in 1853 Sandfield Macdonald, probably with Hincks's help, had
secured for himself and his two brothers the sub-contract to build the
Grand Trunk line from Montreal Island to Farran's Point in western
Stormont county.[18] Now, as co-Premier, he worked with C. J. Brydges
and E. W. Watkin to arrange appropriate legislation to convert some
bondholders into stockholders, thus reducing the interest charges on
the Grand Trunk. He also helped the railway make a number of other
fiscal adjustments, although he ensured that merger talks between
the Grand Trunk and the Great Western came to an end.[19] In addition,
again working with Watkins, Sandfield Macdonald helped develop a
scheme to win a British guarantee for new loans of £3 million to build
an intercolonial railway from the Grand Trunk terminus at Rivière du
Loup to Halifax. In September 1862 Canada hosted an interprovincial
conference with Joseph Howe and Leonard Tilley to draw up a proposal.
Later, Sicotte and Howland would be sent to Britain to win imperial
approval.[20] This decision lost the government its *Rouge* support;
Dorion stopped attending meetings of the Executive Council in

September and then resigned in October 1862. The failure to win British guarantees led to Canada's hasty retreat from its intercolonial commitments, and this opened the door for a reconstructed Sandfield Macdonald/Dorion government later in 1863.

There would be even less change in the Sandfield Macdonald/ Sicotte government's fiscal policy. Committed to "retrenchment," Howland found it as difficult as Galt to bring expenditures into line with revenue. As a result, he chose to abandon Galt's proposal to reduce tariffs, fearing revenues might decline. When Howland decided in September 1862 to remit funds to Barings and Glyns to clear advances owed, he opted, like his predecessors, for new loans rather than new taxes. There would be one departure, however: Howland decided to borrow from domestic rather than foreign sources.

In October 1862 Howland proposed issuing $2 million in "Provincial Notes" payable in one year at 5 per cent interest. This move, Howland explained, was necessitated by the budgetary deficit combined with the impossibility of selling debentures at acceptable prices in Britain. The Minister also observed that he had received assurances that "Public Securities at short date would be a convenience and advantage to many Public Institutions and individuals in the Province." These "notes" would be dated and issued as required.[21] Despite their name, these were clearly debentures, not notes. Unlike Hincks's small-denomination debentures a decade earlier, these new securities came in $100 and $500 denominations which ensured they would not likely circulate as a paper currency. This did not, however, detract from their marketability; various private and institutional investors quickly purchased these securities.[22]

Although remittances to London corrected the imbalances in the provincial account at Barings and Glyns, this proved to be temporary. Within the month the government once again notified Barings and Glyns that they would have to advance moneys to pay interest on the public debt due 1 January. They were also ordered to sell debentures already in their hands and to reimburse themselves out of the proceeds. Howland noted the recent rise in quotations which ensured that provincial securities were "now selling at about *par*, less accrued Interest," yet in a marked departure from previous government policy, Howland did "not, however, desire to restrict you to that price [par]."[23] Cabinet shuffles and by-elections in Canada, meanwhile, delayed further action.

The improved state of the London capital market increased the quotations for all securities, not just those of Canada. This provided an opportune moment to reduce the total debt of the province by redeeming the Imperial Guaranteed Loan of 1842. In April 1862 Galt observed that the Indian Stock held in the Sinking Fund had risen so much in value that a quick sale would realize a profit greater than the saving in interest if the 4 per cent guaranteed debentures were allowed to run to maturity. Galt also felt that redeeming the guaranteed bonds, and thus ending any liability for the British government, might also improve negotiations then taking place on the Intercolonial.[24] Canada ordered the liquidation of the Sinking Fund and the redemption of the £1.5 million stg guaranteed debentures.[25] Reducing the guaranteed portion of the public debt, however, provided no noticeable easing of financial pressures.

Luther Holton, Galt's partner in Gzowski's railway construction company, soon became the Minister of Finance in the reorganized Sandfield Macdonald/Dorion government, and despite having to fight a "hotly contested" election did manage to get down to the business of his new office. Unable to introduce new fiscal measures with Parliament prorogued, the province faced a serious deterioration in its financial dealings with its London agents. Holton promised to conduct his relations with Barings and Glyns with "unreserved frankness and cordiality" and then observed: "I fear ... we shall be obliged to rely upon your good offices to a greater extent than would otherwise have been necessary, or than it would have been reasonable to ask." Holton promised that as soon as the elections were won Parliament would be recalled to introduce "measures calculated to produce so considerable an increase in revenue as will relieve our finances of all embarrassments," but he gave no hint what these measures might involve.[26]

Holton spelled out the problem in his budget speech of 1863. He projected a deficit on ordinary expenditures of $1.9 million. There was in addition the unfunded debt: "the amount is Startling." The province owed Glyns $1.8 million, owed Barings $1.6 million, owed other creditors $770,000, and on 1 January 1864 would owe $1.5 million in interest payments. Against these liabilities the province had cash balances of $1.7 million. The government needed to come up with $4 million to cover its unfunded loans and another $2 million to cover ordinary expenditures. The problem was, Holton added, that the government was "not in a position to borrow money until we declare our fixed purpose to provide for an annual expenditure from this time forward by increased taxation." Holton noted that the province had been running deficits of roughly $2 million per annum for seven years. It was too late in the year to implement specific tax items, but Holton promised to act shortly. He told Parliament to expect a number of proposals early in the next session. The three-year-old policy of exempting tolls on the canals, he suggested, had been a mistake; the public works should be seen as a source of revenue. Holton promised as well to "look the question of direct taxation sternly in the face." Finally, he asserted that "for the purpose of revenue our Customs tariff was already too high" and lower rates would likely produce more revenue.[27]

In the short term Holton had to rely upon the good graces of Barings and Glyns. Both, as they had in the past, provided the necessary advances and received in turn £250,000 stg in new debentures and £100,000 in sterling exchange to be followed shortly by another £50,000. Holton, meanwhile, assured his London bankers of the government's intention to recall Parliament in August in order to pass a Supply Bill, and "an efficient Militia Law." Not until the next regular session, however, did he intend to introduce "such comprehensive revenue measures as will place the finances of the Country in a sound and satisfactory footing."[28] Later, in September 1863, when it appeared the government might be defeated in the Assembly, Holton assured Barings and Glyns "that whatever changes there may be in the personnel of the Canadian Administration, the policy of our administration to provide by additional taxation for the deficiency in our revenue, will be adhered to." He professed amazement, meanwhile, that quotations for Canadian securities remained low, since the Canadian harvest had been good and government revenue was increasing.[29]

The various "comprehensive revenue measures" adopted in 1863 helped, but they did not solve the province's fiscal problems. Revenue from the tariff rose $400,000 (11 per cent), revenue from Excise rose $330,000 (66 per cent), and revenue from public works rose $157,000 (41 per cent). In 1863 total revenue was up $1.4 million (16 per cent). The government also managed to reduce expenditures by $370,000 (3.4 per cent) despite a near 400 per cent increase in militia spending. The deficit, as a result, was much reduced, yet it remained at nearly $1 million.

In 1864 the government changed its fiscal end-of-year from 31 December to 30 June and for six months ran its first budgetary surplus in nearly a decade. In that half-year the government took in $470,000 more than it spent. Nevertheless, even though the province would run a second budgetary surplus in 1866, this was more than offset by large deficits in 1865 and again in 1867. Between 1858 and Confederation, then, the Province of Canada had rung up a cumulative deficit on its ordinary expenditures and revenue of $22.8 million. To finance these deficits it sold $20 million more provincial debentures than it redeemed. The government stayed but one step ahead of financial disaster.

Holton's "comprehensive" measures had not counted on a crisis at the Bank of Upper Canada, the holder of the provincial account since 1848. The position of the Bank had seriously deteriorated with the depression of 1857. Although it had survived that crisis, the Bank was only limping along and by 1863 could no longer provide sterling exchange to be sent to Britain.[30] Although he had promised to sort out the provincial accounts in London, Holton found himself having to ask for more rather than less accommodation. As Holton explained to Barings and Glyns, a demand upon the Bank "might seriously embarrass, perhaps actually imperil," that institution. Instead of cash, new Orders-in-Council provided another £250,000 stg in debentures for Barings and Glyns. This would bring the total amount of unsold provincial debentures in Barings' and Glyns' hands to £817,000 which would "very nearly cover your account."[31] Holton preferred that Barings and Glyns delay any sales until after Parliament had enacted new fiscal legislation. By July, however, he informed his London agents that he wanted "a considerable portion" of those debentures sold.[32]

The Bank of Upper Canada's position, meanwhile, had become all but hopeless. So compromised was the Bank that it could no longer accommodate the provincial government, and as a consequence lost its one remaining advantage, the government account, which was moved to the Bank of Montreal. The province now began to press the Bank of Upper Canada for moneys owed, but it did not press too hard, and a repayment schedule was soon worked out. The key items of dispute involved a claim by the Bank against the province for £100,000 stg advanced to the Grand Trunk and the balance of public deposits in the Zimmerman Bank.[33] In both cases the government rejected outright the Bank's claims, yet "circumstances surrounding the origin of the transactions themselves warrant consideration."[34] The government accepted a proposal made by the Bank to reduce its debt to the province to $1.5 million by 1 January, and to repay the balance over a number of years at a reduced rate of interest. These were, Holton informed Robert Cassels, "extremely indulgent terms."[35]

Unable to collect moneys owed from the Bank of Upper Canada, the government also found itself unable to market securities in Britain at acceptable prices. Holton uncharitably put the blame squarely on the Bank of Upper Canada and its "inability to meet demand drafts from the large balance it owes the Government."[36] In late 1863 Holton informed Barings and Glyns that he wanted a "considerable portion" of the debentures in their hands sold. The market, however, was not co-operative. Barings and Glyns responded that they would continue to carry the provincial advances rather than risk selling securities at ruinous prices.[37] Holton also had to deal with Howland's one-year Provincial Notes due to mature in December 1863.

The government would have to seek a larger domestic loan to carry it through.[38] As Holton explained to Barings and Glyns:

Ever since my accession to Office, a few months ago, I have been more and more impressed with the importance to the Provincial credit of avoiding, if possible, applications for further loans in England until the repeated promises of successive administrations to equalize by adequate measures of taxation our annual income and expenditure should be fulfilled.

He intended, accordingly, to sustain the province's financial position "by means of our own Provincial resources."[39] Holton found a lender at the Bank of Montreal. In November 1863 that Bank agreed to purchase $1.5 million worth of three-year, 5 per cent debentures and in addition became the fiscal agent of Canada in the province.[40] "The sole object of the change," Holton explained to Barings and Glyns, "is to secure to the Government the services of an institution possessing resources so ample that it can without restricting its ordinary operations, greatly facilitate the financial operations of the Government."[41] A more immediate concern was the maturation of the Provincial Notes issued under Howland's administration in late 1862.

The Bank of Montreal purchased three-year debentures at a 2 per cent discount and paid $1,470,000 into the province's new account. The Bank then redeemed $750,000 worth of Howland's Notes maturing 1 December and 11 December. Another $250,000 would be used to purchase exchange to be forwarded to Barings and Glyns by 10 December. The remaining $470,000 would remain on deposit.[42] This loan allowed Holton to avoid debenture sales in Britain as capital markets there deteriorated rapidly. By November 1863 Holton feared a full-scale financial panic might grip London which would make it "unwise to attempt any sales." If Barings and Glyns could not continue their advances to the province, Holton at least wanted some notice in order "to seek some other arrangement in Canada."[43]

By spring 1864 a new Taché/John A. Macdonald government was in office, and Galt had returned as Minister of Finance. The government seemed also to be bringing in more revenue than it was spending. Although Holton had reported in February that the "finances of the Country, are in a much more prosperous condition, than for several years past," he still feared a budgetary deficit. To deal with this he had promised "to invite Parliament to impose, at an early period of the session," new taxes.[44] Holton's fiscal projections, however, proved for once too pessimistic. For the first time in years, economic and financial prospects seemed on the mend. Galt, who took over the Finance portfolio in March 1864, informed Barings and Glyns several months later that "I am sanguine in the belief that a speedy recovery may be brought about and provision made for the large balances in which the Province stands indebted to your firms." Galt even intended to send remittances to cover the 1 July interest payments on time, although he also had to agree to pay the current Bank of England rate on the provincial account at Barings and Glyns.[45]

The prolonged political log-jam, meanwhile, seemed finally to clear during the spring and early summer of 1864. The failure of the Sandfield Macdonald/Dorion government to reorganize itself led to its resignation on 21 March 1864. There followed a series of discussions between Taché, John A. Macdonald, Cartier, Lord Monck, and others on the possibility of a coalition that would include some Upper Canadian reformers. Partial success in these talks led to a new Taché/John A. Macdonald administration, which announced a vigorous programme but survived its first want of confidence vote on 13 May by the narrowest of margins, 64-62. One month later, on 14 June, Luther Holton moved another want of confidence motion, this time on the charge that Galt as Minister of Finance in the old Cartier/Macdonald government had illegally and corruptly provided the Grand Trunk with a $100,000 grant for property in Montreal. The government was then defeated 60–58. Lord Monck in turn pressed his administration to pursue talks for a new coalition with George Brown rather than seek a dissolution. The key issue would prove to be a government commitment to seek a new federal constitutional solution in an expanded British North America Union. Brown, together with Grits William McDougall and Oliver Mowat, joined a reorganized administration under Taché's leadership on 22 June 1864. The drive for Confederation had begun.

In July 1864 John A. Macdonald outlined the government's new commitment to British North American union to ally James Vrooman. Confederation, he commented, would "prevent anarchy," and would "settle the great Constitutional question of Parliamentary Reform." It would also "restore the credit of the Province abroad." The very existence of the Great Coalition, as Macdonald observed, helped improve Canada's image in London, which had "been sadly shaken by our domestic dissensions."[46] George Carr Glyn agreed that "these repeated changes [in government] are most detrimental both externally and internally to the country."[47] A more direct solution, however, would come with the annexation of the west and the restoration of an agricultural frontier. That frontier might be developed, as in the past, by promoting immigration and railways. Confederation promised to recreate the conditions of frontier growth that had sustained Canadian economic and financial policies for a quarter-century and more. But union would be difficult to achieve. Although at Charlottetown and Quebec Maritime representatives committed themselves to the scheme, within a year the project seemed to founder on the shoals of Atlantic particularism; it would take another two years for the scheme to come to fruition. In the meantime, the Province of Canada had to soldier on with its financial burden. It did so with the help of a new and powerful ally, the Bank of Montreal. The Bank, meanwhile, grew larger and considerably more powerful as a result of its new government liaison.

As Galt prepared for Charlottetown all seemed well at the Finance Department. The budget produced a surplus for the first six months of 1864 despite, as he pointed out to Barings and Glyns, the delay in implementing the new taxes enacted during the session. With those new fiscal measures in force, "there can be no doubt whatever that the means of the Province will be more than adequate to meet all our current engagements."[48] Those new taxes did boost revenue; total revenue for the fiscal year ending 30 June 1865 was almost $1 million higher than in the fiscal year ending 31 December 1863. Expenditures, however, also jumped, a result of a near $800,000 increase in public works expenditures. The deficit in 1865 turned out to be over $1 million. The financial situation which seemed on the mend in 1864 again began to take on crisis proportions as the government ran yet another deficit.

In late 1864 Barings and Glyns pressed the government to deal with the overdrawn provincial account. Under the circumstances Galt turned to the Bank of Montreal for assistance. In August he informed J. R. Christian at the Bank that he needed £150,000 stg exchange in two instalments for 3 and 10 September. He went on to warn that the government would soon be demanding more: "The nature of my advises from England renders it absolutely necessary that I should remit as largely as the state of the balance in this country will permit."[49] For the moment this was possible because the provincial account at the Bank of Montreal showed a healthy surplus; moneys held in other banks could be transferred, and all moneys owed the government could be deposited. The concentration of government funds in the Bank of Montreal, however, created a number of problems for other banks, who were quick to blame the provincial agent for the "stringency" in domestic capital markets. Galt promised to do all in his power to deal with the problems, but recognized that money was tight and flowing into the Bank of Montreal.[50]

Galt also explored a new option to deal with the provincial account in London. Galt recognized that "the quotations of our securities are now so low as manifestly to make it inexpedient to cover the amounts due to your firms by the sale of the debentures," and suggested the province be given a special two-year loan on the expectation that the money market would improve over this term. Although little came of this suggestion, Galt would make a similar proposal for a special loan the following year. In the meantime he promised to send remittances "as our incoming revenue may enable me to make from week to week."[51] By September £240,000 stg had been sent by the Receiver General.

Unable to negotiate a special two-year loan, Galt preferred simply to continue the advance. In case Barings and Glyns were unwilling, the Executive Council authorized Galt to negotiate a £400,000 stg "temporary loan for not more than six months" to cover the balance owed. Galt informed Barings and Glyns that the remittances for the January interest payments would be sent soon, although if for some reason he was unable to remit funds "the government will desire to use a portion of the usual credit which they have with your firms."[52] Galt received a positive response; the advance would be continued for six months at the Bank of England rate — or not less than 5 per cent — but only on condition that remittances "are regularly made" and the "advance" did not exceed £400,000. Galt pointed out that the account was already overdrawn for £454,000 and that, although he accepted the conditions for the loan, he could not cover the amount over £400,000 stg. He had, however, already forwarded £100,000 to cover the January interest payments and another £200,000 would shortly follow.[53] To pay for these remittances, Galt secured a $500,000 short-term loan with the Bank of Montreal, which would run until 1 April 1865 and would cost the government 7 per cent interest.[54] The province was not reducing its debt or even keeping it in check. It was simply borrowing money necessary to meet interest payments as they fell due from a domestic rather than a British bank.

The financial situation got worse before it got better. By January 1865 the government was running critically short of cash. The balance of the earlier $1.5 million loan from the Bank of Montreal had been exhausted, and, as E.H. King* pointed out, after all outstanding credits and debits the government account stood at only $43,000. Understating the gravity of the situation, King commented: "I don't suppose you want to keep the a/c [sic] so bare as it will be otherwise."[55] Galt, however, had little choice. By the end of February he could still hope that spring revenue from customs would provide enough funds to cover the two loans of $250,000 and $500,000; more realistically he suggested he would probably need another $250,000 loan.[56]

Everyone connected with the Finance Department pinned their hopes on an expected bonanza in customs revenue. Revenues for 1864 had been much higher than expected and new specific duties enacted late in the parliamentary session would now be in force. As customs receipts began coming in, the government moved quickly to repay the $500,000 loan which fell due 1 April.[57] Later in the month, however, it was clear that expectations for rapidly increasing receipts

* Manager at the Bank of Montreal.

were to remain unrealized. Galt headed for London, authorized to make whatever arrangements were necessary to deal with interest payments and the advances still due Barings and Glyns. Before he left he negotiated a new $1 million loan from the Bank of Montreal to cover remittances to Britain for the July interest payment. On this occasion the Bank demanded that £200,000 stg in Canadian securities be placed in their hands as security for the loan.[58]

In England Galt received little satisfaction as Barings and Glyns became increasingly reluctant to carry indefinitely large unfunded balances in favour of the province. Galt convinced his London agents to extend their advances until 31 December 1865, but he also had to agree that after that date both would be "at liberty to realize on the best terms in your power the securities now held by you." Galt attempted to qualify this "liberty" and suggested a 10 per cent discount was the lowest price acceptable for these bonds. Like Howland before him, Galt had no choice but to break with the long-standing government policy that no new debentures could be sold below par. Under severe financial pressure, Galt would "be glad to see the balances covered at any time before the 31st December" if these bonds could be sold at 90. An offer of 90, however, would be hard to get; the current quotation for Canadian 5 per cent debentures stood at only 84. Everyone hoped that an expected drop in the Bank of England discount rate would help improve quotations.[59] During the summer and fall the discount rate did fall, yet quotations for Canadian fives rose only slightly to 85.5 by July. This remained critically low and significantly below the 90 figure which Galt considered a minimum. Galt's options were narrowing; he would need more credit from domestic sources to avoid a serious financial crisis. Domestic credit could be developed in two ways: the government could seek more accommodation from domestic banks, or it could revive the question of a provincial bank of issue.[60]

Sydenham had originally proposed a bank of issue as an easy, if partial, solution to Upper Canada's debt problem. Even fiscal conservatives like John Macaulay had recognized the advantage of such a "clever scheme," by which a capital of £1 million could be created.[61] Yet despite support from Reformers like Francis Hincks, both the Banks and too many of Sydenham's conservative backers opposed his plan. "For my part," John Macaulay explained in December 1841,

I have cherished a great feeling of distrust and doubt with regard to it — Possibly it might work well — but according to my impressions, it is not called for by our circumstances — Our present Banks, with capital moderately increased, would furnish us with a wholesome circulating medium — & bear the charge of keeping it a convertible currency — The scheme of a Bank of Issue would burthen us with the responsibility of maintaining Bank paper at par value.[62]

Although the government left to the banks the right to issue notes and the obligation to protect their value, it did introduce legislation charging a one per cent tax on all notes and bills in circulation.[63]

Hincks did not revive the question of a bank of issue during the financial crisis of 1847–1849, yet he accomplished as much with his proposal for small denomination debentures. Hincks intended these debentures to circulate like notes, the only difference being that they paid 6 per cent interest.[64] In 1862 William Howland, as we have seen, also proposed issuing $2 million in "Provincial Notes" payable in one year at 5 per cent interest.[65] Unlike Hincks's small denomination issue, however, the $100 and $500 denomination ensured they would not circulate "in lieu of money."

Throughout the Union period, note issue remained the prerogative of the chartered banks, a prerogative that some of the larger institutions believed was being abused. D. Davidson of the Bank of Montreal, for example, complained in 1859 about the number of new banks being chartered. According to Davidson,

> The Banks already in operation (irrespective of those under the Free Banking System) have 5 millions of dollars of their capital still unpaid. . . . In several instances charters have been granted without any provision whatever which would prevent the issue of notes before any capital was actually paid up.[66]

Cayley for one favoured some change in the system, which he described as "a cutthroat game" that made "a shuttle cock of the credit and business of commercial men in the hands of the Banks in their struggle to secure a circulation for their notes."[67] In addition to providing a new source of capital, a bank of issue might have the double advantage of better controlling and regulating note issue and circulation.

Desperate for new sources of credit, Galt now proposed issuing $4 million in provincial notes. Unable to proceed with this initiative until the new year, Galt sought to renegotiate his deal with Barings and Glyns. He asked for a new one- or two-year loan of £750,000 stg at not more than 6 per cent to pay advances owed as well as the £200,000 stg owed the Bank of Montreal.[68] As part of the deal the Bank of Montreal would delay repayment of its $1 million loan, but only on condition that a second loan of $300,000 be settled.[69] Barings and Glyns agreed, and Galt arranged for payment to the Bank of Montreal. Before any of these arrangements could be finalized, however, the new British loan collapsed.

At the end of July 1865 the Bank of England discount rate stood at 3.5 per cent. Once the £750,000 stg deal had been struck in mid-August, however, the rate began to increase sharply. The rate hit

6 per cent in mid-September and then 7 per cent in October. "It is thus self-evident," Barings and Glyns reported, "that in the present state of the money market, no loan can be made at your limits." Nor did Barings or Glyns expect any improvements in the near future.[70]

Quotations for Canadian securities, as expected, tumbled from an already low 85.5 in July 1865 to 77.5 in March 1866.[71] Under the circumstances the government authorized Barings and Glyns to seek the loan on whatever terms could be arranged.[72] Barings and Glyns in turn suggested that it might be possible to raise £750,000 at 7 per cent, but this would require the issue of new debentures to be held as security. Barings and Glyns soon upped the ante to 8 per cent.[73]

The attempt to raise a loan for Canada even at 8 per cent interest, Barings and Glyns commented, "proved to be one of the greatest difficulty, and demonstrates, as it is our duty to observe, that Canada must depend not upon temporary expedients but upon its own resources." Galt in turn reminded his London agents that "we think you have scarcely given consideration to the fact that our revenue has latterly been largely augmented by increased taxation, that we have not appeared as borrowers in your market for several years, and that our present resort to the Expedient of a temporary loan mainly arises from our fear to take any step which might increase the difficulties in the way of Confederation."[74] Galt was in a querulous mood and objected to the "tone of your last letters" which had "caused remarks to be made in Council which induce me to write a few private lines to put the matter through without further delay."[75] In this private correspondence Galt suggested that Glyns' position was hardly justified by the "facts." Galt pointed out that over the last six years the province had borrowed only £600,000 with which they had purchased back £140,000 as investments in Sinking Funds. Galt also warned that if a British loan could not be secured, the government would have no choice but to deal with the Bank of Montreal "which would not be agreeable to you," undoubtedly a reference to Glyn's interest in the Bank of Upper Canada.

The Bank of England rate, meanwhile, hit 8 per cent in the new year, and Barings and Glyns reported they had been able to arrange loans for only £255,000 stg at 8 per cent on security of £339,400 provincial debentures. As an "inducement to others" Barings and Glyns lent another £90,000 of their own money secured by £120,000 in debentures.[76] This was far short of the £750,000 required, and Galt had no choice but to fall back on the "resources" of the country, in this case the credit resources of the Bank of Montreal.

The collapse of the £750,000 stg loan in Britain forced the government to renegotiate all of its loans with the Bank of Montreal just weeks before these loans fell due. In addition, the government had to come up with remittances to meet interest due 1 January in London. Galt asked that the $1 million loan be extended until the end of December. He requested as well a new $1,250,000 loan at 7 per cent interest to run until 2 April 1866 and to be used to pay the January interest. This loan would be secured by the deposit of £300,000 to £350,000 stg 6 per cent debentures which the Bank could sell after 2 April. E. H. King agreed to these terms but on condition that the government agree to keep a minimum of $400,000 on deposit at the bank.[77]

Despite the difficulties that followed in the wake of the collapsed British loan, Galt found some reason to be pleased. As he told George Carr Glyn, "I was balked in what I desired to do in regard to our currency last session, and *now* I shall have my own say."[78] There had been considerable initial opposition in Cabinet to his proposal to issue provincial notes. As he explained to Glyns in 1865, "I have found it impossible to obtain the consent of my colleagues to the introduction this Session of the measures I wish, respecting the Currency of the Country."[79] Later, when commenting on George Brown's resignation from cabinet, Galt observed that Brown had opposed everything in Council and had been continually threatening resignation, and "[b]y this means he balked my Bank of Issue last session."[80] The issue that provoked Brown's resignation, Galt believed, was the question of reciprocity and the fact that the Cabinet, including Howland, had backed his proposals and did not include Brown among the delegates to be dispatched to Washington for talks.[81]

Although the proposal for an immediate issue of provincial notes was blocked in 1865, Galt had won a small victory, as evidenced by the Executive Council approval of the proposal to seek at the next parliamentary session legislative authority to issue such notes "with or without interest." Cabinet wanted the delay until the winter session "in the belief that from the abundant harvest and probable revival of trade it will be a more favourable period for these contemplated arrangements."[82] By the opening of Parliament Galt was ready to implement his plans. He also had the advantage of having run, as he noted in his budget speech, a $596,000 surplus during the previous fiscal year. This surplus made his task considerably easier.[83]

In 1866 Galt reported on the economy as well as on the budget. When he delivered his 1866 budget speech the repeal of Reciprocity was certain. The loss of the Treaty, he believed, undermined Canadian exports to the United States. It was critical in these circumstances to seek new markets in the Maritimes, France, the West Indies, and Latin America.[84] Moreover, repeal, Galt suggested, had hurt agricultural interest, and this required the government to adjust duties to "cheapen to a great extent the articles which go into consumption of the vast body of the people." This involved some general reductions, yet revenue needs demanded as well heavier duties "on those articles which will furnish a larger amount of revenue with less cost of collection." Galt looked to new excise taxes on spirits and tobacco and new taxes on liquor, tea, and sugar. He also proposed an export duty on sawn lumber to offset the American duty.[85]

Galt reduced the general tariff rate. Articles in the 25–30 per cent list would now be charged between 15 and 20 per cent. Duties on articles on the 10 per cent list would be phased out. Not only would this reduce the cost of living, it would reduce the input costs of manufacturers. This in turn would encourage manufacturers to expand and, more importantly for Galt, to export:

> while they will be able to supply our own people with goods five per cent cheaper than under the existing tariff, the manufacturers will be placed in a more favorable position than now with regard to competition in foreign markets.

Galt suggested that had the government's fiscal condition been stronger, he would have reduced the general rate to as low as 12.5 per cent. Galt concluded his comments by asserting, "with regard to all manufactured goods, I have no hesitation in expressing my individual wish, sir, that we were in a position now to abolish Customs duties on all of them (Loud cheers)."[86]

Galt pinned his hopes for the future on economic growth that would lead to a rapid increase in exports. Economic growth stimulated by a vibrant export sector would lead to strong imports, which could be taxed at a lower level to produce sufficient revenue. This would have the advantage of lowering the cost of living, and, as Galt observed, cheap prices and low taxation attracted immigrants.

There could be little faulting the basic objectives outlined in Galt's budget speech, yet there remained problems. In particular, the Minister's belief that new excise and other taxes could generate sufficient revenue relative to expenditures seems starkly unrealistic. Certainly Galt's expectations were not realized. Between 1866 and 1867 revenue from excise increased $100,000 to just under $2 million. Revenue from customs, meanwhile, fell by over $300,000 to only $7 million. There was also the question of the government's existing short-term liabilities.

Galt outlined those liabilities at the end of his budget speech. The $1.5 million loan from the Bank of Montreal would shortly mature. The final £140,000 on the Imperial Guaranteed loan would also mature, although in this case the assets of the Sinking Fund offset the liability.

This could not be said of the $2.6 million Welland Canal debentures against which the Sinking Fund held only $681,000. There was, in addition, the $3.1 million "floating" debt owed Barings and Glyns, all of which was secured by the deposit of debentures. Of the debt owed Barings and Glyns, £520,000 stg cost the government 8 per cent interest. To this could be added another $750,000 special loan owed the Bank of Montreal. Against these "floating" loans the government had but $674,000. The government, in short, needed on 1 July an additional $3.2 million to meet its unfunded liabilities falling due and $5.1 million to meet its maturing debentures. With Canadian debentures quoted at 20 per cent discounts in London, it would be impossible to raise the necessary funds in the usual manner. Galt proposed instead issuing $5 million worth of provincial notes redeemable in specie in Montreal and Toronto. The government, however, would not itself create a bank of issue. Rather it would negotiate an agreement with an existing bank willing to surrender its own power to issue notes.[87] The holder of the government account already had the inside track. The Bank of Montreal had become a valued ally of the provincial government; for an appropriate fee, the Bank was both willing and able to accommodate the government's needs.

In 1866 the government's fiscal position had improved significantly and enough of the £750,000 stg British loan had been raised to clear its old debts with the Bank. By April even the $1 million loan originally due in November 1865 had been settled.[88] Although the province had to request a special loan again in June 1866,[89] financial relations between the government and its provincial agent were quite healthy when Galt opened negotiations on the provincial note issue.

After the introduction of appropriate legislation, Galt invited King to Ottawa in July "finally to settle matters." Discussions progressed slowly, but by the end of August all was ready for the implementation of the programme on 10 September 1866.[90] Under the agreement the Bank surrendered its power to issue its own notes; for this it would be compensated at 5 per cent per annum based on its circulation on 30 April 1866. The government in turn would deliver to the Bank the full amount of authorized provincial notes and would pay 0.25 per cent commission on all notes in actual circulation. The government also agreed never to overdraw on its issue account and to provide debentures as security in the case of an unusual demand for redemption of provincial notes. The government also agreed to provide six months' notice if the agreement was to be terminated.[91] The total amount authorized was $8 million.[92]

At the same time the government returned to the Bank of Montreal seeking additional "accommodation." In early August the Executive Council authorized new advances for $1.5 million to cover remittances to Barings and Glyns as well as extensions on a $750,000 loan due 1 September.[93] Later in November the government ordered this loan paid out of the provincial notes held by the Bank. As part of the original deal, $600,000 in provincial debentures would be redeemed by the government and for this purpose a loan was to be negotiated. Finally, another $1.5 million was to be borrowed to cover sterling exchange sent to Britain to pay the 1 January 1867 interest.[94]

No sooner had these arrangements been made than Receiver General Belleau requested authority to negotiate another $500,000 to cover current accounts. Large and unexpected militia expenditures had depleted the government's cash balances in its ordinary accounts.[95] Belleau had only $306,000 available, there was no likelihood of significant revenue receipts in the near future, and large disbursements would soon come due. Belleau also reminded the Executive Council that agreements with the Bank of Montreal required them to keep a $400,000 balance in the government account. Although the Note Account contained $629,000, this was unavailable to meet other expenses, since it would be required to repay other advances due the Bank.[96]

Although the government managed to repay a $1.1 million loan in January 1867 and half of a $1.5 million loan in May,[97] it immediately sought a new advance. On 18 June 1867 the Executive Council authorized a new loan of $1.25 million.[98] By this point the original credit in the Issue Account had been exhausted repaying earlier loans, and the balance in the ordinary account was far below the agreed-upon minimum. Indeed, the issue account by the end of February 1867 showed a deficit rather than the surplus Howland had expected.[99]

Belleau believed that the situation demonstrated that "under the existing agreement we are more or less in the hands of the Bank. . . . The Government does not have at present, in my opinion, any proper control over its own circulation." Belleau believed that the Bank had, in effect, been holding the government hostage. With millions in provincial notes locked in its vaults, the Bank of Montreal demanded payment of loans in cash. When offered provincial notes, the Bank threatened to redeem them immediately in specie. Under the circumstances the Bank had in effect forced new loans on the government and was, Belleau argued, lending the government its own money at 7 per cent interest.[100] The government had become the prisoner of its unfunded debts.

Nor had there been any improvement in the situation in London. Both Barings and Glyns had managed to arrange a few loans following the collapse of the 1865 agreement. Against these loans provincial debentures had been deposited as security.[101] This was a risky operation, as repayment might prove difficult and a forced sale of these debentures would be at ruinous prices. In June Galt acknowledged the "severe monetary crisis" gripping financial markets which dragged quotations for Canadian 5 per cent debentures down into the 70s, yet remained convinced his new provincial note initiative would provide a solution.[102] In the meantime, the government authorized $2 million worth of new 6 per cent, three-year debentures to be sold in Canada.[103] This was later altered; domestic issues would pay 7 per cent and mature in two years. Barings and Glyns proved more than willing to extend their various special loans at 8 per cent interest but demanded they be secured by the new provincial 7 per cent debentures.[104] The government still needed additional money. In September the Executive Council accepted par bids for $853,000 worth of the new debentures and agreed to make additional sales at par.[105] This money did not go very far, however, as the government redeemed $1.3 million debentures between October and December 1866.[106]

The new provincial note issue did not, as we have seen, produce the expected boon for the government. With no new moneys forthcoming, Barings and Glyns became increasingly nervous. In December they sent a worried communication to Howland, the recently appointed Minister of Finance:

> In view of the approaching period when the dividends fall due on the Canadian 5 and 6 per cent Loans, and being without remittances or communications from the Government on the subject, we should feel obliged by your giving us instructions on the matter as there are no funds in our hands to meet the payments maturing on the 1st Jany [sic] but as you are aware a considerable amount stands at the debit, in our accounts with the Government.[107]

Thus on the eve of Confederation the Province of Canada had come full circle. It had been born in a financial crisis and it ended its constitutional existence in the same condition.

As celebrations for Confederation were being planned, the financial position of the Province of Canada was as precarious as at any time in its history. During its last year the provincial government ran a budgetary deficit of over $500,000, the eighth deficit in the ten fiscal years since 1858. During the last decade of its existence Ministers of Finance repeatedly promised to introduce new revenue measures to correct this basic problem. Avoiding direct taxation, they juggled customs duties, increased excise taxes, and held increases in expenditures in line. The promised budgetary surplus, however, never materialized. The government repeatedly blamed their budgetary problems on the

American Civil War. The War, successive Ministers of Finance observed, disrupted trade, which undermined government revenue, while at the same time it forced Canada to increase its spending on the militia. Both of these arguments are of dubious value.

Despite the arguments of successive Ministers of Finance, trade statistics do not indicate a disruption. Both imports and exports increased during the war years, and Canada's balance of trade actually improved during the first years of the war. Militia spending, meanwhile, was hardly an overwhelming burden. Indeed, in 1862 militia spending was significantly less than in 1858, although spending then increased dramatically to almost $500,000 in 1863 and to $760,000 in 1865. The Fenian raids, on the other hand, really did increase spending on the militia; in 1866 the government spent $1.6 million on defence. Even in 1866, however, the militia accounted for only a small portion of total expenditures, and total expenditures increased only marginally despite a doubling in defence spending.

The war had not caused the problem; accumulated debts combined with trade and budgetary deficits had. After a very successful marketing of Consols during Galt's first term as Minister of Finance, capital markets contracted. Unable to sell new debentures at reasonable prices, the province scrambled to meet its debt service charges. Unable to borrow abroad to pay interest abroad, the government returned to domestic capital markets to raise money to meet obligations. With the adoption of the Provincial Note Act and the issuance of new domestic debentures in 1866, the government was exploiting the full range of its credit options. Despite this, it was not reducing liabilities, it was simply maintaining a holding pattern.

Unlike the original loans contracted in the 1830s, 1840s, and 1850s, this capital was not recycled within the domestic economy; it flowed out to meet obligations abroad. This could have devastating consequences for a country that continued to import more than it exported. In 1867 the Province of Canada ran a trade deficit as large as at any time in its history. The public debt, which had gone a long way to offset balance of trade deficits between 1840 and 1857, had now become a burden contributing to a rapidly deteriorating balance of payments.

The Canadian economy as then structured had become unworkable. E. H. King at the Bank of Montreal certainly understood the problem, even if he viewed it as a short-term apparition rather than a long-term systemic crisis. In 1864, Galt had borrowed money from the Bank to be sent to London to meet interest on the public debt. At the time Galt hoped that the operation would not create "stringency" in Canadian capital markets. King responded in a surprisingly defensive and strident tone. King was incredulous: how, he asked, could Galt imagine that sending £150,000 stg to Britain would have any other result than to remove these funds from the capital available to merchants in Canada? King denied that the "stringency" complained of had anything to do with the policies of the Bank of Montreal and blamed instead poor economic conditions and the trade deficit. "A reference to the Bank Statements published in the Official Gazette," he wrote,

> will afford ample explanation of the necessity that has arisen for a contraction of loans. The increase in the Bank Discounts of Canada in July 1864 compared with that month of 1863, is very large, and if to this be added the $1,500,000 advanced to the Government by the Bank of Montreal, and allowance made for the alteration in the figures of the Bank of Upper Canada return, it will be found that the Banks have now employed a sum exceeding $6,000,000 greater than last year. This is the state of matters, with an increase of interest Deposits of over $5,000,000, a reduction in specie of $1,500,000, an enormous stock of timber on hand and in the woods, heavy and increasing importations particularly of dry goods, stimulated by the abundance of money for some time past, a grain crop likely to be under an average, low and unrenumerative prices for both timber and breadstuffs, and high rates of interest in England with a prospect of higher. In the presence of all these facts can a doubt remain of the urgent necessity for caution and restriction upon the Banks of Canada.[108]

The failure to make any dent in the basic problems of debts and deficits ensured that something more radical would be required. Confederation, involving as it did the death of the old Province of Canada, was certainly radical. Whether it would prove a solution was a moot point.

Notes

1.   "Report of the Minister of Finance of Canada," Sessional Paper No. 10, *Sessional Papers*, 1863.

2.   ECO, R.G. 1 E 1, State Book T, Vol. 82, Minute, 10 August 1858, 62.

3.   "Report of the Minister of Finance," Sessional Paper No. 10, *Sessional Papers*, 1863.

4.   Finance, R.G. 19, Vol. 2756, Hincks to Barings, 8 November 1848. Earlier in September Hincks had addressed letters to both Barings and Glyns, requesting an advance of £40,000 stg. Also see Hincks to Barings, 7 September 1848, and Hincks to Glyns, 7 September, 25 October, 1 November, and 22 November 1848.

5.   Finance, R.G. 19, Vol. 2756, Hincks to Barings, 20 December 1848.

6.   Finance, R.G. 19, Vol. 3376, Galt to Glyns and Barings, 23 November 1858, and ECO, R.G. 1 E 1, State Book T, Vol. 82, Minute, 7 January 1859, 438. Advances would

fall due on 15 June and 15 December. Barings and Glyns could sell debentures given as security after those dates, failing other settlements.

7.   In March 1861 Galt ordered Barings and Glyns to sell up to £150,000 stg of the 5 per cent debentures to settle outstanding balances due their firms. See Finance, R.G. 19, Vol. 3376, Galt to Glyns and Barings, 21 March 1861. Then in June 1861 the Cabinet authorized another £300,000 of the 5 per cent debentures to cover expenses under the Supply Bill. Half of these were ordered sold in October. The government also sold a number of the new debentures to domestic banks. See ECO, R.G. 1 E 1, State Book W, Vol. 85, Minutes, 13 June, 2 October, 8 November, and 15 November 1861, 242, 423, 480–481, 503–504; Finance, R.G. 19, Vol. 3376, Galt to Barings and Glyns, 14 June and 2 October 1861, Galt to T. Douglas Harrington, Deputy Receiver General, 7 November and 14 November 1861, Vol. 1165, Harrington to Glyns, 13 September and 10 October 1861.

8.   Quotations for Canadian 5 per cent debentures had slipped marginally below par in late 1860. By September 1861 the government was selling new issues at 99, although the price rose to 101 in November. By mid-1862 quotations were down to 98.5. See Finance, R.G. 19, Vol. 1164, Harrington to C. Alleyn, Provincial Secretary, 4 October 1860, and Vol. 1165, James Morris, Receiver General, to Barings, 4 July 1862; Vol. 2765, William Dickinson, Acting Deputy Inspector General, to Barings and Glyns, 11 November 1861, and Vol. 3376, Galt to Barings and Glyns, 12 September 1861.

9.   Finance, R.G. 19, Vol. 3376, "Private," Galt to William Hamilton Merritt, 19 November 1861. Merritt, always the promoter, had requested government assistance to develop a "Propeller line." Galt turned him down, pointing out that the government was having enough problems balancing its budget. Galt also commented that his recent optimism had been shattered by the war to the south. Galt was convinced that the decline in quotations for Canadian debentures in London resulted from the impact of the war on American capital markets. To Barings and Glyns Galt commented that it was "a subject of regret though not of surprise." Galt to Glyns and Barings, 20 December 1861. By January 1862, however, the crisis appeared to have passed, and Galt was glad to see that the decline in quotations "has not been permanent." He still feared, however, a decline in trade and, as a result, prepared to propose new specific duties in the 1862 parliamentary session. Galt to Barings and Glyns, 6 January 1862. Also see *Baring Papers*, M.G. 24, I D 21, Vol. 3, George Carr Glyn to Thomas Baring, 23 February 1862.

10.   ECO, R.G. 1 E 1, State Book X, Vol. 86, Minute, 10 June 1862, 289, Finance, R.G. 19, Vol. 1165, Morris to Glyns, 12 June 1862, Morris to Barings, 12 June 1862, and Vol. 3376, Howland to Barings and Glyns, 19 September 1862. Galt, earlier in the year, had mentioned sending £350,000 stg in debentures. See Finance, R.G. 19, Vol. 2765, Galt to Barings and Glyns, 19 May 1862, Dickinson to Barings and Glyns, 7 June 1862.

11.   Finance, R.G. 19, Vol. 1165, Harrington to "The Honble. The Minister of Finance," 8 August 1862. None of these bonds had been sold by September "in consequence of the decline in their value." Howland announced he had made arrangements to remit $1 million as a better alternative to selling debentures below par. Finance, R.G. 19, Vol. 3376, Howland to Barings and Glyns, 19 September 1862.

12.   See Finance, R.G. 19, Vol. 1165, Morris to Cashier, Bank of Upper Canada, 2 September 1862, Harrington to W. Dunn, Cashier, Quebec Bank, 8 September 1862, Harrington to Cassels, 8 September 1862, Morris to Henry Starnes, Manager, Ontario Bank, 17 September 1862, Harrington to C. S. Ross, President, Commercial Bank, 17 September 1862, [Harrington] to Thomas Kirby, Manager, Commercial Bank, 18 September 1862.

13.   See Finance, R.G. 19, Vol. 1165, Morris to Glyns, 18 September 1862, and Morris to Barings, 18 September 1862.

14.   Finance, R.G. 19, Vol. 3376, Howland to Barings and Glyns, 19 September 1862, and Vol. 1165, Morris, "Memorandum," 24 November 1862. Also see Harrington to the Provincial Secretary, 19 September 1862, Harrington to Starnes, 24 September 1862, Harrington to Barings, 26 September 1862, Harrington to Glyns, 26 September and 29 September 1862, Harrington to Barings, 29 September 1862, Harrington to the Provincial Secretary, 29 September 1862, Morris to Glyns, 3 October 1862, Morris to Barings, 3 October 1862, Harrington to the Provincial Secretary, 3 October 1862, Harrington to W. Farwell, Cashier, Eastern Township Bank, 17 November 1862, Morris to Starnes, 20 November 1862, Harrington to the Provincial Secretary, 20 November 1862, Morris to Glyns, 21 November 1862, Morris to Barings, 21 November 1862, Morris to Starnes, 22 November 1862. The total cost of these remittances was $1,194,666.67, which was charged against the Consolidated Revenue Fund. See ECO, R.G. 1 E 1, State Book Y, Vol. 87, Minute, 24 November 1862, 122.

15.   See Bruce W. Hodgins, *John Sandfield Macdonald, 1812–1872* (Toronto, 1971), 54–55.

16.   Bruce W. Hodgins, "John Sandfield Macdonald," in *The Pre-Confederation Premiers*, 266.

17.   *Ibid.*, 267.

18.   *Ibid.*, 257.

19.   Hodgins, *John Sandfield Macdonald*, 58–60.

20.   See Morton, *The Critical Years*, 123; Hodgins, "John Sandfield Macdonald," in *The Pre-Confederation Premiers*, 270–271; Hodgins, *John Sandfield Macdonald*, 60.

21.   ECO, R.G. 1 E 1, State Book X, Vol. 86, Minute, 24 October 1862, 619–620, State Book Y, Vol. 87, Minute, 24 November 1862, 122, and Finance, R.G. 19, Vol. 1165, Harrington to George Mathews, Engravers, Montreal, 14 November 1862, Morris "Memorandum," 24 November 1862, Harrington to Mathews, 1 December and 18 December 1862.

22.   See Finance, R.G. 19, Vol. 1165, Harrington to A.M.J. Durnford, Collingwood, 24 November 1862, Harrington to Horace Kilborn, Newboro, 24 November 1862, Harrington to James F. Brown, Toronto, 24 November 1862, Harrington to D. Fisher, Cashier, Ontario Bank, Bowmanville, 24 November 1862, Harrington to D. G. Baillange, Quebec, 24 November 1862, Harrington to A. LeMoine, Treasurer, Trinity House, Quebec, 24 November 1862, Harrington to Starnes, 1 December and 3 December 1862, Harrington to C. J. Smith, Manager, Bank of British North America, Quebec, 22 December 1862, and Harrington to E. B. Lindsay, 12 January 1863. In December 1862 Receiver General Morris used over $493,000 worth of these notes to purchase £100,000 stg exchange from the Bank of British North America. Morris to Smith, Acting Manager, Bank of British North America, Quebec, 11 December 1862. From the correspondence it is not clear whether this was part of or in addition to the $500,000 in notes provided later in the month. The Ontario Bank in Montreal, meanwhile, purchased $200,000 of these notes on its own account, and an additional $400,000 which it would sell on behalf of the province. The Bank, however, returned unsold $345,000 of these notes in March 1863. See Harrington to Starnes, 3 December 1862 and 5 March 1863, and Harrington to the Provincial Secretary, 7 March 1863.

23.   Finance, R.G. 19, Vol. 3376, Howland to Glyns and Barings, 19 December 1862. Howland was in London at this time.

24. This strategy had been suggested by Thomas Baring, who believed that an announcement of the government's intention to redeem the guaranteed loan would undermine opponents of a British contribution to the Intercolonial who had been suggesting that claims "on the Province were not secure and that Great Britain might be called on to pay her contingent for Canada as well as her own for the Intercolonial Railroad." *Galt Papers*, M.G. 27 I D 8, Vol. 2, Thomas Baring to Galt, 13 March 1862, and *Baring Papers*, M.G. 24 I D 21, Vol. 3, Galt to Thomas Baring, 29 March 1862.

25. Galt, "Memorandum," 15 April 1862, in ECO, State Book X, Vol. 86, Minute, 17 April 1862, 183–185. Back in 1858 the government had insisted that the Sinking Fund be invested in securities that paid higher rates than Consols. Although it had originally intended to shift these funds from Consols to provincial securities, disagreements with the Treasury delayed action. Most of the funds held in the Sinking Fund were eventually invested in the new India Stock. See Finance, R.G. 19, Vol. 3376, Galt to Barings, [10] January 1859, Galt to Barings and Glyns, 7 March, 14 March, 16 May, 6 June, 14 July and 12 November 1859, Galt to Glyns, 12 November 1859. [This is a second letter of the same date.] *Galt Papers*, M.G. 27 I D 8, Vol. 1, Thomas Baring to Galt, 21 April 1859, ECO, R.G. 1 E 1, State Book T, Vol. 82, Minute, 31 August 1858, 102, and State Book U, Vol. 83, Minute, 23 November 1859, 461. Although the Treasury agreed to the new Canadian proposal to sell the India stock, it delayed acting. Not until late December were Barings and Glyns ordered to begin redeeming the first £300,000 stg debentures of the guaranteed loan which matured 1 January 1863. See ECO, R.G. 1 E 1, State Book X, Vol. 86, Minute, 24 October 1862, 632–633, and Finance, R.G. 19, Vol. 3376, Howland to William Gladstone, Chancellor of Exchequer, 3 December 1862, Howland to Sir Frederick Rogers, Colonial Office, 8 December 1862, Howland to George A. Hamilton, Treasury, 19 December 1862, Howland to Barings and Glyns, 20 December 1862, and Vol. 1166, Harrington to Glyns, 23 October 1863. Later in 1864 there would be some difficulty as the price of India stock fell, making it "impracticable" to raise the £300,000 required for redemptions that year by sales of securities held in the Sinking Fund. See Finance, R.G. 19, Vol. 3376, L. H. Holton, Minister of Finance, to Barings and Glyns, 12 February 1864 and Galt to Barings and Glyns, 4 May 1864. Within the month, however, Barings and Glyns reported the sale of £217,000 of the India Stock. Finance, R.G. 19, Vol. 1166, E.-P. Taché, Receiver General, to Glyns, 24 June 1864, Taché to Barings, 24 June 1864, and Harrington to Barings, 13 January 1864. By the end of the year Galt was "glad to notice the prices realized [by the Bank of England for the India Stock] will afford considerable profit upon that transaction." Finance, R.G. 19, Vol. 3376, Galt to Barings and Glyns, 6 December 1864.

26. Finance, R.G. 19, Vol. 3376, Holton to Barings and Glyns, 22 May 1863.

27. *Galt Papers*, M.G. 27 I D 8, Vol. 9, Holton, "Budget Speech," [1863]. The canals had been built to entice the trade of the western states to the St. Lawrence system, and some believed with William Hamilton Merritt that reciprocity too would encourage American farmers to choose the St. Lawrence route. See Masters, *The Reciprocity Treaty*, 3–4. The St. Lawrence canals, meanwhile, were very cheap, yet little American traffic was diverted. The 1860 decision to rebate 90 per cent of the Welland tolls if a ship subsequently stopped at a St. Lawrence port produced only a decline in revenue rather than an increase in traffic. See McKee, "Canada's Bid for the Traffic of the Mid-west," 31–32. Officer and Smith suggest that the trade of the St. Lawrence did very poorly as a result of reciprocity, and that during the early years of the treaty "Montreal lost steadily" relative to Buffalo and Oswego. Officer and Smith, "The Canadian–American Reciprocity Treaty," 619–622.

28.   Finance, R.G. 19, Vol. 3376, Holton to Barings and Glyns, 10 July 1863, Vol. 1166, Harrington to Glyns, 5 June 1863, Harrington to Barings, 5 June 1863, Harrington to the Provincial Secretary, 11 June 1863, Harrington to Glyns, 12 June 1863, Harrington to Barings, 12 June 1863, Harrington to Glyns, 17 July 1863, Harrington to Barings, 17 July 1863, Harrington to the Provincial Secretary, 17 July 1863, and ECO, R.G. 1 E 1, State Book Y, Vol. 87, Minute, 29 May 1863, 554–555. By July 1863 quotations for Canadian 5 per cent debentures had fallen to between 95.5 and 96.5. Finance, R.G. 19, Vol. 3376, Holton to Barings and Glyns, 24 July 1863.

29.   See Finance, R.G. 19, Vol. 3376, Holton to Barings and Glyns, 18 September and 25 September 1863. Holton's mood was as volatile as the London market and the political situation in Canada. He was more confident and a little happier later in October as quotations rose and the government successfully weathered another want of confidence motion. By November, however, the mood had changed again as he began to fear a "panic" developing in the London capital markets. See Holton to Barings and Glyns, 2 October, 9 October, 16 October, and 24 November 1863.

30.   Under an agreement of May 1851 the Bank of Upper Canada was to reimburse Barings and Glyns for interest payments in Britain, and they would in turn be reimbursed by the provincial government at the rate of .5 per cent above the current New York exchange rates. In effect the Bank was providing short-term loans to the provincial government. See ECO, R.G. 1 E 1, State Book L, Vol. 74, Minute, 16 May 1851, State Book M, Vol. 75, Minute, 10 May 1852, and Baskerville, *The Bank of Upper Canada*, cix, passim.

31.   Finance, R. G. 19, Vol. 3376, Holton to Barings and Glyns, 29 May 1863, and ECO, R.G. 1 E 1, State Book Y, Vol. 87, Minute, 29 May 1863, 554. In addition to the debentures, the Bank of Upper Canada promised to remit at least £100,000 stg exchange, and Holton expected soon to forward a similar amount. Between 25 September 1863 and 9 October 1863 the government remitted £150,000 stg, half to Barings and half to Glyns. This cost the government $735,000. See Finance, R.G. 19, Vol. 1166, Howland, Receiver General, to Barings, 25 September 1863, Howland to Glyns, 25 September 1863, Harrington to the Provincial Secretary, 25 September 1863, Howland to Glyns, 2 October 1863, Howland to Barings, 2 October 1863, Harrington to the Provincial Secretary, 2 October 1863, Howland to Glyns, 9 October 1863, Howland to Barings, 9 October 1863, Harrington to the Provincial Secretary, 9 October 1863.

32.   Finance, R.G. 19, Vol. 3376, Holton to Barings and Glyns, 17 July and 24 July 1863.

33.   See Baskerville, *The Bank of Upper Canada*, cxxv. On the Zimmerman Bank, see J. K. Johnson, "'One Bold Operator': Samuel Zimmerman, Niagara Entrepreneur, 1843–1857," *Ontario History*, LXXIV (1982), 26–44.

34.   Finance, R.G. 19, Vol. 3376, Holton to Thomas Street, Hon. L Wallbridge, and Cassels, 26 November 1863.

35.   Finance, R.G. 19, Vol. 3376, Holton to Street, Wallbridge, and Cassels, 26 November 1863, Holton to Cassels, 11 December 1863 and 8 January 1864. The terms of this agreement with the Bank can be found in ECO, R.G. 1 E 1, State Book Z, Vol. 88, Minute, 8 December 1863, 265–267. As part of the deal the Bank was required to "abandon the pretension" that it was not liable for the £100,000 stg Bill of Exchange of the Grand Trunk or the government's claim on the Zimmerman Bank. The government also insisted that it maintained the right to demand payment of the full amount owed "if the public Interest" required.

36.   Finance, R.G. 19, Vol. 3376, Holton to Cassels, 7 November 1863. In his budget speech that year Holton put the blame where it properly belonged, on budgetary deficits. See *Galt Papers*, M.G. 27 I D 8, Vol. 9, Holton, "Budget Speech," [1863].

37.   Finance, R.G. 19, Vol. 3376, Holton to Barings and Glyns, 8 January 1864.

38.   See *Galt Papers*, M.G. 27 I D 8, Vol. 9, Holton, "Budget Speech," [1863], and Finance, R.G. 19, Vol. 3376, Holton to Cassels, 7 November 1863.

39.   Finance, R.G. 19, Vol. 3376, Holton to Glyns and Barings, 11 November 1863. Also see *Galt Papers*, M.G. 27 I D 8, Vol. 9, Holton, "Budget Speech," [1863].

40.   See Finance, R.G. 19, Vol. 3376, Holton to E. H. King, General Manager, Bank of Montreal, 21 November 1863, and ECO, R.G. 1 E 1, State Book Z, Vol. 88, Minutes, 19 November 1863, and "Copy," Holton, "Memorandum," 18 November 1863, 222, 224–227. There were two separate Orders-in-Council dated 19 November covering the loan, agency, and the initial use of the funds.

41.   Finance, R.G. 19, Vol. 3376, Holton to Glyns and Barings, 11 November 1863.

42.   *Ibid.*, Holton to King, 21 November 1863, and Vol. 1166, Harrington to Matthews [sic], 9 November and 19 November 1863, Harrington to King, 25 November and 29 December 1863. The redemptions in fact cost $817,900, $39,000 of which was interest. See Vol. 1165, Harrington to the Provincial Secretary, 1 December 1863.

43.   Finance, R.G. 19, Vol. 3376, Holton to Barings and Glyns, 24 November 1863.

44.   *Ibid.*, 26 February 1864. Also see Holton to Barings and Glyns, 26 December 1863.

45.   See ECO, R.G. 1 E 1, State Book AA, Vol. 89, Minute, 20 May 1864, 26, and Finance, R.G. 19, Vol. 3376, Galt to Barings and Glyns, 4 May and 20 May 1864. Galt informed King at the Bank of Montreal that he would require £140,000 stg by 15 June which would "run down our balance to a somewhat low figure." This was later reduced to £120,000 stg. See Vol. 3376, "Private," Galt to King, 3 May and 6 May 1864. George Carr Glyn, meanwhile, reminded Galt that the original conditions of the provincial account had "not been adhered to" and demanded the higher rate of interest as a result of the "heavy loss" incurred on the provincial account. See *Galt Papers*, M.G. 27 I D 8, Vol. 2, "Private," George Carr Glyn to Galt, 6 May 1864. When Galt took the Finance portfolio in March he immediately informed Barings and Glyns that he wanted to avoid all sales of debentures in their hands. See Galt to Barings and Glyns, 31 March and 24 June 1864. Galt also assured his London agents that the inclusion of George Brown in the new government guaranteed passage of necessary fiscal proposals. He would later blame Brown for blocking a number of his initiatives.

46.   NAC, *Macdonald Papers*, M.G. 26 A, Vol. 571, File No. 1, Letterbook 6, Macdonald to James Vrooman, 7 July 1864, cited in J. K. Johnson, "John A. Macdonald," *The Pre-Confederation Premiers*, 222.

47.   *Galt Papers*, M.G. 27 I D 8, Vol. 2, "Private," George Carr Glyn to Galt, 20 April 1864.

48.   Finance, R.G. 19, Vol. 3376, Galt to Barings and Glyns, 26 August 1864. Galt had kept Barings and Glyns well informed as to the progress of his new tax measures as they moved through the Assembly. He remained optimistic that not only would these new taxes balance the budget, but "I trust that the unanimity which has been displayed by Parliament in thus providing for the deficiency in our Revenue will have a good effect on our Securities in London." See Galt to Barings and Glyns, 3 June 1864. Also see Galt to Barings and Glyns, 16 May 1864.

49.   Finance, R.G. 19, Vol. 3376, Galt to J. R. Christian, Bank of Montreal, 24 August 1864 and "Private and Confidential," Galt to King, 29 August 1864.

50.   *Ibid.* For King's response see below, 203.

51.   *Ibid.*, Galt to Glyns, 26 August 1864. Quotations for Canadian 5 per cent debentures sank to 89 in May 1864. See Finance, R.G. 19, Vol. 3376, Galt to King, 6 May 1864.

52.   Finance, R.G. 19, Vol. 3376, Galt to Barings and Glyns, 29 September 1864, and ECO, R.G. 1 E 1, State Book AA, Vol. 89, Minute, 23 September 1864, 296–297.

53.   Finance, R.G. 19, Vol. 3376, Galt to Glyns and Barings, 11 November 1864.

54.   *Ibid.*, Galt to King, 10 November and 14 November 1864. In the letter requesting the loan Galt also asked for £100,000 stg exchange for 10 December and informed King he would need another £100,000 for 15 December. Also see Finance, R.G. 19, Vol. 1166, Harrington to King, 15 November 1864, and Harrington to Christian, 18 November 1864. Between 18 November and 16 December 1864 the government drew $600,000 against its new account to pay for exchange. See Harrington to the Provincial Secretary, 18 November, 25 November, 2 December, 9 December, and 16 December 1864.

55.   *Galt Papers*, M.G. 27 I D 8, Vol. 3, "Private," King to Galt, 23 January 1865. King offered to provide an additional advance of $250,000 until customs receipts began arriving in March.

56.   Finance, R.G. 19, Vol. 3376, Galt to King, 20 February 1865.

57.   See Finance, R.G. 19, Vol. 1166, Harrington to Christian, 1 March 1865, Harrington to the Provincial Secretary, 1 March 1865, Harrington to Christian, 1 April 1865, Harrington to the Provincial Secretary, 1 April 1865, Harrington to Christian, 11 May 1865, and Harrington to the Provincial Secretary, 11 May 1865. The government repaid the whole $600,000, plus $14,000 interest.

58.   Finance, R.G. 19, Vol. 3376, Galt to King, 8 April 1865; Galt to King, 11 April 1865, [Galt] to Taché, 11 April 1865; Vol. 1166, Harrington to Christian, 10 May 1865, Harrington to the Receiver General, 17 May 1865, Taché to Galt, 19 May 1865; *Galt Papers*, M.G. 27 I D 8, Vol. 3, King to Galt, 10 April 1865, and ECO, State Book AB, Vol. 90, Minutes, 6 April 1865 and 17 May 1865, 270, 533. The Bank of Montreal requested that the £200,000 stg debentures be placed to its credit with the Union Bank in London. See Finance, R.G. 19, Vol. 3376, Galt to Glyns and Barings, 5 June 1865.

59.   Finance, R.G. 19, Vol. 3376, Galt to Glyns, 9 June 1865. There are two different letters of this date, the first more official in tone and stating the terms of the arrangement, the second more informal stating Galt's hopes for improvements in the money market. Also see Vol. 1166, Taché to Glyns, 21 April 1865, N. F. Belleau, Receiver General, to Glyns, 11 August 1865; Vol. 1167, Harrington to Glyns, 21 September, 12 October, and 23 November 1865, Glyns to Taché, 10 June 1865, Barings to Taché, 6 July 1865, Barings and Glyns to Galt, 13 June 1865, and Glyns to Taché 22 July 1865. The only sales of debentures came in May 1865 when the province sold 5 per cent India Stock at 106.25 and purchased Canadian fives at between 82.5 and 83.5. See Vol. 1158, Barings and Glyns to Galt, 16 May 1865, Galt to Dickinson, 27 May 1865, George Forbes, Bank of England, to Barings, 16 May 1865, Mullins, Marshall and Company to [?], 15 May 1865, Barings and Glyns to Galt, 20 May and 26 May 1865.

60.   See McIvor, *Canadian Monetary, Banking and Fiscal Development*, 51–53.

61.   *The Arthur Papers*, Vol. 3, Macaulay to Arthur, 9 August 1841, 441–444. R. D. Jackson, meanwhile, suggested that "the circulating medium in this Country is no doubt

restricted, but this arises not from any want of facilities in the issue of notes or Bills intended to pass for money, but from the want of Capital to be represented by such Bills or notes." See GGO, R.G. 7 G 12, Vol. 59, Despatch No. 51, R. D. Jackson to Lord Stanley, 16 December 1841.

62.   *The Arthur Papers*, Vol. 3, Macaulay to Arthur, 4 December 1841, 477–479. On Hincks, Macaulay commented: "He is among the shrewdest of his party — the great object he now wishes to carry is the Bank of Issue — by which the Government would become the sole maker of paper money — this was Lord Sydenham's favourite measure."

63.   See GGO, R.G. 7 G 12, Vol. 62, Despatch No. 101, Bagot to Stanley, 6 May 1842.

64.   See above, Chapter 3, 72–73, passim.

65.   See above, 186.

66.   Finance, R.G. 19, Vol. 3368, D. Davidson, Bank of Montreal, to Galt, 19 March 1859.

67.   Finance, R.G. 19, Vol. 3369, Cayley to Galt, 20 October 1859. Although Cayley opposed the creation of a provincial bank of issue, there was some considerable, if cautious, support for the idea. D. L. Macpherson, for example, reported that the Toronto Board of Trade thought it a very good idea. The Board would support such a government initiative except that it feared a government bank would be controlled by "party 'Hacks'" who would put patronage ahead of business. See *Galt Papers*, M.G. 27 I D 8, Vol. 7, "Confidential," D. L. Macpherson to Galt, 10 April 1860.

68.   *Galt Papers*, M.G. 27 I D 8, Vol. 10, "Confidential," Galt to George Carr Glyn, 15 August 1865; ECO, R.G. 1 E 1, State Book AB, Vol. 90, Minutes, 16 August and 19 September 1865, 533, 615–616, Finance, R.G. 19, Vol. 3376, [Galt] to Barings and Glyns, 14 August 1865. Galt also withdrew his earlier authorization to sell Canadian debentures at 90.

69.   Finance, R.G. 19, Vol. 3376, Galt to King, 14 September and 21 September 1865, Galt to Barings and Glyns, 22 September 1865, and ECO, R.G. 1 E 1, State Book AB, Vol. 90, Minute, 19 September 1865, 615. For the earlier renewals of the $300,000 loan, see Finance, R.G. 19, Vol. 1166, Harrington to Christian, 1 June 1865, Harrington to the Provincial Secretary, 6 June 1865, Harrington to Christian, 19 June 1865, Harrington to King, 22 June and 24 June 1865, Harrington to the Provincial Secretary, 6 July and 4 August 1865, Harrington to King, 17 August 1865, and Harrington to the Provincial Secretary, 22 August 1865. The loan was repaid with interest in late September 1865. Reiffenstein to W. MacDougall, Provincial Secretary, 20 September 1865.

70.   See Finance, R.G. 19, Vol. 1158, Glyns and Barings to Galt, 12 October 1865. Also see Glyns to Taché, 27 July 1865, and Glyns to Belleau, 28 September 1865.

71.   See Finance, R.G. 19, Vol. 1158, Glyns to Taché, 22 July 1865, and Barings and Glyns to Galt, 22 March 1866. Quotations for Canadian 5 per cent debentures remained under 80 for the rest of the year.

72.   ECO, R.G. 1 E 1, State Book AC, Vol. 91, Minute, 9 November 1865, 61. If the rate of interest was over 6 per cent the loan was to be of short duration and not extend beyond 1 October 1866. Also see Finance, R.G. 19, Vol. 3376, Galt to Barings and Glyns, 10 November 1865.

73.   Finance, R.G. 19, Vol. 1158, Glyns and Barings to Galt, 25 November, 30 November, 7 December, and 14 December 1865; Vol. 3376, Galt to Barings and Glyns, 15 December and 21 December 1865.

74. See Finance, R.G. 19, Vol. 1158, Glyns and Barings to Galt, 30 November 1865, and Vol. 3376, Galt to Barings and Glyns, 21 December 1865.

75. See *Galt Papers*, M.G. 27 I D 8, Vol. 10, "Private," Galt to George Carr Glyn, 21 December 1865.

76. Finance, R.G. 19, Vol. 3376, Barings and Glyns to Galt, 4 January 1866, and Barings and Glyns to Galt, 11 January 1866.

77. Finance, R.G. 19, Vol. 3376, Galt to King, 10 November 1865, and ECO, R.G. 1 E 1, State Book AC, Vol. 91, Minute, 9 November 1865, 60–61. The Bank of Montreal would be called on to advance more money to the province over the course of the next several months, most often supplying Barings and Glyns with sterling to meet drafts of the Receiver General. See ECO, R.G. 1 E 1, State Book AC, Vol. 91, "Copy," Galt, Minister of Finance, 4 January 1866, 199–200, included in Minute, 6 January 1866, 198–199.

78. *Galt Papers*, M.G. 27 I D 8, Vol. 10, "Private," Galt to George Carr Glyn, 21 December 1865.

79. *Ibid.*, "Confidential," Galt to George Carr Glyn, 15 August 1865.

80. *Ibid.*, "Private," Galt to George Carr Glyn, 21 December 1865.

81. *Ibid.*, Vol. 3, Galt to Amy Galt, 21 December 1865.

82. See ECO, R.G. 1 E 1, State Book AB, Vol. 90, Minute, 16 August 1865, 533, and Finance, R.G. 19, Vol. 3376, [Galt] to Barings and Glyns, 14 August 1865.

83. *Galt Papers*, M.G. 27 I D 8, Vol. 6, Galt, "Budget Speech, 1866," 3–4.

84. *Ibid.*, 5–6, 13–17.

85. *Ibid.*, 11–12, 17–21.

86. *Ibid.*, 23–26. Galt discussed at length his faith in the ability of Canadian manufacturers to produce for export markets.

87. *Ibid.*, 28. The legislation creating provincial notes called for the issue of $5 million, redeemable in specie and payable on demand. Banks that surrendered their power to issue their own notes would also be freed from the requirement of holding provincial debentures. Those debentures could be exchanged for additional amounts of provincial notes as long as the total issue did not exceed $8 million. Against these notes the government was required to hold specie equal to 20 per cent of the notes issued up to $5 million and 25 per cent of the value of notes issued in excess of the $5 million limit. The balance was to be held in debentures which could be used to redeem notes if necessary. All proceeds from the notes became part of the Consolidated Revenue Fund. See "An Act to provide for the issue of Provincial Notes," *Provincial Statutes of Canada*, 29–30 Vic. cap. 10, 1866.

88. In January the government had repaid the balance of the $1 million loan; this was followed by two instalments on the $1.5 million loan in early April. See Finance, R.G. 19, Vol. 1167, Harrington to the Provincial Secretary, 10 January 1866, Harrington to Glyns, 5 January 1866, Harrington to Barings, 5 January 1866, Harrington to King, 5 January 1866, Reiffenstein to MacDougall, 3 April 1866, Harrington to the Provincial Secretary, 5 April 1866, Harrington to A. MacNider, Manager, Bank of Montreal, Ottawa, 6 April 1866, Harrington to the Provincial Secretary, 2 May 1866, Harrington to A. Drummond, Bank of Montreal, Ottawa, 3 May 1866. The £200,000 provincial debentures held as security against the $1 million loan were turned over to Barings and Glyns. See Harrington to R. B. Angus, Manager, Bank of Montreal, Montreal, 5 May 1866. Another

special loan for $750,000 was repaid in July. See T. D. H[arrington] to the Provincial
Secretary, 2 July 1866, and Harrington to Drummond, 3 July 1866.

89.   Finance, R.G. 19, Vol. 3376, Galt to King, 5 June 1866. The government asked for
between $500,000 and $750,000. King insisted that the government would have to pay
more than 7 per cent interest and that the loan should mature on 1 September. He
worried, meanwhile, that the loan might drain reserves and leave the bank vulnerable.
King demanded and Galt agreed that £200,000 stg debentures would be deposited with
the Bank's London agents as security against the loan, although Galt hoped King would
change his mind and "not consider this necessary." See "Private," Galt to King, 11 June
and 12 June 1866.

90.   Finance, R.G. 19, Vol. 3376, "Confidential," Galt to King, 11 July and 27 August
1866. In August the government arranged for the British North American Bank Note
Company to begin production on the new notes. See Vol. 1167, Harrington to British
North American Bank Note Company, 17 August 1866, Harrington to R.S.M. Bouchette,
Chairman, Board of Customs and Excise, 18 August 1866, and ECO, R.G. 1 E 1, State
Book AD, Vol. 92, Minute, 16 August 1866, 55–59.

91.   ECO, R.G. 1 E 1, State Book AD, Vol. 92, "Memorandum of proposed Arrangement
between the Government and the Bank of Montreal for the Surrender of its power to
issue Notes by the Bank and thereupon being appointed the Agent of the Province for
the issue and redemption of Provincial Notes, 25 August 1866," 111–118, and Minutes,
29 August 1866, 13 September 1866, 110, 149–151.

92.   ECO, R.G. 1 E 1, State Book AD, Vol. 92, Minute, 13 September 1866, 149–151.

93.   ECO, R.G. 1 E 1, State Book AD, Vol. 92, Minute, 10 August 1866, 29-30. The
government would pay 7 per cent interest on these loans. Also see Finance, R.G. 19,
Vol. 1167, Harrington to King, 17 August 1866, Harrington to Glyns, 7 September 1866,
Harrington to Barings, 7 September 1866. The $750,000 loan was extended for one
month and repaid on 1 October 1866. See Harrington to Langton, 20 September 1866,
Harrington to Angus, 20 September 1866, Harrington to Langton, 25 September 1866,
Harrington to Angus, 25 September 1866.

94.   See ECO, R.G. 1 E 1, State Book AD, Vol. 92, Minute, 7 November 1866, 401–403.
Also see Finance, R.G. 19, Vol. 1167, Harrington to Langton, 1 December 1866. The
arrangement to cover the $600,000 debentures led to considerable confusion. Harrington
found it strange that the agent of the province could exchange debentures for notes and
then present the notes to itself for payment charged against the Receiver General. For
Harrington, it "seems like a quick way of making the finances of the Country subserve
the peculiar interests of the Bank of Montreal by forcing on loans at a high rate of
interest." This may have been the case, but it was equally true that the government
had no other means of redeeming those bonds. Harrington believed that the Bank should
not present the notes for payment but should simply hold them. As he admitted, if the
Bank did present the notes, the government would have to seek another temporary loan
for at least $600,000. The effect would be to force the province to pay 7 per cent interest
to meet an obligation that had previously cost only 5 per cent. See Finance, R.G. 19,
Vol. 1178, Harrington to Belleau, 4 February 1867. Eventually the Bank was ordered
to send the bulk of these debentures to Barings and Glyns and payment was provided
out of the ordinary account rather than the provincial note account. See ECO, R.G. 1
E 1, State Book AE, Vol. 93, Minute, 18 June 1867, 285–286.

95.   Between 1865 and 1866 expenditures on the militia doubled from $760,000 to over
$1.6 million and then declined to $1.4 million in 1867.

96.   See ECO, R.G. 1 E 1, State Book AD, Vol. 92, Minute, 18 December 1866, 551–552, Finance, R.G. 19, Vol. 1167, Belleau to the Minister of Finance, 12 December 1866, and Harrington to King, 14 December 1866.

97.   Finance, R.G. 19, Vol. 1167, Harrington to Langton, 14 January 1867, and Harrington to King, 15 January 1867, Harrington to John Simpson, Assistant Auditor, 1 May 1867, Harrington to King, 2 May 1867, and Harrington to Drummond, 2 May 1867.

98.   ECO, R.G. 1 E 1, State Book AE, Vol. 93, Minute, 18 June 1867, 285–286. Also see Finance, R.G. 19, Vol. 1167, Harrington to Langton, 18 June 1867, Harrington to Angus, 18 June 1867, and Harrington to Langton, 21 June and 2 July 1867.

99.   Finance, R.G. 19, Vol. 1178, Belleau to Howland, 21 February 1867.

100. *Ibid.*

101. By March 1866 Galt had to despatch another £100,000 to cover these loans. ECO, R.G. 1 E 1, State Book AC, Vol. 91, Minute, 17 March 1866, 320–321, and Finance, R.G. 19, Vol. 1167, Harrington to Barings, 22 March 1866, and Harrington to Glyns, 22 March 1866. A total of £520,000 stg of the original £750,000 was raised.

102. See Finance, R.G. 19, Vol. 3376, [Galt] to Barings and Glyns, 7 June 1866. Quotations for Canadian fives fell from 79 in May to 76 in August 1866. See Vol. 1158, Glyns to Belleau, 24 May and 9 August 1866.

103. ECO, R.G. 1 E 1, State Book AD, Vol. 92, Minute, 3 August 1866, 8–9.

104. Finance, R.G. 19, Vol. 1167, Belleau to Barings and Glyns, 10 August 1866, and Vol. 1158, Barings and Glyns to Belleau, 30 August 1866.

105. ECO, R.G. 1 E 1, State Book AD, Vol. 92, Minute, 14 September 1866, 161–162, and Finance, Vol. 1167, Belleau, "Memorandum," 14 September 1866. The government had received offers to purchase another $74,000 worth of debentures at below par.

106. See Finance, R.G. 19, Vol. 1167, Harrington to the Provincial Secretary, 1 October 1866, Harrington to the Auditor, 29 October 1866, Harrington to Angus, 30 October 1866, Harrington to Drummond, 3 November 1866, Harrington to H. H. Whitney, Secretary, Montreal Harbour Commissioners, 17 December 1866, Harrington to Angus, 18 December 1866, Harrington to Langton, 10 January, 18 January, and 31 January 1867, Harrington to the Auditor, 19 February and 5 March 1867, and Harrington to Simpson, 27 March 1867.

107. Finance, R.G. 19, Vol. 1158, Barings and Glyns to Howland, 20 December 1866. Loans from banks in Canada provided sterling exchange to meet interest charges, but the Canadian account at both Barings and Glyns remained overdrawn. See Barings and Glyns to Howland, 21 December 1866, and Barings to Belleau, 10 January 1867.

108. Finance, R.G. 19, Vol. 3376, "Private and Confidential," Galt to King, 29 August 1864, and *Galt Papers*, M.G. 27 I D 8, Vol. 2, King to Galt, 31 August 1864.

Chapter 9
Conclusion

*Such was the origin of that debt which
has since become the greatest prodigy that
ever perplexed the sagacity and
confounded the pride of statesmen and
philosophers. At every stage in the growth
of that debt the nation has set up the same
cry of anguish and despair. At every stage
in the growth of that debt it has been
seriously asserted by wise men that
bankruptcy and ruin were at hand. Yet
still the debt went on growing; and still
bankruptcy and ruin were as
remote as ever.*
— Thomas Babington Macaulay,
The History of England[1]

At the stroke of midnight on 1 July 1867 a huge bonfire lit the skies above Major's Hill in Ottawa. As the crowds which had been gathering for over an hour shouted cheers to "The Queen" one hundred guns of the Ottawa Field Battery fired a salute from their drill hall in Lower Town. Bells rang out lustily from all parts of the city, accompanied by rockets and roman candles. The next morning at 11 o'clock in ceremonies in the East Block, Lord Monck became the first Governor General of the Dominion of Canada. Outside, numerous celebrations continued throughout the day and into the night. Similar, if less elaborate, demonstrations occurred throughout the old Province of Canada.[2] As *The Ottawa Citizen* reported,

> Nothing could more thoroughly testify the satisfaction given to the change just completed by their representatives than the universal determination evinced on Monday to celebrate its inauguration with the greatest eclat.[3]

In Toronto, which had greeted the Union so half-heartedly 26 years earlier, "the day was one continued succession of rejoicings," according to the *Globe*.[4]

As everyone celebrated the birth of the new Dominion, few thought to mourn the death of the old Union of the Canadas. *The Globe* noted that the new Dominion was "stamped with a familiar name, which in the past has borne a record sufficiently honourable to entitle it to be perpetuated," but the name went back far beyond the Union. Moreover, what emerged from the old Canada was not the union of eastern and western sections, but the older separate world of the Upper and Lower provinces. Unlike New Brunswick and Nova Scotia, the Province of Canada ceased to exist as a geopolitical entity of altered status. The financial legacy of the old Province of Canada, however, was more than a public debt now assumed by the new Dominion. In truth, much had been accomplished during the 26 years of the Union.

The financial history of the Union provides a critical element in the broader history of state formation in British North America.[5] When Upper and Lower Canada ended their separate constitutional existence, neither possessed political or administrative structures adequate to control the development and execution of modern economic policies. There was no Minister of Finance in the modern sense of that term, and the Receiver General was a British appointee. Although the process of change had already begun by the late 1830s, reform accelerated rapidly with the arrival of the Union and its dynamic Governor General. Lord Sydenham's administrative and political initiatives ensured that the Executive Council would soon begin asserting its political authority. From a financial point of view, Canada achieved responsible government long before 1848. Canada may not have had all of the constitutional trappings of a sovereign state, but the limits on its autonomy lay outside the domain of financial and economic policy.

With political control of economic policy lodged firmly in the hands of the Executive Council, the province soon developed the means to exercise effective administrative control. As often as not, reform involved a slow process of learning by doing. Receivers General, Inspectors General, and Ministers of Finance rarely anticipated problems; rather, they reacted to a series of crises and difficulties. Reform, as a result, may have been haphazard, yet it remained inexorable. By 1849 the province had a clearly defined development strategy, which brought together various elements of land, trade, transportation, and financial policies. The government developed specific programmes designed to achieve its objectives. When Hincks's vision proved a bit too grand, renewed financial crises led subsequent governments to introduce new initiatives, including the adoption of more modern accounting practices and a modern currency. The demands of inherited debts and slower growth also led to new policies for managing the public debt. These involved, among other things, a more sophisticated manipulation of the tariff in an attempt to maximize benefits for both revenue and trade. With the introduction of provincial notes in 1866, the government of Canada was in possession of a modern administrative bureaucracy, able to exploit the full range of options open to a small country. Despite the difficulties, Canadians were in control of their own destiny.

In charge of their own fate, Canadians nonetheless appear to have made a mess of public finance. During the last half-dozen years of the Union, a succession of Finance Ministers and provincial governments scrambled to make ends meet, able, it seemed, to cope but not really to command. Yet this is too pessimistic a view. The government may have been "strapped" for funds with its credit options narrowing, yet the province had hardly exhausted its considerable resources. From a financial point of view, the provincial government managed hard times reasonably well. In addition to debts and difficulties, they left a permanent legacy of canals and railways which, if overcapitalized,[6] remained a vital component of a modern economy that produced a relatively high standard of living for most of its citizens.

In the nineteenth century many pessimists believed the rising British debt would with time undermine the economy. Optimists such as Thomas Babington Macaulay responded that these "prophets of evil" suffered from a "double delusion." They "erroneously imagined" that the debt of a state was analogous to that of an individual, and "they made no allowance for the effect produced by the incessant progress of every experimental science, and by the incessant efforts of every man [sic] to get on in life." As Macaulay observed, "They saw that the debt grew; and they forgot that other things grew as well as the debt."[7] A nineteenth-century Canadian might have added that other things grew because of the debt.

Public spending of borrowed moneys did indeed stoke the fires of economic growth during the first 15 years of the Union period. Yet there remained a critically weak link in the financial chain. Macaulay noted that the public debt differed fundamentally from individual debt, because in the latter case the individual borrowed from someone else and in the former case society borrowed from "a part of itself."[8] In Canada's case society had borrowed from someone else.

If the economy had an Achilles' heel it was its large and near-permanent trade deficit. Some of that deficit represented investments in productive assets, which stimulated economic growth; some represented consumption in excess of productive capacity. The process of state formation so clearly visible in the history of public finance was less a product of choice than of necessity. The modern Canadian state emerged when the imperial state ceased playing its traditional economic role of underwriting the colonial economy and, in essence, financing the colony's trade deficit. During the 1830s imperial spending stopped balancing accounts. Although there was no conscious policy decision to this effect, the Canadian state assumed the imperial role. Unwilling to cut imports substantially, the state began to pay the tab with borrowed funds.

Canadian historiography has traditionally stressed the role of the state in directing economic change.[9] Beginning with Harold Innis and the staple trade model and continuing through later "Laurentian" and "metropolitan" variations, the interpretive emphasis has been placed on the interrelated problems of tariffs and transportation policies which influenced patterns of development.[10] The critical role played by the state, however, went beyond tariffs, canals, and railways; the state also kept this economy going. If it is unwise to venture into counter-factual history, it remains true that the economic history of the Union would have been very different indeed had not the Canadian state balanced the country's trade deficit by importing capital. No other institution was capable of playing this critical role.

The Canadian government ignored for the most part its trade deficit, believing that the natural resource endowment of the country provided near unlimited potential for growth. Canada, everyone believed, could outgrow deficits. The state developed programmes and poured resources into schemes designed to realize this potential sooner rather than later. For the most part this involved doing the same things in greater quantities — settling more land, growing more grains, cutting more timber — rather than diversification. Canada's potential was certainly great, but it was not as great as the vision of contemporaries.

Canadian development strategies not only involved realizing domestic potential, they involved capturing a larger share of the economic activities of the continent. Canals, everyone preferred to believe, could not fail to win at least part of the trade of the western states, and this would make them self-financing. The reality fell far short of expectations. Not only would the canals not pay for themselves, the removal of tolls failed to attract significant trade away from New York and into the St. Lawrence. Similarly, the metropolitan dream of significant railway through-traffic never materialized. Perhaps more damaging to the dreams of Hincks and others, valuable crown lands had long since been alienated. Much of what remained of the public domain consisted of an empire of precambrian rock. Although huge tracts of wild land had yet to feel the plough, the dreams of agricultural expansion at the heart of the province's economic strategy could never be fully realized within the confines of the St. Lawrence/Great Lakes watershed. As Doug Owram observes, "The problem was that Canada's past growth had depended to a large extent on the existence of an untapped frontier"; new frontier land, however, was now harder to find.[11]

This more modest economic reality ensured that the catalyst of economic growth during the first 15 years of the Union might become the yoke around Canada's economic neck. After firing the economic engine between 1840 and 1856, the public debt threatened to sap whatever inertia remained from the years of rapid growth. Between 1840 and 1855 the state had become one of the primary vehicles by which capital was imported into the Canadian economy. Between 1856 and 1862 the government borrowed more in London, but now the capital was increasingly being spent in London to service the accumulating debt. Unable after 1862 to raise large sums abroad, the Canadian government began borrowing domestically to meet interest payments on its external debt. The public debt no longer helped balance a trade deficit. After 1862 the debt contributed instead to a growing balance of payments problem. Rather than fueling economic expansion, the Canadian state became one factor contributing to slower growth.

No doubt the economic conditions that produced the extraordinary growth of the early 1850s could not be sustained indefinitely, yet Canadian economic performance during the 1860s remained well below expectations at a time when a number of factors should have generated more rapid growth. Although the initial boost to the economy provided by the construction phase of railway development had passed, the longer term and more substantive contributions of railways in reducing transportation costs and integrating larger markets were being felt by the 1860s.[12] The railways had also become major manufacturing enterprises as well as carriers of freight; this provided another boost to growth and diversification. The construction phase of railway development, meanwhile, brought a rapid increase in imports, which contributed to a massive jump in Canada's trade deficit between 1851 and 1854. The passing of the construction phase helped reduce imports, while the development of manufacturing capacity opened the prospect of domestic substitution for previously imported products. No doubt the American Civil War contributed to a credit squeeze that sent discount rates up and debenture quotations down, yet the Civil War also brought much potential for profit. United States inflation during the war years ran at 25 per cent compared to only 7 per cent in Canada. This gave Canadian exporters an advantage; exports increased in both volume and diversity. In particular, there was a marked increase in non-reciprocity exports to the United States.[13] All of these factors ensured that the Canadian economy continued to grow during the 1860s, but it grew at a much reduced rate.[14]

Despite evidence of economic growth, a gloomier mood developed in the 1860s, centred less on an appreciation of the general economic environment than on the general political environment and the government's financial difficulties. The new pessimism, undoubtedly as exaggerated as earlier optimism, contributed enormously to the drive for British North American union. Richard Cartwright captured the mood in the Confederation debates:

> [T]hree changes of Ministry within the space of a single twelve months; the fate of cabinets dependent on the vote of a single capricious or unprincipled individual, in a House of 130 members; a deficient revenue and a sinking credit; all useful legislation at a standstill. . . . I speak of facts patent and known to all.[15]

Similarly, John A. Macdonald believed that one of the great objects of Confederation was a solution to the province's financial difficulties. Confederation would provide a wider tax base, would hopefully improve trade performance, and would, everyone believed, restore an agricultural frontier. In so doing, Confederation would re-create on a grander scale the preconditions that had helped fuel the growth ethic of the 1840s. It would re-create those visions of grandeur waiting to be realized through immigration and settlement, stimulated by the transportation projects that an expanded state would encourage.

Alexander Galt held the vision of the western plains before his colleagues and then observed that

> The reason why we have not been able to assume possession of that territory and open it up to the industry of the youth of this country who, in consequence of the want of some such field for the employment of their energies, have been obliged to go off to the States in thousands, especially to those states possessing the boundless resources of the great North-West, is because the resources of Canada — great as they have been, considering the disadvantages under which she has labored — have been inadequate for the development of this great district.

Galt promised that "one of the first acts" of the new Dominion would be "to enter into public obligations for the purpose of opening up and developing that vast region, and making it a source of strength instead of a burden to us and the Mother Country also."[16] It was fitting that once Confederation had been accomplished, none other than Francis Hincks should return to his old bailiwick at the Ministry of Finance. He undoubtedly felt very much at home. With a few revisions in details his "Memorandum" of December 1848 could serve again as a guide for Canadian economic and financial policy.

Notes

1.   Thomas Babington Macaulay, *The History of England, from the Accession of James II*, Vol. IV (New York, 1887), 325.

2.   See, for example, *The Ottawa Citizen*, 5 July 1867, *The Globe*, 2 July 1867, or *The Montreal Gazette*, 2 July 1867.

3.   *The Ottawa Citizen*, 5 July 1867.

4.   *The Globe*, 2 July 1867.

5.   There is a growing scholarly interest in the emergence of the "institutional state" in British North America. This was reflected in the Workshop on Social Change and State Formation: British North America, 1830–1870, held at the University of Toronto in February 1989. Papers from that conference can be found in *Colonial Leviathan: State Formation in Mid-Nineteenth-Century Canada*, ed. by Allan Greer and Ian Radforth (Toronto, 1992). Other examples can be found in Michael Katz, "The Origins of the Institutional State," *Marxist Perspectives* (1978), 6–22, R. D. Gidney and D. A. Lawr, "Bureaucracy vs Community? The Origins of Bureaucratic Procedure in the Upper Canadian School System," *Journal of Social History* 13 (1981), 438–457, and Bruce Curtis, "Preconditions of the Canadian State: Educational Reform and the Construction of a Public in Upper Canada, 1837–1846," *Studies in Political Economy: A Socialist Review* 10 (1983), 99–121.

6.   A. W. Currie long ago noted that the nominal value of stocks and bonds issued far exceeded the real costs of assets. Often, cash was raised by sale of bonds while shares were given away to promoters. Currie cites Robert Giffen who, in 1873, observed that "in England, money was wastefully spent but still it was spent whereas in the American case the addition to the nominal capital is transparently without equivalent. It represents no real expenditure." Robert Giffen, *American Railways as Investments* (London, 1873), 13, cited in A. W. Currie, "British Attitudes toward Investment in North American Railways," *Business History Review* XXXIV (1960), 203. Also see McCalla, "Railways and the Development of Canada West, 1850–1870," in *Colonial Leviathan*, 198.

7.   Macaulay, *The History of England*, Vol. IV, 328.

8.   *Ibid.*, 328.

9.   See, for example, Michael Bliss, "'Rich by Nature, Poor by Policy': The State and Economic Life in Canada," in *Entering the 1980s: Canada in Crisis*, ed. by W. P. Ward and R. K. Carty (Toronto, 1980), H.G.J. Aitken, "Defensive Expansion: The State and Economic Growth in Canada," in *Approaches to Canadian Economic History*, ed. by W. T. Easterbrook and M. H. Watkins (Toronto, 1967), or J.M.S. Careless, "Frontierism, Metropolitanism, and Canadian History," *Canadian Historical Review* XXXV (1954), 1–21.

10.   The best example of this interpretation can be found in Easterbrook and Aitken, *Canadian Economic History*, 350–408.

11.   Canada's new-found interest in the Northwest at the end of the 1850s resulted from this realization. As early as 1855 the *Globe* began to worry about "confinement." Doug Owram, *Promise of Eden: The Canadian Expansionist Movement and the Idea of the West, 1856–1900* (Toronto, 1980), 43.

12.   For a general assessment of the economic impact of railways on Canada West see McCalla, "Railways and the Development of Canada West, 1850–1870," in *Colonial Leviathan*, 192–229.

13.   See Officer and Smith, "The Canadian–American Reciprocity Treaty," 603.

14.   Real GNP increased from $406 million in 1850 to $582 million in 1860, an increase of 43 per cent. By 1870 real GNP reached $764 million, an increase of 31 per cent. See Table 1: 2 "Long-Run Trends in GNP, Real GNP and Real GNP Per Capita, 1850–1970", in Marr and Patterson, *Canada: An Economic History*, 6.

15.   Canada, Legislature, *Parliamentary Debates on the Subject of the Confederation of the British North American Provinces*, 1865, cited in *The Confederation Debates in the Province of Canada/1865*, ed. by P. B. Waite (Toronto, 1963), iv.

16.   Alexander Tilloch Galt, *The Confederation Debates in the Province of Canada/1865*, ed. by Waite, 56. Also see den Otter, *Civilizing the West*, 25–27, passim, and Owram, *Promise of Eden*.

Appendix I: Public Accounts for the Province of Canada, Consolidated Revenue Fund, 1842–1857 (£1,000 cy)

	1842	1843	1844	1845	1846	1847	1848	1849
Expenditure								
Interest on Public Debt	79.7	96.4	123.6	143.7	148.0	151.1	169.2	182.7
Civil government	48.7	35.0	28.8	33.0	29.2	33.5	33.8	32.3
Administration of Justice	64.0	47.0	56.6	54.7	59.1	63.1	68.1	64.3
Provincial Penitentiary	3.5	6.5	19.3	13.0	16.9	12.8	15.0	13.8
Legislature	17.0	29.3	35.9	50.7	52.8	49.0	29.2	60.7
Education	22.9	18.8	68.3	79.6	58.1	61.8	64.8	39.6
Agriculture	2.7	2.7	3.3	7.5	8.9	8.4	9.4	8.6
Hospitals and Charities	11.5	8.2	13.4	14.0	14.8	16.5	12.7	12.5
Public Works	51.9	22.7	11.6	77.2	83.0	46.2	12.2	3.5
Militia and Enrolled Forces	2.0	2.0	3.1	2.4	4.0	3.0	1.8	2.0
Light Houses and Coastal Services	2.5	2.4	5.1	4.9	5.5	4.4	4.8	4.9
Emigration	2.7	0.6	7.0	2.4	3.4	0.9	0.8	0.6
Pensions	12.7	14.8	13.5	12.3	11.8	10.9	10.8	12.8
Indian Annuities							6.7	6.7
Sinking Fund	47.3		54.1				15.0	
Miscellaneous	5.7	6.4	56.6	27.9	27.5	18.5	20.2	32.2
Total Expenditure	374.8	292.8	500.2	523.3	523.0	480.1	474.5	477.2
Revenue								
Customs	265.4	218.9	429.7	419.0	391.2	381.1	304.4	412.6
Excise	31.9	30.5	34.4	20.3	18.6	28.8	28.5	21.1
Revenue from Public Works	16.4	26.1	25.6	27.5	48.5	42.6	24.1	42.6
Territorial	25.8	27.2	5.2	22.9	23.5	25.8	3.2	9.6
Bank Imposts	10.3	7.6	10.5	13.0	15.9	16.0	12.5	10.8
Casual	15.9	10.6	10.4	21.7	15.3	12.6	7.0	16.7
Total Revenue	365.7	320.9	515.8	524.4	513.0	506.9	379.7	513.4
Balance	−9.1	28.1	15.6	1.1	−10.0	26.8	−94.8	36.2

Appendix I — Continued

	1850	1851	1852	1853	1854	1855	1856	1857
Expenditure								
Interest on Public Debt	202.1	225.4	215.4	227.4	226.1	219.5	225.2	281.0
Civil government	34.0	40.1	39.6	39.7	43.0	72.5	60.3	64.6
Administration of Justice	86.6	85.3	86.8	89.7	103.9	111.3	123.2	137.7
Provincial Penitentiary	10.0	5.8	6.7	7.0	5.0	15.0	14.9	17.9
Legislature	49.4	49.7	47.8	68.5	89.2	100.5	118.5	129.0
Education	53.7	66.2	60.4	101.4	71.3	106.7	97.5	110.0
Agriculture	13.1	12.9	13.8	15.9	18.2	17.7	18.5	22.5
Hospitals and Charities	15.0	17.6	13.9	27.4	22.1	39.8	41.3	46.6
Public Works	5.5	6.7	8.5	17.6	33.4	116.3	99.6	93.3
Militia and Enrolled Forces	2.3	1.9	2.1	2.1	2.2	32.5	43.7	48.7
Light Houses and Coastal Services	6.0	6.2	8.2	17.6	21.5	34.1	28.6	34.3
Emigration	0.8	0.9	0.8	0.8	17.7	2.5	9.8	5.8
Pensions	10.0	9.5	10.6	11.6	10.7	11.5	9.8	11.7
Indian Annuities	10.9	7.8	7.8	7.8	6.7	9.9	8.8	8.9
Sinking Fund		73.0	219.0	73.0	73.0	85.2	60.8	73.0
Miscellaneous	42.4	38.4	69.5	70.0	205.9	136.7	144.7	179.3
Total Expenditure	541.8	647.4	810.9	777.5	954.9	1111.7	1105.2	1264.3
Revenue								
Customs	583.5	703.7	705.5	986.6	1168.0	813.8	1028.9	898.9
Excise	20.0	20.2	22.4	22.5	17.2	16.8	20.5	27.0
Revenue from Public Works	52.6	65.0	71.4	77.6	50.5	36.2	51.8	34.7
Territorial	21.7	20.0	32.2	64.1	71.2	76.3	25.7	34.6
Bank Imposts	13.3	15.8	19.0	23.1	26.8	22.5	22.1	18.8
Casual	13.1	17.5	29.9	21.2	35.6	53.4	89.7	56.3
Total Revenue	704.2	842.2	880.4	1195.1	1369.3	1019.0	1238.7	1070.3
Balance	162.4	194.8	69.5	417.6	414.4	−92.7	133.5	−194.0

Source: "Public Accounts for the Province of Canada for the Year 1857," *Appendix to the Journals of the Legislative Assembly*, 1858. All calculations are my own.

Appendix II: Public Accounts for the Province of Canada, 1858–1864 ($1,000)

	1858	1859	1860	1861	1862	1863	1864	1864	1866	1867
Expenditure										
Interest on Public Debt	3030.9	3203.0	3766.9	3735.7	3774.3	3717.7	1883.8	3664.4	3590.7	3631.8
Charges of Management	56.7	51.3	216.9	67.3	52.1	42.6	19.5	35.7	66.7	183.5
Exchange	10.8	6.7	3.9	26.7	20.8	19.6	7.5	68.6	53.9	54.2
Sinking Fund	434.9	255.0	6487.3	119.4	167.0	182.7	219.3	116.3	125.1	243.3
Redemption of Public Debt	204.8	2897.8	15885.1	2738.9	279.8	4166.4	2798.1	1239.3	336.0	1813.1
Premium and Discount	30.9		1775.0	13.4	7.1	32.5	97.3			
Civil Government	394.7	390.0	423.1	437.3	486.6	430.5	214.3	458.8	461.1	536.8
Administration of Justice	608.4	682.5	652.1	670.8	664.7	695.3	341.1	749.8	738.6	812.7
Police	41.9	31.6	30.9	30.5	31.2	30.8	11.6	29.4	41.1	37.0
Penitentiary, Reformatories and Inspection	61.6	82.2	101.7	148.0	155.6	152.2	48.7	219.3	190.7	243.8
Legislature	684.4	471.0	472.6	463.1	432.0	627.4	230.6	473.2	398.5	386.0
Education	529.3	526.4	522.8	506.8	533.6	528.4	120.7	570.2	567.5	620.4
Literary and Scientific Institutions	33.4	14.0	17.2	17.9	16.8	14.3	6.3	14.0	15.5	14.8
Hospitals and Charities	195.0	238.4	274.1	272.0	307.7	250.9	111.3	310.1	324.4	348.0
Geological Survey	19.6	21.2	22.0	20.3	17.4	23.7	11.0	19.4	20.6	23.3
Militia and Enrolled Forces	162.4	61.8	107.4	84.7	98.4	481.1	207.8	756.9	1640.6	1412.9
Arts, Agriculture, Statistics	24.6	5.3	27.2	2.3	17.5	11.4	1.7	18.9	5.5	57.9
Public Works	720.4	404.3	811.6	1036.2	421.1	474.7	241.3	881.1	516.4	540.2
Rents and Repairs	38.3	42.2	61.7	39.6	97.0	39.3	18.4	47.2	89.1	109.1
Roads and Bridges	163.3	124.1	188.5	181.7	259.6	119.6	7.4	170.1	219.4	146.1
Census			1.2	118.4	24.6	12.6	4.1			
Agricultural Societies	111.0	70.2	101.5	102.6	108.3	105.7	1.6	108.4	102.2	108.1

Appendix II — Continued

	1858	1859	1860	1861	1862	1863	1864	1865	1866	1867
Light Houswes and Coastal Services	116.6	126.5	120.9	110.5	103.5	102.7	37.3	116.8	113.8	110.5
Ocean and River Steam Services	217.6	270.1	766.8	432.0	507.9	511.4	226.2	307.8	304.3	310.3
Emigration and Quarantine	50.0	37.5	36.0	48.4	54.3	57.4	13.1	51.0	46.6	52.8
Pensions	45.3	42.5	36.9	34.5	42.5	40.5	20.0	42.3	35.1	51.5
Indian Annuities	31.0	40.0	35.3	35.4	26.6	43.8	17.3	40.2	22.1	35.4
Fisheries	15.6	14.1	22.5	27.3	25.2	22.8	16.2	18.6	22.4	36.8
Seigniorial Tenure Redemption	298.4	136.8	213.0	224.1	379.8	222.6	101.6	199.2	190.5	200.8
Cullers' Office	50.2	63.7	63.1	68.4	68.6	76.8	19.3	85.3	64.3	65.0
Railway and Steamboat Inspection	14.8	13.8	13.0	15.1	15.0	10.6	5.5	10.4	10.7	10.6
Township Indemnity								18.1		105.6
Advances and Repayments	163.3	284.3	1238.2	231.7	223.5	89.5	12.3		22.0	148.2
Municipalities' Fund	344.5	153.7	374.2	446.0	313.4	142.3	0.7	104.9	79.5	108.6
Investments for Trust Funds	270.9	133.9	40.0							
Indian Fund	113.0	90.8	150.0	99.7	112.8	131.9	63.3	139.2	133.6	148.3
New Coinage	340.7	6.9	10.7							
Removal of the Seat of Government		104.3	6.0					12.2	177.5	7.8
Secret Service										42
Miscellaneous	66.0	217.1	266.1	109.0	64.1	68.5	49.8	277.7	123.2	152.6
Subsidiary Lines	263.6	17.8		340.0	80.6					

Appendix II — Continued

	1858	1859	1860	1861	1862	1863	1864	1865	1866	1867
Bursar of University				179.9						
Collection, Management and Other Charges on Revenue										
Customs	341.9	332.8	351.6	363.4	379.4	364.9	178.1	397.1	405.7	627.6
Excise	16.3	22.8	34.0	31.8	35.2	36.6	22.3	174.4	109.9	140.7
Post Office	565.6	391.4	633.5	442.5	436.6	431.9	167.6	483.3	655.5	559.2
Public Works	270.6	234.8	235.6	279.0	313.8	236.8	108.6	246.8	239.5	267.5
Territorial	221.3	190.1	152.4	277.5	135.8	79.8	74.5	134.8	71.5	133.4
Other	29.1	51.9	132.0	113.3	104.0	78.7	52.7	79.0	86.8	89.6
Total Expenditure	11403.6	12556.6	36882.5	14743.1	11395.8	14908.9	7789.8	12890.2	12418.1	14727.4
Revenue										
Customs	3368.2	4456.3	4756.7	4774.6	4652.2	5171.1	3074.8	5660.7	7328.1	6973.3
Excise	138.8	343.9	306.5	344.7	500.3	829.8	519.4	1303.0	1888.6	1950.7
Post Office	295.4	333.2	330.9	357.0	391.4	438.8	236.8	468.5	524.9	409.8
Ocean Postage			74.5	100.7	17.3		189.3	72.3	97.0	57.4
Revenue from Public Works	400.7	311.5	264.2	324.6	383.7	539.9	129.4	394.9	417.5	408.4
Provincial Steamers			22.0	30.6	37.8	35.9	3.1	34.6	35.2	33.2
Territorial	415.4	482.2	644.8	678.9	629.9	682.8	261.9	830.9	628.5	776.4
Casual	12.9	14.4	88.9	22.1	11.2	11.8	12.9	15.3	11.8	16.5
Quebec Loan	0.7	0.2	0.4	0.7		0.3	0.8		0.1	0.1
Interest on Investments	189.5	157.6	448.8	489.3	394.7	362.8	88.2	154.3	158.6	87.5
Premium, Discount and Exchange		15.7		18.9	3.4	157.8	108.9	49.8	25.4	16.2

Appendix II — Continued

	1858	1859	1860	1861	1862	1863	1864	1865	1866	1867
Bank Imposts	45.2	37.4	49.5	52.4	26.4	15.4	10.9	11.9	16.9	18.0
Law Fees	42.2	54.4	40.9	32.5	30.3	29.5	17.1	36.4	28.9	25.4
Fines and Forteitures	20.8	42.0	19.7	24.3	22.3	14.4	8.7	18.2	18.7	12.9
Bill Stamps								119.8	90.2	104.0
Speical Revenues	178.3	287.0	244.9	268.5	252.1	287.0	101.1	403.1	334.8	352.3
Debentures	2199.6	2422.5	30425.7	2764.0	2222.1	4622.2	2662.9	1074.6	0.4	3986.9
Open Accounts	2963.7	1615.2	1897.1	2371.8	1054.0	1183.0	700.8	1073.6	1067.2	1109.1
Total Revenue	10271.4	10573.5	39615.5	12655.6	10629.1	14382.5	8127.0	11721.9	12672.8	16338.1
Balance	−1132.2	−1983.1	2733.0	−2087.5	−766.7	−526.4	337.2	−1168.3	254.7	1610.7

Source:
"Public Accounts for the Province of Canada," *Appendix to the Journals of the Legislative Assembly*, 1859, and *Sessional Papers*, 1860–1868. All Calculations are my own. Figures for 1858–1863 cover 12 months ending 31 Dec.; for 1864, six months ending 30 June; for 1865–1867, 12 months ending 30 June.

Index

Achevé d'imprimer
en mai 1992 sur les presses
des Ateliers Graphiques Marc Veilleux Inc.
Cap-Saint-Ignace, Qué.